COOK
YOUR WAY
TO THE
LIFE
YOU WANT

Christina Pirello

HPBOOKS

HPBooks
Published by The Berkley Publishing Group
A division of Penguin Putnam Inc.
375 Hudson Street
New York, New York 10014

HPBooks hardcover edition: November 1999
HPBooks trade paperback edition: June 2002

HPBooks trade paperback edition ISBN: 1-55788-374-2

Visit our website at
www.penguinputnam.com

The Library of Congress has catalogued
the HPBooks hardcover edition as follows:

Pirello, Christina
        Cook your way to the life you want / Christina Pirello. — 1st ed.
        p.   cm.
        Includes bibliographical references and index.
        ISBN: 1-55788-351-1 (trade hc)
        1. Cookery (Natural foods)   I. Title.
     TX741.P5638   1999
641.5'63—dc21   99-42896
                                                              CIP

Printed in the United States of America

10   9   8   7   6   5   4   3   2

COOK
YOUR WAY
TO THE
LIFE
YOU WANT

*To my mother and father, Tonia and Albert, for giving me
life and doing the best they knew how*

CONTENTS

PREFACE

It happens to most everyone. You've either met someone, read a book, or perhaps seen a movie that had a profound effect on your life. Whether it was a chance meeting or even the result of something you didn't want to do, the outcome was life changing. There was no turning back.

When speaking about Christina to someone who has yet to meet her, I often tell the person or people I am talking with that meeting my wife, Christina Pirello, will change their life forever. It's a combination of her presence and what she has to say. Her presence is so powerful, you know she's in the room; and what she has to say (especially about food and how it affects each of us), and the way she says it, makes so much sense that you want more of what she has to offer.

To this day, whether I'm watching Christina on television or listening to her lecture to a thousand food-service buyers for the Defense Department, I am mesmerized by her ability to communicate and, more importantly, by her ability to inspire. I call it the "magic of Christina."

I've always believed that food creates who you are, both physically and spiritually. Like us, it has both a physical quality, that which we see, and an energetic quality, that which makes up its very essence, its character. Christina, and her magic, makes it real, makes it life changing. Christina says, "The food you choose to eat today creates the person who opens the door and goes out to face the world tomorrow."

As you read the pages of this—her second—book, make the recipes, and study the philosophy of the energy of food, you'll no doubt agree, and your life will change forever.

—Robert Pirello

ACKNOWLEDGMENTS

I'd like to bypass the typical acknowledgments that accompany a book—editors, friends, loved ones. I'm hoping that all of the people in my life who have been a part of this adventure know who they are and know how grateful I am for their love and support.

I'd like to acknowledge, instead, all those brilliant teachers, philosophers, health practitioners, alternative care providers, and enlightened medical professionals who have come before me and from whom I continually draw inspiration, knowledge, and strength.

Beginning with Hippocrates and moving through history, healers and philosophers have paved the way for free thinking and for us to maintain control over our lives and our health. Without remembering every name through the ages, suffice it to say that without incredible minds like Galileo and Leonardo da Vinci, we would have remained in the dark about life's energies for a long time.

Our modern world is no different. With Georges Ohsawa, alternative healing and our realignment with nature was reborn. Michio and Aveline Kushi continue to work tirelessly to educate people about the connection between diet and overall well-being. Those who came after these great thinkers took the precious ancient teachings of the East and the knowledge of the West and created a modern way of viewing healing that can appeal to any culture, with little mystery or mysticism, just practical, sensible information that can be applied to any lifestyle. Teachers like my own macrobiotic mentors—William Tara, Murray Snyder, Diane Avoli, and Geraldine Walker—and those who have touched my life with their written wisdom—Herman and Cornelia Aihara, Edward and Wendy Esko, Meredith McCarty, Denny Waxman, AnneMarie Colbin, Mary Estella, Molly Katzen, Frances Moore Lappé, Steve Gagne, Patrick Riley, and countless others—have helped shape the world of wholistic healing.

And to those enlightened medical professionals who have taken wholistic healing out of the world of snake-oil salesmen and hucksters into the light of legitimacy, where it belongs (most of it, anyway)—Andrew Weil, Neil Barnard, and Dean Ornish, to name a few: Thanks for paving the way for free thinking and free choice and for being responsible for our health.

My gratitude to all who have come before me, who have taught me what little I know and who continue to inspire me daily.

None of what I have achieved in the last couple of years would be possible without the support of my most devoted sponsor and friends at Eden Foods. Their dedication to organic growing and sustainable agricultural practices, along with their commitment to creating and maintaining the purity of our food supply, inspires me every day. To Michael Potter and Sally Gralla, my heartfelt gratitude.

To my husband whose nobility and unconditional love continues to bring out the best in my nature and inspires me always. To John Duff and Jeanette Egan for their brilliant editing and infinite patience. And to my students, with deep gratitude, for all they teach me. And finally, to Jane Suttel for the most beautiful clothing I have had the honor to wear and to Sue, the best cheerleader a girl ever had. Thanks.

INTRODUCTION

For me, cooking is a complete experience, not a chore to be endured. I am convinced that for us to create the life we want we must begin to see food and cooking in a new light. We must remember that the act of cooking is the act of nourishing ourselves; so to say that we hate to cook—or we don't have time to cook—is to deny that we are of any value, to ourselves or anyone else. No wonder we all have self-esteem issues. We have forgotten how to feed ourselves, to feel satisfied and content.

I spend a lot of time in the kitchen. It's my job. And I love every second of it. Having worked as an artist in my earlier years, I love the creative outlet I now find in cooking—developing recipes, creating beautiful presentations, discovering new (to me) combinations of food, and, of course, always discovering how the energies come together to create the dance of life. But, in truth, I love everything about cooking and nourishing. I love planning each menu, even if it's just in my head as I wander the produce section of the market, checking out what's fresh. I love shopping, choosing each and every ingredient that will come together in my meals. I am always struck by the beauty of fresh produce as the colors complement and coordinate with each other in the kind of splendor that only nature can provide. It makes me pause in wonder—even on those days when I'm so busy I can barely stop to take a breath.

I love the action of the kitchen . . . every step in the process of creating a meal. I love watching clear water sliding, glistening, over the vegetables I am about to prepare. I love the feel of my knife in my hand as I slice and dice my way through the ingredients. I love the sputtering of the pressure cooker, as it softens my grain and beans. I love simmering stews and bubbling casseroles. I love the sizzle of a sauté as I move the veggies around the skillet, shiny with oil. I love the seasonings—the variety of flavors I can create with a pinch or a sprinkle. I love the fragrances of a meal in progress.

I love the challenge of creating meals that will help us meet our goals. I love the variety of ingredients, techniques, and cooking styles that I have available to me. I love the daily self-discovery of seeing how the energy of food works in me to make me the person I am. I love playing with the energy of food and seeing how I differ each day.

I love serving meals every evening. I love setting the table and deciding which serving bowls will look best with each dish. I love the social aspect of the meals that I serve, as we catch up with each other in the evening after our busy days. It's a time for us to slow down and remember each other and what life is really all about. It's the most rejuvenating time of the day. (If you haven't cooked and eaten a meal with loved ones lately, give it a go; you'll be amazed at how splendid it is.)

I love cleaning up. You heard me right. I love cleaning up after dinner. It's not a hassle for me, because I clean pots and pans and utensils as I work to prepare the meal. So it's not like I face a sink of crusty pots and pans after a relaxing dinner. When we sit down to eat, my kitchen is clean and reorganized, and peaceful, not a chaotic wreck. So cleanup just involves our serving pieces and dinner dishes. But the act of cleaning up after a meal is such a great meditation, such a mindful act, if you let yourself get into it. Now, I'm not some New Age ex-hippie, lost somewhere between Earth and Mars, zoning out over the kitchen sink, staring at soap bubbles. Cleaning is meditative in its symbolism. As I wash and rinse dishes, it's a quiet time that I use to reflect on the day I've had. It's a time that signifies for me the end of the day—and the beginning of a restful evening, cleansed of the day's challenges.

Have I had to rethink my priorities to create the space in my day to cook meals? You bet I have. Have I seen the fruits of that reorganization? You bet I have. I face daily challenges just like everyone else. I have bad days and cranky days and low days just like everyone else. I get overwhelmed just like everyone else. But through the preparation of daily meals and the ever-continuing observation of how food affects us, I have created the life that I want. I work very hard—and have the strength for that work. I face business stress every day—and I handle it with grace and balance. And I can let go of it when it's done. The way I choose to eat has opened many doors for me, not only maintaining my health but giving me the clarity of mind to see my way through any situation, to make decisions, and to be responsible for the outcome.

I think that understanding the energy of food—and how that energy behaves in our bodies, creating the people that we are—has given me freedom. Being responsible can be seen as either a burden or, as it is defined, the ability to respond. Isn't that a liberating thought? Just think about it: The food we choose to eat can either enslave us to its tyranny, dominating our thoughts and actions, or can serve us as we strive to achieve our dreams of health and well-being. We live in a world that loves to steal our dreams. We get caught up in the day-to-day routine of survival in a world that seems to move faster and faster, threatening to leave us behind. It's time to stop and think and care for ourselves, so that we have the strength to ride the roller coaster of life each day, so that we remain an oasis of calm in the maelstrom of daily challenges.

And that's what this book is about. It's not just another plan or system to achieve the perfect body, shiny hair, perfect health, and eternal youth. Lots of books promise us the moon, implying that we can have a problem-free life if only we read this book, follow one more plan, or implement one more system.

What I offer you in these pages is simply my perception of what I think is the truth. And that truth is that, as a part of nature, we can either fit in, contributing to the harmony of the planet, or we can go against the natural law, creating disharmony in our environment and creating struggle for ourselves as a result.

Drawing from the ancient wisdom that are the foundations of every culture, I have given you, I hope, the tools to nourish yourself, your friends, and your family in a deliciously healthy way. I hope that you come to have a better understanding of who you are (and what made you that way) and how the food you choose affects the body, mind, and spirit. I hope that these pages free you from all the dietary constraints that enslave you—from energy bars, diet plans, gram counting, and portion measuring.

And finally I hope that your eyes will be opened to the wondrous possibilities that there are—and that will give you the ability to respond positively and creatively to whatever challenges may be presented to you.

To your health!

FINDING THE BALANCE IN YOUR LIFE

IT'S REMARKABLE HOW much we think about, talk about, read about, and obsess about food. But even with all the studies, statistics, information, and data bombarding us daily, do we really *understand* food? I don't mean grams and vitamins and calories; we have *that* down to a science. But do we get it? While we may have a deep understanding of what is *in* the food we eat, we appear to have forgotten *why* we eat.

Somewhere along with our dependence on technology, we lost our way completely and, as a result, seem always to be searching. Every self-help book that can find its way to a shelf becomes a bestseller, proclaiming to have the answer. And we dutifully go on each quest—for our inner child, our authentic self, our true spirit. We trek off to groups; we write in our journals; we examine our deepest selves. And it seems that the more we struggle, the more the answers elude us, even with valid and valuable life exercises.

And then there are the diets. We've embraced low fat, high protein, low protein, high carbs, low or no carbs, grapefruit, cabbage soup, and the champagne and grape diet. We weigh food, reconstitute food, drink chemical-laced shakes, eat energy bars, and measure and count portions. We move food cards around our little folders, so we'll know when we've had our allowances. I think there may be more diet programs than religious affiliations. Yet we just keep getting fatter, and more miserable.

So we drive to the gym where we can get on a treadmill to go for a walk. We take the elevator to the floor that houses the stair machines. We lift, pull, push, jump, step, and spin, cramming our physical activity into one intense hour each day.

And then we wonder why we are all so depressed. With all this frantic activity, we have lost the essential ingredient to success and happiness. We have forgotten *what* we are.

We are fundamentally products of nature, subject to the same laws that govern all living organisms. But what makes us human is our unique ability to create what we visualize in our minds. Unfortunately, we have become enchanted with that ability and enslaved by the results. The sophisticated technology that we've created has alienated us from our true natures and insulated us from the essential life forces that nourish us. In setting ourselves against nature, we have created an imbalance and, in so doing, promoted conditions of physical, emotional, and spiritual malaise.

We have ignored the basic precept that the human structure is not only the physical bone, muscle, and tissue of the body but also the life force or energy that animates it. Understanding the energy interactions is fundamental to recognizing how everything we do, including eating, creates the life we have. Understanding can also help us create the life we want.

THE FORCES OF LIFE

The universe in which we live is an endless interplay of opposing forces, changing from physical matter to energy to physical matter and back to energy in a continuing cycle of construction and destruction, of expansion and contraction. The interaction of these two forces, called yin and yang by Chinese and other Asian healers, creates an unending pattern of action, which is evident throughout nature. Yin is symbolic of energy that is primarily expansive in nature, outward in its movement, going from physical to the nonphysical. Yang, on the other hand, is symbolic of energy that is primarily contracting or constricting in nature, inward in its movement, from the nonphysical to the physical. Yet these energies aren't distinct or separate from each other. They come together to form one energetic interaction, constantly changing from one to the other and back, expanding and contracting. This interaction of opposites is what makes nature come alive; this is the pulse of life as we know it.

The basic concept of yin and yang forms the foundation for much of Eastern philosophy in which all of nature is part of one whole, meaning that no one phenomenon is independent of any other. All things are linked, forming one continuing pattern of action. As well, everything in nature is in a constant state of change or motion. Nothing is static; a state of flux is the norm, even if we can't see it. Both expansion and contraction exist in all things, complementing each other as they interact, opening, closing, appearing, and disintegrating. And finally, in any phenomenon, both yin and yang are present, but one or the other will be the dominant energy. Every organism, phenomenon, or system will seem either expansive or contracted in its apparent character, while its opposite nature may be minimal or even dormant. Rocks appear hard, and water soft—but rocks can be ground into powder and water frozen into ice. This is energy changing from one form to another.

The idea that all physical matter is made up of energy is one that is completely accepted in the scientific world of physics, but once we remove the idea from science, we tend to shroud it in mysticism. As individuals, we find it hard to accept the world as energy, because we have lost touch with the rhythms of nature. We live in increasingly arti-ficial environments: in air-conditioned or overheated homes, in windowless offices, in cars. We can go for days without feeling the power of the earth under our feet. So, of course, we lose touch with nature and its rhythms feel foreign to us.

For our ancestors, understanding the environment was the key to survival. Knowledge of the rhythms of nature—like when the cold winds were expected, when the monsoon season would start, or when the drought was likely to occur—was essential to a successful harvest or hunt. It meant the continuance of their cultures. Although no longer vital to our physical survival, understanding nature is vital to our health and our ability to be responsible for ourselves and the health of our families, our society, and ultimately our planet.

Yin and Yang in Action

When we use our perceptive abilities to explore our environment, we experience an expansive, more emotional or spiritual awareness of our surroundings. This quality is characteristically yin. When our physical senses allow us to take in our environment, to gather information and nutrition, to increase our physical control over our environment, the quality is yang. Depending on our activity, location, and purpose, one or the other energy will dominate the moment, so we get the most useful information for the situation and can act appropriately.

The Basics of Yin and Yang

Characteristic	Yin	Yang
Nature	Expansive, moving to liquid, gas	Contracted
Physical character	Nonmatter, energy	Physical matter
Energy	Possibilities	Physical, active
Basic nature	Passive	Active
	Intellect	Physical
	Resting	Moving
	Leisurely	Aggressive
	Slow	Quick
	Alkaline	Acidic
In the body	Upper body, moving to the head	Lower body, moving to the feet
	Kidneys, liver, lungs, heart, spleen	Bladder, gallbladder, stomach, intestines
Body energy	Blood	Ki
Time of day	Evening, night	Morning, day
Temperature	Cool, cold	Warm, hot
Season	Autumn, winter	Spring, summer
Sexuality	Female	Male
Movement	Active to passive	Passive to active
	Potential to reality	Reality to potential
	Building	Breaking down
	Resting energy	Moving energy

Digestion is a simple physical example of yin and yang in action. The digestive system is a series of hollow organs (yang) whose job is to absorb nutrients by breaking down the dense, physical (yang) food we take in, transforming it to yin energy. Our nervous system, on the other hand, is an organized, compact, complicated (yin) system that allows us to scope out our environment, to perceive the energy and natural rhythms that surround us, and to transform them to yang information that we can use. These two systems, although opposite, work hand in hand to nourish us on all levels—physical and sensual.

As human beings, it is important to understand that the sensory information that we receive, and how we process that information, is key to the quality of our existence. What we see, hear, feel, touch, and smell has the ability to benefit us, or not. Truly healthy people feed themselves by assimilating lots of information—both physical and nonphysical. They continually seek "nourishment" by seeking challenges, by placing themselves in situations that create a deeper understanding of life. This adaptability and vitality may be thought of as a curiosity; but in reality, it creates a healthy mind and body. But as we've grown farther away from nature, we have lost our innate ability to connect with our natural environment. To return to our true human selves, we must reconnect to nature and understand the vital rhythms that govern us.

Then we can be fully responsible and in control of how we feel and how we fit in the world.

THE FIVE TRANSFORMATIONS OF ENERGY: THE DYNAMIC CYCLES OF NATURE

The Five Transformations of Energy is the theory that outlines the energetic and physical relationships that are basic to all of nature. In modern thinking, we place our focus almost completely on the physical—tissue formation, cell structure, organ systems—but there's more to us than that. The more traditional approach, as articulated by the practitioners of Chinese medicine, attempts to understand not only the individual's relationship to nature but the energetic qualities of the world and how the individual relates to them. Ancient cultures maintained a very sophisticated understanding of the body and the location and function of the organs. They recognized that all physical matter was composed of energy and that what we perceive as differences in form are simply energies existing at different levels, or different densities, if you will. There have been many theories about how ancient peoples developed such a profound understanding of the universe, but it seems evident that they were simply so in tune with nature, so keyed in to the

Seasons, Time, Organs, and Tastes Associated with Each Transformation of Energy

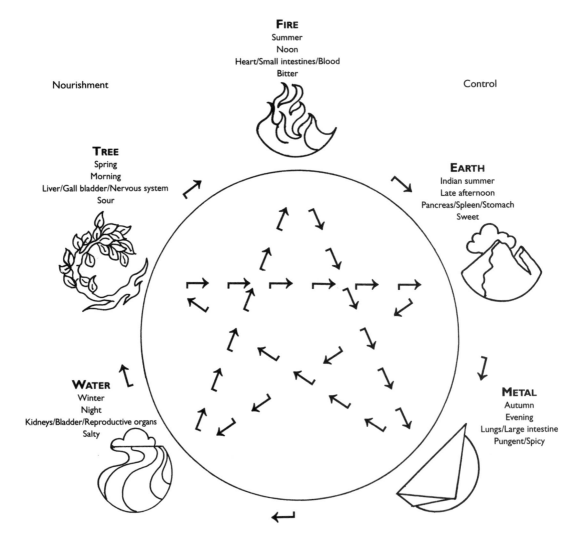

FIRE
Summer
Noon
Heart/Small intestines/Blood
Bitter

Nourishment

Control

TREE
Spring
Morning
Liver/Gall bladder/Nervous system
Sour

EARTH
Indian summer
Late afternoon
Pancreas/Spleen/Stomach
Sweet

WATER
Winter
Night
Kidneys/Bladder/Reproductive organs
Salty

METAL
Autumn
Evening
Lungs/Large intestine
Pungent/Spicy

rhythms of their surroundings, that their intuition allowed them to see reality. They didn't invent the laws of nature; they simply observed them. And in seeing humanity as a part of a great whole, subject to the same laws as the rest of life in the universe, they respected this reality.

The basic classifications of energy come in the form of yin and yang, but the constant interplay of opposites isn't black and white. Energy doesn't normally abruptly expand or contract itself. Just as day gradually becomes night or summer becomes fall, changes occur gradually as energy moves from one form to another. The physical world can be viewed simply as a reflection of the way energies interact with each other as they shift and change.

In their attempts to make the workings of nature clearer, ancient philosophers assigned physical characteristics to these points of interaction, creating a way to explain natural phenomena. The five classifications that make up the Five Transformations of Energy theory—earth, metal, water, tree, and fire—are physical assignments of energy transformation as yin changes to yang to yin and on and on.

Interestingly, this view doesn't contradict contemporary ideas—it simply adds another dimension to them. In addition to the physical structure of the body, the Eastern view accepts the influence of nature's energies on the body, like sunlight passing into us without our conscious knowledge, except as a delicious, enlivening warmth. The Five Transformations of Energy theory is an attempt to describe the energetic qualities that exist in the process of yin changing to yang. Although each of the five stages of transformation is unique in its distinguishing characteristics, it is not an individual phenomenon. All five make up a chain of energy shifts that are manifested throughout the universe. They are evident in the rhythms of the seasons, in the body's own cycles, and in the inner working of all creation.

Earth

 Earth is used to illustrate the point at which movement begins to settle, to gather, to condense. It is where energy begins to fall inward toward the center. As it continues to settle, the energy grows more firm, more concentrated. Think of plants decomposing and settling into the earth, creating soil as they sink. The Earth Transformation is associated with the season of late summer.

Within this transformation lies a calm, centered energy, with its influence affecting the function of the spleen, stomach, and pancreas. Earth's signature flavor is sweet.

❖

Metal

 As energy condenses and settles, growing firmer, it reaches the stage of complete physical materialization. Most closely associated with autumn, the Metal Transformation is the phase of energy change that is the most compact, the densest. Think of ore or stone. In this phase, when energy is at its most concentrated, there exists the most potential for movement. When energy can contract no further, it seeks release.

Within this transformation lies a deep, stable energy—organized and detail oriented. Its influence governs the function of the lungs and large intestines. A spicy, pungent flavor is its signature.

Water

 The strong contraction of metal energy must find release. But rather than explode into motion, the release comes in the form of a gentle, multidirectional floating energy, akin to flowing water. This is the beginning of yin, or expansive movement. Think of water spilled on a tabletop. It gently flows in many directions, viscous, yet moving.

Within this transformation lies a flexible, adaptable energy—easygoing, able to adjust to any situation. Its influence governs the strength of the kidneys, bladder, and reproductive organs; a salty taste is its signature; and it makes us strong and yet moveable. Water is the transformation of winter.

Tree

 Energy movement takes on a specific direction in its expansion in the Tree Transformation phase. Imagine water evaporating. This phase reflects energy ascending, moving upward and gently expanding. A further expansion of water energy, tree energy is more controlled and directed. Think of sprouting plants growing from the earth toward the sun. Tree energy reflects spring.

Within this transformation lies a strongly moving energy that still remains rooted in the earth, giving us focus and direction. Its influence governs the liver, gallbladder, and nervous system; a sour taste is its signature flavor; and it keeps us sharply focused on our goals, and yet compassionate and flexible.

Fire

The explosive energy of ignition resides in the symbol of fire. The greatest potential for opposing energy exists in the Fire Transformation. Fire's warmth and flames radiate outward from the source, moving rapidly in all directions. In the process, however, fire consumes itself, leaving ashes behind. It demonstrates the extreme yin expansion as it explodes, yet it reduces itself to ash, condensing into the earth, beginning the cycle of transformation again and again. Fire is the transformation associated with summer.

Within this transformation lies the extremes of both movement and calm. Herein lies the explosive energy of roaring flames and the low, calm energy of simmering. Its influence governs the function of the heart and small intestines; bitter is its signature flavor; and it gives us great vitality and charisma, yet allows us to find our deeply calm center of strength.

Each transformation of energy is essential to the next one. This cycle of energy is not a series of unrelated phenomena, but a continuing pattern of movement as energy shifts and changes, expanding and contracting, creating physical matter and dissolving itself back into energy.

Within this theory of energy transformation, all of nature has a place. This is natural law. All of nature, including humans, is animated by these energies—organ systems and function, biological life, emotional and spiritual health. Time of day; the seasons; tastes; colors; and all foods, cooking styles, cutting techniques, and food combining are influenced by yin and yang.

This simple theory clearly establishes the link between physical matter and energy and explains how that interaction affects our ability to act and be in the world. Within this understanding, we can choose appropriate foods, plan menus, observe our own energies, understand our moods, make ourselves comfortable, and affect how we behave. This is the key to understanding our own health, to being responsible and creating the life we want.

THE NOURISHING CYCLE

Just as life moves smoothly through the daylight to the night and from spring to summer to autumn to winter, so does energy move through us in an orderly, gently expanding, and contracting movement, with each transformation nourishing the next. This creates a smooth flow of energy through the body, resulting in efficient organ function and an overall feeling of well-being. In other words, in good health, your life force suffers no blockages, so you feel alert and vital.

The cycle of nourishment is simply a way to understand how one transformation of energy moves to and becomes the next. It works by analogy of physical characteristics, like this: Fire burns to ash, decomposing to become (and nourish) the energy of Earth. Earth, with its gathering strength, will continue to contract until it is as hard as stone, or metal. Metal, as contracted as energy can get, has nowhere to go but to begin to expand (remember, all things turn into their opposites). Rather than explode, though, Metal energy will open up to a gentle, floating energy, like flowing water. Water, by its very nature, will rise as it evaporates. This ascending energy, rooted in the earth, replicates the

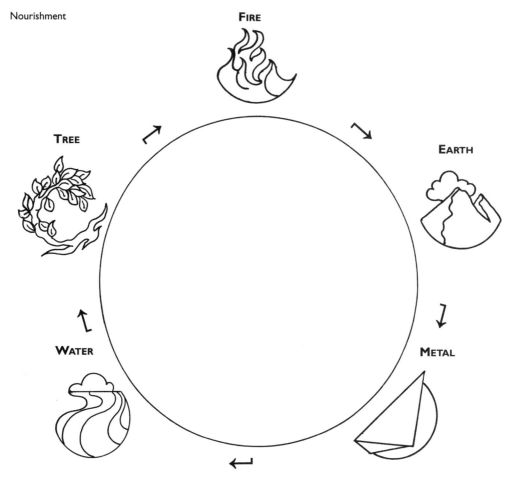

FIRE

TREE

EARTH

WATER

METAL

movement of plant growth, creating the energy known as Tree. Remember that water nourishes plants and trees naturally. Tree energy, in its turn, nourishes the transformation of Fire—you burn wood to create fire. Fire decomposes to ash, nourishing Earth—and so the cycle continues, with night turning to day and the seasons flowing from one to the next, the pulse of life continuing from one stage, or transformation, to the next, providing the basis of the interdependence of all living matter.

If energy becomes blocked or agitated, the body will suffer an imbalance of one sort or another—either too much or a deficiency. For example, if you consume large quantities of salty snacks, you overstimulate Water energy (where salty taste resides), resulting in overactive kidneys and bladder. Water energy, however, transports life force to the liver and gallbladder. So an overstimulation of Water energy—while overworking the kidneys and bladder—also results in the liver (Tree energy) becoming overtaxed, because Water nourishes Tree. The initial symptoms would manifest as irritability and short temperedness. If the kidneys continue to be overstimulated, they weaken, making you timid and tired. And over time, as the liver continues to be overworked, it becomes tired, resulting in dizziness, vision disorders, muscle and tendon pain, and an overall lack of vitality.

Ideally though, good health is maintained when all of the Five Transformations of Energy are evenly and actively nourishing each other, assisted by food and lifestyle choices. Not only must we nourish each stage, but we must be conscious of the flow of energy to maintain balance. To do so, we must be aware of the influences that each transformation has on its counterpart. This is where the *controlling cycle* comes into play.

The Controlling Cycle

Nature loves balance and so, within the Five Transformations of Energy, there is a natural control or limiting cycle—a natural system of checks and balances, if you will. In this cycle of energy movement, each stage serves to regulate and control its counterpart, preventing it from becoming excessive or stagnant, holding too much energy, and creating deficiencies and excesses in various organ systems. This controlling aspect of the Five Transformations regulates smooth organ function in the face of any excess, maintaining order within the grand scheme of things.

Each transformation of energy has an opposing, or complementary, energy working to maintain balance and stability of the energy flow through the body.

It goes like this: Fire energy (heart and small intestines) controls Metal energy (lungs and large intestines)—remember fire melts metal. Metal energy controls Tree energy (liver, gallbladder, nervous system)—think of an ax chopping wood. Tree energy controls Earth energy (spleen, pancreas, stomach)—think how plants draw nutrients from the earth. Earth energy controls Water energy (kidneys, bladder, reproductive organs)—earth absorbs water, creating mud. Water energy controls Fire energy—water can extinguish flames.

Within this check-and-balance system, excessive energy can be damped down and deficient energy can be made more active to create balance. Using both nourishing and controlling energies, you work to maintain smooth transformation of energy through the body. For example, if your kidney (Water) energy is weak or depleted, you feel tired and timid, and your skin has a washed-out look. To counter this, you nourish your Water energy by choosing foods with a Metal character, because Metal is the *supporting* energy of Water. If, however, the kidneys are overstimulated, so you have an excess of energy there— you feel jittery, inflexible, anxious, and unable to sleep. To settle things down you look to Water's *complementary* energy, Earth, because it can override excessive Water energy.

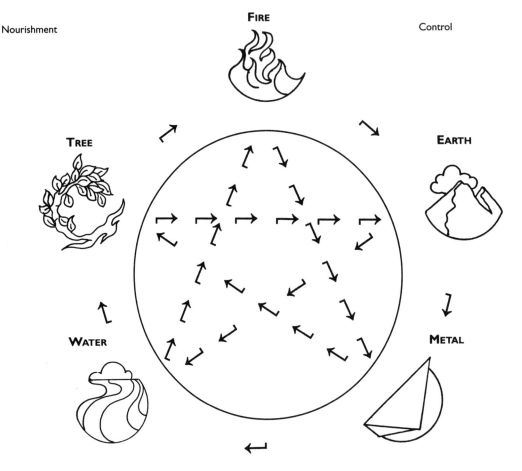

Nourishment

Control

FIRE

TREE

EARTH

WATER

METAL

When applied to our bodies in daily life, the Five Transformations of Energy show us how energy moves through us and how it affects each of our organs and its functions. Based on centuries of experience, practitioners of Chinese medicine have developed an understanding of the use of food, exercise, herbs, and other specifics to maintain our health and to change and heal various conditions, restoring our vitality.

Yin and yang, Five Transformations of Energy, nourishing and controlling cycles—you're probably wondering what all this has to do with the quality of your daily life and, specifically, your food. Life has many ups and downs, little adventures that keep us on our toes. If you are living in a more balanced state, these challenges are easier to handle. The way we live in the modern world violates nature at every turn. We live flat out, all or nothing, live hard, party hard—creating chaos in the process. When we live at a crazy pace, we create erratic energy, making balance harder to achieve. Think of it like this. Picture yourself standing on a seesaw. Which is easier—trying to balance with your feet perched at the outer ends of the planks or standing with your feet planted securely on either side of the center point? Although there is no such thing as perfect balance (or perfect health, for that matter), you can hover close to the center, maintaining a delicate fluctuation of movement, as you allow the world to gently expand and contract around you, with you an integral part of it all.

You can apply this thinking to everything in your life. If you live in extremes, the body becomes exhausted. You can choose to thrash wildly between these extreme points or you can rock gently back and forth, staying vital, alert yet calm. You can't completely avoid extremes in life. There will always be challenges like job stress, family issues, and too much work. Extreme living exacts a high toll; but if you generally live your life in a centered manner and take responsibility for what you can control, you will be prepared for the roadblocks that life throws in your path.

You can't control a lot of what happens in your daily life—not the weather or the traffic or the behavior of those around you. The one aspect of your life over which you do maintain complete and total control is your food choices. Only you decide what to put in your mouth from moment to moment. You may be influenced by lots of things—ancestry, habit, cultural images, and convenience; but ultimately, you make conscious (or unconscious) choices of what to eat. And the foods you choose determine who you are, how you feel, and the health of your body and emotions.

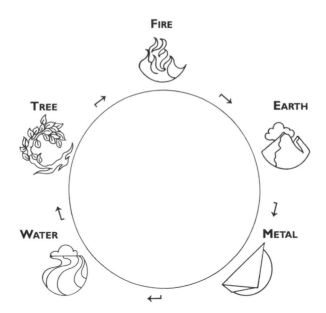

FIRE

TREE

EARTH

WATER

METAL

YOU ARE WHAT YOU EAT
THE FIVE TRANSFORMATIONS OF ENERGY

THE FIVE TRANSFORMATIONS of Energy theory is a system of approaching balance that is steeped in thousands of years of Chinese medicine. But what does that have to do with modern life? And more important, how can we apply it to our own lives in a practical manner? Let's look at the basis of the theory.

One of the most important tools in a wholistic approach to health, the Five Transformations of Energy theory was developed to reveal and explain the mysteries of life. Governing everything from time of day to seasons to organ function to health and agricul-

ture, this theory is a way of explaining yin and yang in terms that humanity can use in practical ways. The basis of Chinese medicine, this theory is the underlying influence of most wholistic modalities in use today, guiding the diagnosis, the recognition of imbalances, and the restoration of health and vitality.

So if this is natural law, why does the theory seem so foreign to us—and so difficult to understand? Simple. There is absolutely nothing in Western philosophy or thought remotely like the Five Transformations of Energy—nothing. Western culture does not use the wholistic approach to health and medicine. We have difficulty understanding that humanity and nature are united, and that body, mind, and spirit are unified. We tend to see them as three separate items housed in one organism, and think that humanity lives *on* its surroundings, instead of being a part of the greater scheme that makes up nature. Eastern thought professes, instead, that every phenomenon, visible or not, is connected, is one—from the ends of the galaxy to the simplest cell structure. That is a very big, and esoteric, view of nature.

In Asian thought, there is a life force that supports all phenomena—yin and yang, the natural shift of energy as it expands and contracts, appears and disappears. Western thought embraces that thought as well; we call it physics. In Chinese medicine, the Five Transformations of Energy are symbolic of the natural balance and order in nature. This balance is evident in every aspect of life. Once we understand and begin to apply this thinking to our own lives and health, the theory becomes quite simple and practical.

With the Five Transformations of Energy theory, yin and yang begin to break through the mysticism, becoming practical guides to seeing imbalance and regaining and maintaining health. With both flexibility and precision, the Five Transformations of Energy can be used to understand every aspect of our lives.

But how did we arrive at the particular structure that makes this theory work? Did the sages of Asia arbitrarily choose illustrations that suited them? Chinese scholars saw the transformation of energy from expansion to contraction as a process of change. The five transformations actually reflect five stages of change, as energy moves from phase to phase, contracting and expanding. Chinese healers saw each stage as a specific step in the ongoing process of change as an orderly process, a natural progression through five stages of energy shifts.

In general terms, the Five Transformations of Energy simply describe the process of change—as it occurs—expansion to contraction and back again. Each of the energy phases is an illustration of the forces that are shaping the shift that is happening—from season changes to time of day to health imbalances to any other phenomenon we call nature.

Within the Five Transformations of Energy theory, there are five points at which the shift of energy is tangible, noticeable. Each of these phases is unique, with many layers making up its character. Each stage of change is quite well defined, with characteristics so specific to its nature that it can never be confused with another phase. Knowing this, Asian scholars learned to use the theory to guide them in every aspect of life—from understanding the nature of nature to diagnosing and healing conditions of health.

Because the forces of life are so strongly evident to us in nature, Asian scholars used examples from nature to illustrate how the phases of energy change, nourish, and control each of the other phases in the continuum of balance. The Five Transformations of Energy as we know them are most clearly shown in the change of seasons—and so the examples used to explain the shifts in energy during expansion and contraction are drawn directly from shifts in nature as it moves through seasonal changes.

Take a look at the Fire phase. It doesn't take strong powers of deduction to see that this phase would be the illustration of summer, when the plants, trees, and flowers are at their most expanded phase of development, with their stalks at full height and leaves and flowers in full, lush bloom. It is also a time of expansion for us, with more time outdoors, more leisure, with vacation season in full swing. We open to the sun, just as plants do. With the sun high and strong, fire is the natural element to illustrate this season.

Next is the Earth phase. Asian scholars saw the short season just after high summer and before chilly autumn as a time with its own unique character. We, in North America, call it Indian summer. It's a very short period of time, sometimes lasting only days, almost like a pause between seasons. It's a calm time—we still spend time out of doors, but we are more inclined to be at home, to come indoors earlier. It's like the fire of summer has reduced to a simmer. Late summer is a time when life is calm. The earth itself seems on

hold, as the dramatic Fire energy of summer settles into the gathered, grounded time of autumn.

Metal energy shows itself in autumn. The opposite of summer, this season has the life force of earth retreating, withdrawing into the soil, contracting and gathering into itself, holding the potential for spring and the blossoming of plants deep in the earth. The air is cold and gray, causing us to hunch inward as we walk and move our lives more indoors.

With Water energy, we see winter. In this dormant phase of energy, the life forces of nature have completely retreated and are well hidden. Everything about this season seems like water—from the weaker sunlight to ice and snow. Everything seems to be resting—think how peaceful snowfall can be. But even a blizzard reflects that energy. We say that snowstorms are paralyzing to our ability to move about. Really, they just help us rest, by keeping us close to home.

And then there is Tree energy, the perfect picture of spring. Life bursts forth from the dormant earth. New life sprouts everywhere, with delicate shoots breaking through the soil, which will develop into the full-blown plants of summer, continuing the cycle into infinity.

So how does this apply to our bodies and daily lives? Asian scholars saw these illustrations of the shifts in energy as metaphors for the mysteries of life. Each energy phase contains within its character all the information we need to balance our lives and keep ourselves healthy (or regain our health). Through many years of study and observation of humanity, they discovered that during each season, certain parts of the body were more enlivened than they were at other times of the year, concluding that our bodies, just like other phenomena in nature, were specifically affected at certain times of the transformation of energy. What this means to us is that we can learn to use life's energies to change and redirect our own bodily functions, smoothing the path for organ function to be efficient and healthy.

So in the Five Transformations of Energy theory, each organ is paired with a related organ and categorized with the season or energy phase that best supports and nourishes their function.

Earth energy governs and enlivens the function of the spleen, stomach, and pancreas, organs that represent our "center." Its settled, calm energy is like late summer and keeps these organs on an even keel.

Metal energy governs and enlivens the function of the lungs and large intestines, organs that represent our potential, drawing our energy in like autumn. This is where our "gutsiness" comes from as well as our ability to "take a deep breath and push on."

Water energy governs and enlivens the function of the kidneys, bladder, and reproductive organs, the seat of our life force, where all of our energy lays in wait, to be tapped into and brought to the surface, not unlike the energy of winter.

Tree energy governs and enlivens the function of the liver, gallbladder and nervous system, the organs and systems that allow our bodies to open and relax by removing toxins and sending out feelers to our surroundings. Like spring, the energy here is clean, sprouting, moving energy.

Fire energy governs and enlivens the function of the heart and small intestines, the organs that are the seat of our passions, our will, and our personality. In this energy, like during the summer season, we blossom forth in all our glory.

When applied to human life and body functions, the Five Transformations of Energy theory can be a useful tool for figuring out how and why certain things are happening.

THE EARTH TRANSFORMATION

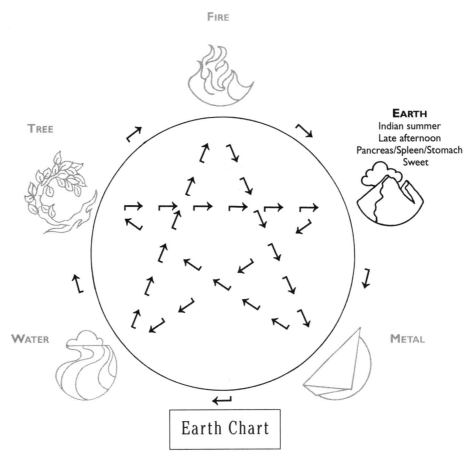

FIRE

TREE

EARTH
Indian summer
Late afternoon
Pancreas/Spleen/Stomach
Sweet

WATER

METAL

Earth Chart

Energy

    Earth energy is considered the center of everything. The epitome of stability, Earth energy is seen as one of the most balanced states of the cycle of energy movement. Earth represents grounded, centered energy, as well as perseverance and resourcefulness.

Season

    Indian summer (harvest)

Time of Day

    Late afternoon

Organ Systems

    Pancreas

    Spleen

    Stomach

Color

    Yellow

Taste
    Mildly sweet

Cooking Techniques
    Boiling
    Simmering
    Stewing

Expression
    Humming
    Singing

Emotions
    Compassionate
    Self-assured
    Thoughtful

Grain
    Millet

Bean
    Chickpea

Vegetables
    Cabbage
    Parsnip
    Pumpkin
    Rutabaga
    Winter squash

Fruits
    Cantaloupe
    Currants
    Honeydew
    Raisins
    Sweet apples
    Sweet cherries
    Sweet grapes
    Tangerines

Sweeteners
    Barley malt
    Brown rice syrup
    Wheat malt

Nuts
    Almond
    Pecan

The stable nature of Earth has many faces. Seen as the beginning of energy gathering together, Earth is animated during the season of late (Indian) summer, as we harvest, and during the late afternoon, as we gather together in the home as the day comes to a close. The organs associated with Earth—the spleen, pancreas, and stomach—are active during this time of day. The color associated with this energy is yellow, the color of early autumn.

Mildly sweet (not sugar sweet, but the *natural* sweet of food) is the flavor that animates this energy; sweet foods relax the body and make us comfortable. Let me explain natural sweet taste. As a culture, we think of sweet as being dessert sweet. By *sweet*, I mean satisfying and satiating. You know the feeling when you are nourished to the core of your being. You sit back from eating, completely contented. So when I refer to foods such as chickpeas and winter squash as tasting sweet, I refer to their natural ability to make us feel deeply nourished. Of course, dessert sweet resides in this energy as well, using grain sweeteners and some fruits to create deeply nourishing treats.

Stewing and boiling, cooking techniques that warm and relax us, are associated with this energy transformation. The sound that supports and nourishes Earth energy is humming or singing, which, as we know, relaxes and nourishes our spirits, in many cases moving us deeply.

When Earth energy is strong and balanced, we possess a great capacity for compassion and consideration for the feelings of others. A strong sense of Earth energy makes us thoughtful, with an innate ability to maintain a sense of direction in our lives. Sure of our abilities when earth is in strong balance, we have the luxury of generosity of spirit, because we know how deep our own capacities run. On the downside, however, should Earth energy become stagnant, blocked, depleted, or excessive, we experience life quite differently.

With an imbalance of Earth energy, we fall into the depths of self-pity. We begin to lose our capacity to deal with life on any level—mundane demands placed on us leave us depleted and overwhelmed. Dreams remain important to us, but we can no longer cope. We no longer have the energy to rise to the challenge to make our dreams a reality. We begin to expect to fail—and so we do.

When our Earth energy remains depleted or blocked, we begin to look to others to feed us energy. Earth's nature is to *give* compassion; but if that energy is depleted or stagnant, we seek compassion from those around us—in fact, we demand it. We feel neglected and victimized if others don't respond as we think they should. We take on the persona of the whining, complaining, weak victim.

We grow increasingly concerned about our health; as a result, we begin to become alienated from those around us. Our neediness causes others to avoid us. As we become more isolated, we grow cynical and suspicious of human sincerity, always looking for people's dark side, rarely seeing the goodness in our community of friends and acquaintances. As the imbalance becomes more acute, we become jealous of everyone else's happiness and see ourselves as martyrs, sacrificing our lives to a cold, unfeeling world. At its worst, an Earth imbalance can find us consciously (while unconscious of the imbalance) placing ourselves in jeopardy to elicit sympathy from those around us.

These are outward, physical signs of Earth imbalance, and the deeply disturbing emotional symptoms can indicate an internal energetic imbalance that requires our attention.

With an Earth imbalance, we tend to have loose, weak muscles, especially in the legs. Women with this imbalance tend to hold weight in the lower body, bulking up in the buttocks and thighs. Men hold the weight in their midsection, looking soft and doughy. Interestingly, the loose muscle tone will show in the face, with ill-defined features and slack facial expressions. The face is slightly puffy and washed out. It appears to lack clear sharp expressiveness.

Even bodily gestures seem to lack definition. With an Earth imbalance, we'll make gestures that just seem to trail off, with no completion—almost as though we didn't have the strength to finish. It's as if limbs are too heavy for us to use them expressively.

The voice may be where we notice the most dramatic characteristics however. When Earth energy is imbalanced, our voice takes on a whining quality, with our sentences often trailing off at the end, without completion. There are lots of sighs in between words, and the voice may rise in pitch at the end of the sentence, as though we were so unsure, we couldn't make a definitive statement, questioning everything.

Here's how it works physically. The spleen, pancreas, and stomach serve as the storage organs for the blood supply to the body. They also serve as an integral part of the lymphatic system, protecting the body from infection. Further, the spleen stores elements that are taken from damaged cells for use later when the body needs them. Note that all these functions have to do with the *gathering* of resources, storage for us to draw on as the need arises.

The pancreas regulates the blood sugar levels, which is the body's way of controlling our stored resources of energy. When the pancreas overworks, becomes aggravated and depleted, our body functions are altered.

Here's the connection: Earth energy, it is said in Asian medicine, activates the function of the spleen, pancreas, and stomach. Because we, as human beings, have a conscious connection to our body and how we feel, we are aware of our resources and how full or low our stores are. So we realize on an intuitive level when we are low, stagnant, depleted. As a result, when we recognize that we have little energy on which to draw, we do not extend ourselves. We can no longer rise to a challenge, growing increasingly dependent on other people to meet our needs.

The condition known as hypoglycemia, or an abnormal decrease of sugar in the blood, is a good example. As a culture, we eat tremendous amounts of simple, refined sugars, which break down very quickly and enter the bloodstream almost immediately upon consumption, altering the blood chemistry instantly. As a result, blood sugar levels will rise and drop dramatically, creating extreme levels of nervous energy alternating with lethargy and weakness. When the blood sugar drops, leaving us with no reserves to draw on, we grow weak; our limbs tremble; and in more serious cases, we become disoriented. The solution? We take in more sugar—candy, chocolate, cookies, orange juice—to raise the blood sugar quickly to a normal level and to get the body functioning. Simple sugars, however, do not create any *stores* of energy to be used to keep the blood sugar levels on an even keel. As we continue this pattern, the dramatic shifts in blood sugar levels weaken the organs, especially the pancreas. We find that the periods of elated feelings of energy that we get from sugar become shorter and shorter, requiring more and more sugar to create the illusion of normal function. As this continues, we begin to exhibit the emotional behavior that goes along with an Earth imbalance.

So what do we do? How do we restore and maintain our Earth energy to keep it nourished and moving smoothly through us? Although we do need to draw from all of the Five Transformations of Energy so that they transition from one to the next smoothly, each person has different needs and natural desires. To strengthen and rebalance Earth energy, we choose foods animated by it, and supplement with foods animated by Fire energy, the transformation that supports and nourishes it.

Sweetly Stable Earth Characters

Foods that enhance, nourish, and support Earth energy come from all of the plant world—grains, beans, vegetables, and fruits—but some of these foods are more Earth oriented, if you will.

Ceres, the Roman goddess of agriculture, gives us the word *cereal,* referring to the family of grasses known to us as cereal grains—the most important food of humankind.

Most grasses are perennial; their flowers have no petals. Grains are the fruit as well as the seeds of the plant. They have within them the ability to rebuild themselves by using the materials of their own construction. Cereal grasses contain the most highly evolved seed of any food plant, meaning that their embryologic roots, stems, and leaves have the same patterns as those of mature, fully developed plants. So choosing whole grains creates in us a similar energy. By consuming foods that contain within them the patterns for growth from embryo to maturity, we create within us the same energetic quality. You might say that one energy reinforces the strength of the other. This growth process can be likened to that of humans—our embryo stage contains all the patterns needed for full maturity.

Grains that enhance Earth energy nourish and relax the middle of the body—the spleen, pancreas and stomach—making its function efficient and smooth. When this part of us is relaxed, our emotional stability follows in suit. The grain best suited to this task is millet, a tiny yellow grain that produces no stomach acid, so it is digested quite easily, leaving us feeling relaxed and comforted.

Beans are also a good choice for nourishing Earth energy, especially chickpeas. These round, mild, nutty beans are a bit fattier than other beans, thus their relaxing nature. And because they relax us and open us to others around us, they are thought to be aphrodisiacs in some cultures.

Vegetable choices come from those that grow close to the ground and have mild characters—but when cooked, sweeten deliciously. Vegetables that grow close to the ground and are filled with seeds (squash and cucumbers) or wrap their leaves around their core (cabbage) have energy that focuses on the middle of the body, keeping us centered, like its own core or seed bowl. That kind of calm, grounded feeling brings us not only clear focus but also a relaxed serenity that allows us to see clearly, so we can act decisively, but with compassion. Winter squash, (including butternut, buttercup, acorn, hubbard, pumpkin, and Hokkaido), artichokes, parsnips, rutabagas, and green cabbages serve us best to create Earth energy in us.

Mildly sweet fruits, even though they are simple sugar, can be enjoyed on occasion without creating too much havoc to your system. Sweet apples, sweet grapes, cantaloupe, honeydew, raisins, tangerines, currants, and sweet cherries are the best choices. Cook these fruits with a pinch of salt to soften them, to make them easier to digest, and to gentle the sugars a bit. Keep in mind what fruit is and the function it performs in nature, and you may see it in a new light. Fruit has the important job of making sure the seed is carried safely to the ground in a vessel (the fruit) that will degenerate quickly and turn into fuel for the seeds' growth (sugar). So in Asian medicine, fruit is likened to the phase of life just before decay. Too much fruit, therefore, can make you weak. Yet you can still enjoy fruit now and then—nature has provided it, after all. Just enjoy it moderately.

For sweeteners, which are nourished most strongly in this energy phase, avoid simple and refined sugar—including sugar, confectioners' sugar, brown sugar, raw sugar, date sugar, organic sugar, cane juice, molasses, honey, maple syrup, fructose, dextrose, and maltose. Even those so-called natural sugars are simple in structure and will affect our health negatively. Use only sweeteners made from whole grains, such as rice syrup, barley malt, and wheat malt. These sweeteners, although still sugar, began their journey to glucose conversion (when they become our fuel) as complex carbohydrates and so break down in the blood relatively slowly. As a result, they don't alter the blood chemistry quite as dramatically as simple sugars, which affect the blood chemistry almost instantly upon ingestion, upsetting the glucose balance in the bloodstream. The resulting roller coaster of moods and energy levels is a minor inconvenience compared to the fact that each ingestion of simple sugar *suppresses immune function for five hours*.

For added energy and vitality, choose almonds and pecans for a pick-me-up that strengthens Earth nature. In nature, nuts hold the imprint for entire trees in them, so they pack a wallop of energy and vitality—eaten in moderation, anyway. If you consume large quantities of nuts, you'll develop nervous energy. Know what your food does before you eat it.

As you work with the Earth recipes, remember that—although other energy transformations may be a part of the recipe (*everything* contains all five, you'll recall)—dishes that fall under this transformation have the effect on us that they do because the Earth nature is most predominant.

THE METAL TRANSFORMATION

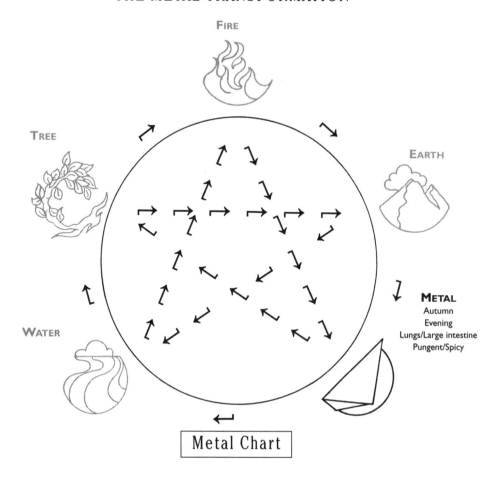

Metal Chart

Energy

Metal energy symbolizes the most contracted, compact of the energy phases. Within Metal energy resides condensation and accumulation—it is the realization of all our potential, with all our possibilities to be achieved. It is the root of our energy; it's where we pull together our resources and figure out how to apply them.

Season

Autumn

Time of Day

Evening

Organ Systems

Large intestines
Lungs

Colors

Gray
White

Taste

Sharply pungent

Cooking Techniques

Pressure cooking
Baking
Roasting

Expression

Weeping

Emotions

Self-discipline
Optimism

Grains

Brown rice
Sweet brown rice
Mochi

Beans

Soybean
Tempeh
Tofu
White beans

Vegetables

Bok choy
Carrot
Cauliflower
Celery
Chinese cabbage
Cucumber
Daikon
Ginger
Leek
Lotus root
Onion
Shallot
Turnip
Watercress

Fruits

Apricots

Peaches

Pears

Nuts

Walnuts

Metal energy displays itself in nature in many ways. The most condensed, descending energy phase, Metal is typified by the color white. Autumn and the evening animate this energy phase. Autumn, while a time of harvest, holds within it the promise of the seasons. Evening holds the expectation of night. The expression that is associated with Metal energy is weeping, a sound that softens our hearts and opens us to many potential feelings.

With a sharp, pungent flavor as its signature, and baking, roasting, and pressure cooking as the techniques that most nourish Metal energy, we create a sense of deep strength and capacity. Sharp, pungent taste would be like that of daikon or ginger—warm, peppery, but earthy, not the kind of spicy taste you would get from chili peppers, which give you a fiery, opening heat and energy. The organs associated with this energy are the lungs and large intestines, which represent the seat of our strength. Without lung function, we can't breathe. If we can't assimilate and use food, we can't live and remain strong. Lungs and large intestines are where we build our

potential, by refreshing and nourishing our body.

Balanced Metal energy manifests itself as self-discipline and optimism. This stage of transformation holds within it the capacity to use our past experiences to create the potential of our future. Asian medicine holds that the large intestines propagate the right way of living as well as generating evolution and change. True to the Asian nature, living right means more than eating the right foods; it means developing the capacity to learn from life and then create the life one is meant to live—to the fullest potential.

With balanced Metal energy working in us, we are positive, organized, detail oriented, and able to rise to any challenge that comes our way. We maintain discipline, with an open, positive view of life's potential.

In the theory of the Five Transformations of Energy, the lungs and large intestines are associated with assimilation and elimination—not only of physical food but of past patterns and habits. Just as our lungs and large intestines take in what is needed from our environment and release what is not necessary, so go our emotions. Our ability to let go of negative thoughts and emotions, memories and past experiences that can hold us back is reflected in the health of our lungs and large intestines. Strong, balanced Metal energy allows us to operate on an even keel, with a positive acceptance of life and its adventures. We can learn from the past and let go of the memories and experiences that prevent us from moving forward in our lives.

As Metal energy becomes deficient, excessive, stuck, or aggravated, it produces "sinking" feelings in us; we grow more introverted and indecisive. Depression and lethargy follow as the imbalance continues. With a Metal energy imbalance, we lose our ability to cope with even the smallest challenge. We become frozen, incapacitated, unable to face even the slightest adversity. If Metal energy is out of balance when we are presented with a problem, we can't see any positive way out of any situation. Confused thinking comes into play.

Different from when Earth energy is out of kilter, Metal energy imbalances cause us to blame ourselves, instead of the world at large, for our problems. There must be something seriously wrong with us to have become so pathetic in life. We see ourselves as a burden to those around us; we are in the way of life. If we allow the imbalance to worsen and deepen, we grow increasingly introverted, losing interest in our environment totally. We grow unresponsive, immobilized, and consumed by negative thoughts.

Physical signs of Metal energy imbalances are most evident in the body's movements—or lack of them. When this energy is off, we lack animation. Our hand gestures are minimal. Weak upper arms, with an inability to lift things, is characteristic of this imbalance. With slouched, rounded shoulders and the head bent forward, a Metal energy imbalance makes us look as if we have the weight of the world on us. Our complexion becomes white and chalky, and our skin has a slightly loose quality.

The voice takes on a monotonous quality, with little affect or inflection. We seem to drone on, rather than speak. It's almost as though by removing animation from our speech, we reinforce our own warped self-image of not being important. The breathy quality in the voice sounds like we have pressure on the chest and are unable to take in sufficient air. As our weakness deepens, we become self-absorbed and overly protective of what we see as our limited vitality.

Because within Metal energy there lies potential for anything, an imbalance can show itself in a tight, contracted, rigid nature. Imbalanced Metal energy can lead to an overly controlling attitude. The control freaks of the world live here. We may push ourselves as though we had no limits. We ignore pain and deny ourselves pleasure. We push through fatigue, hunger, and stress. Food is only fuel, not something to be enjoyed; it serves just to keep us going. Muscles and joints grow stiff and immovable; we see ourselves as machines.

Emotionally, a Metal energy imbalance is evident when we hold on to the past and any slight that was ever visited on us. We see things only in extremes: black and white, right or wrong, good or bad. We resist change as being too painful to bear, growing bitter and unrelenting in life.

Here's how the physical part works. The large intestines serve not only as our major excretory organ but also as the regulator of fluid in our body, and are the primary area of fluid absorption. Consider the importance of moisture regulation to the lungs. If excess liquid gathers in the lungs, then oxygen absorption is inhibited and carbon dioxide is not released. Remember that it is oxygen that nourishes the brain to create the thought that results in constructive action, moving us forward.

If the brain is regularly deprived of oxygen, we can't think clearly. We become confused. Because the body is focused on sustaining our most basic functions, we find it hard work to maintain our level of concentration. If the lungs aren't functioning at top capacity, then the blood isn't well oxygenated and the brain is undernourished. If the lungs are operating at optimum levels, then we can think clearly and take action. It's worth noting that people who we describe as depressed or overtired tend to breathe deeply or sigh excessively.

Our capacity to be propelled into action comes from the strength of our intestines. We often use the term *gutsy* to refer to people who go for it, move, and take action. That strength comes from intestinal fortitude. If the intestines are strong and smooth functioning, then fluid is balanced in the body.

The lungs are working at their peak, and the brain is receiving the right amount of oxygen. Thought is clear, and action is decisive. It all works together.

To balance the strong, contracted Metal energy, choose foods that are animated by it and support it with the nourishing energy of Earth, which will keep Metal energy moving smoothly, keeping us strong and focused on our path.

Strengthening Metal Characters

To keep the gathered, dense energy of Metal strong and balanced, but not frozen and stagnant, we can choose from a variety of grains, beans, vegetables, and fruits.

Of all the grains, brown rice, sweet brown rice, and mochi will keep Metal energy at its most acute. With qualities of endurance and adaptability, rice promotes stamina and focus. Brown rice is perfectly balanced nutritionally, with the added bonus that it has the uncanny ability to regulate moisture in the body. Too much, and it dries us out a bit—too little, and it will not allow us to soak moisture up as needed. Rice behaves in the body as a mild diuretic; its mineral composition and astringent nature help the body release excess fluid that may accumulate in tissues. If, on the other hand, the body tends to be dry, then rice will use its capacity to absorb fluid (just like it does when it cooks) to help body tissues do the same thing.

Remember that cereal grasses contain the most highly evolved seed of any food plant, meaning that their embryologic roots, stems, and leaves have the same patterns as those of mature, fully developed plants, similar to the way we grow from an embryo, with the memory patterns to reach full maturity.

The edible portion of cereal grains is the kernel. It is, in reality, a complete fruit. Grains, like rice, contain the ability to reproduce in great abundance from a single seed, making them highly productive plants. Each whole cereal grain represents both the beginning and end of the plant's life—containing within it all the potential and energy of the entire plant. Because of this unique character, grains, more than any other food, have the greatest capacity for increasing human potential—on all levels of our existence. Their ability to reproduce in great quantity, with very little help—or interference—from us, as well as their adaptability and versatility, make grains—especially brown rice—the most important food for humanity. Cereals, the seeds of nourishment, are the evolution of past, present, and future blood quality that will determine the health of humanity. Whole grains have the ability to finely tune the human nervous system, unifying all organ function into one smoothly operating organism.

The beans that serve us the best in nourishing Metal energy include Great Northern beans, baby limas, navy beans, soybeans, tempeh, and tofu, all of which create a sense of compassion in us, as well as a calm, centered endurance. Their cooling natures relax us and allow us to think creatively to solve any problems we may face. A bean is essentially a single seed that produces a plant and contains within its seed more concentrated amounts of protein, starch, and iron than any other plant. With their incredible natural immune defense, they strengthen and energize us like nothing else. The protein that we get from beans is quite calming and soothing compared to animal protein, which creates internal heat and aggression.

Tofu and tempeh are remarkable foods. Tofu, with its mild character, can be deceiving. Made by pressing the curd that is extracted from cooked soybeans, this simple food comes to life when combined with any number of seasonings and cooking styles, from frying to baking to marinating. High in calcium, protein, and phytochemicals, tofu is essential to a healthy diet.

Tempeh, unlike tofu, is not so mild. Made by fermenting soybeans, tempeh has a meaty, dense texture and strong, earthy flavor, making it ideally suited to stews and casseroles and sandwiches. Marinated, grilled, fried, or simmered, tempeh is a great source of calcium and protein. And its fermented nature helps the body with the digestive process.

The vegetables for Metal energy ground us, center our focus, and sharpen our thinking. Roots of plants are incredibly self-centered, in that their only goal is to nourish and strengthen themselves. They transform mineral into vegetable to nourish the plant. They stabilize the plant and draw nutrients into the plant from the soil. They store nutrients for distribution to the plant as needed. Root vegetables, like carrots and turnips, drill deeply into the soil, firmly planting themselves in the earth, helping us hold our focus. Roots like onion, shallots, and daikon, with their peppery taste, stimulate our circulation, cleansing the blood, giving us clear, sharp, thinking. Cooled and calmed by refreshing energy, leeks, bok choy, cauliflower, celery, Chinese cabbage, cucumber, and watercress allow us to relax and open to the many options before us. Unlike roots that are held tight to the ground, these vegetables are the *beginning* of Metal energy's opening that allow us to realize our potential.

Lotus root, an exotic tuber, is known for its ability to dissolve mucus and hardened fat in the lungs and large intestines. With its many chambers and astringent quality, this potato-like vegetable can increase lung capacity and focus our thought as our blood gets more oxygen to feed our brain.

This section wouldn't be complete without mentioning ginger. Tropical by nature, this underground root is a tuber that thrives in hot, humid climates. It's long been revered for its medicinal powers, because it drives warming energy into the body, improving circulation, in imitation of its downward growth pattern. Stimulating to the middle organs, it is particularly effective in softening and opening the pancreas, liver, spleen, and large intestines, releasing stored energy and digestive enzymes.

Fruits don't really strengthen Metal energy, but choosing the more contracted, less sweet peaches, apricots, and pears can nourish this energy by relaxing our bodies and preventing rigidity, a common imbalance in this transformation. Walnuts, with their pungent flavor, focus our thinking and give us great vitality.

As for all transformations, the recipes under the Metal sign contain more than one energy phase, but they have Metal energy as the controlling influence.

THE WATER TRANSFORMATION

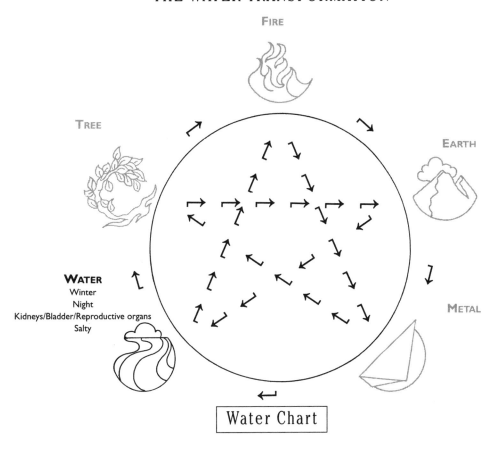

FIRE

TREE

EARTH

WATER
Winter
Night
Kidneys/Bladder/Reproductive organs
Salty

METAL

Water Chart

Energy

Symbolic of the first movement toward expansion, Water is the energy of spontaneity. This is the phase in which we open ourselves to all possibilities. The movement here is floating, viscous, spreading in all directions like flowing water. Flexible, this energy adapts to any variety of conditions, creating our sense of exploration and adventure.

Season

Winter

Time of Day

Night

Organ Systems

Bladder

Kidneys

Reproductive organs

Colors

Black

Deep blue

Purple

Taste

Salty

Cooking Techniques

Salt pickling

Steaming

Expression

Groaning

Emotions

Adaptability

Adventurous

Resourceful

Grain

Kasha (buckwheat)

Beans

Azuki

Black soybean

Black turtle

Kidney

Pinto

Vegetables

Burdock

Radicchio

Red cabbage

Sea vegetables

Agar

Arame

Dulse

Hiziki

Kombu

Nori

Wakame

Shiitake mushrooms

Water chestnuts

Fruits

Blackberries

Blueberries

Chestnuts

Cranberries

Sour grapes

Watermelon

Condiments

Miso

Sea salt

Soy sauce

Tamari

Umeboshi plums

Umeboshi vinegar

Water energy is responsible for holding our deepest life force, dispersing our essence to the rest of the body and nourishing and supporting our vitality. Considered to be at the core of our being, Water energy is responsible for survival and fear, as well as being the very root of our will.

Water energy has within it great flexibility and is thought to be the start of ascending energy. The colors associated with this changeable phase are black, deep blue, and purple, all colors that have great potential, depth, and adaptability. It is easy to see why winter and nighttime are the season and time of day that support this energy. In the dark of night, we go indoors, resting and gathering our energy, reflecting on our goals. In the cold weather of winter, we are more adventurous with sports like skiing, cross-country hiking, and other outdoor activities that demand our courage. This is the perfect illustration of the polarity that can exist in Water energy. On one hand, this flexible energy allows us to be introspective, resting, like the energy of winter. On the other hand, Water energy makes us adaptable and open to possibilities, nourishing our adventurous side. Seems paradoxical—and it is; but it is the nature of nature. Associated with ears and hearing, the sound that supports Water energy is low moaning.

Moderately salty flavor supports this energy phase, because it is essential to strong blood, lymph, and other body fluids. Salt is essential to cooking. It makes food taste like itself, bringing forth the strengths and flavors to the surface, opening the food to all possibilities; however, food should never taste salty. Salt's job is to make food shine, which is why we miss it so much when it's not there. So salty taste is simply about using salt to enhance the characters of other foods. The ascending energy of steaming and the salty flavor of pickling are the most nourishing cooking styles of this powerful energy phase. Governing the vitality of the kidneys, bladder,

and reproductive organs, rest and rejuvenation are key. In our modern culture of all-or-nothing living, we tend to overburden our kidneys, with little concern for gathering and refreshing their strength. If that is missing, Water energy will evaporate, leaving the body tired and weak.

With Water energy in balance, we can realize our adventurous side. Strong Water energy shows itself in our ability to rise to a challenge, to meet situations head on and deal with them. This phase, in balance, gives us the capacity to extend ourselves beyond the familiar. It creates in us a curiosity and desire to experience all that the world has to offer. It creates the confidence we need to face, with grace and style, the little adventures life throws our way.

If the Water phase becomes imbalanced, either deficient, stagnant, excessive, or aggravated, we experience this energy in a different manner. Diminished or stagnant Water energy will leave us feeling inhibited and tentative about life, developing deeper fears as the imbalance continues. Anxious—with a lack of confidence—and even fearful are the characteristic behaviors of Water energy imbalance. We begin to see the world as a threatening, terrifying place and ourselves as weak and vulnerable to any number of harmful influences.

When this energy is low or diminished, we fear for our very survival, seeing the world as filled with danger. The sense of adventure is lost to us. Change becomes intolerable, and we hold on to our current environment as if it were a life raft. Unlike the inability to act that goes with a Metal energy imbalance, we take action. We grow increasingly controlling of our surroundings, developing all sorts of phobias. Acute, clinical fears come when Water energy is dangerously depleted.

Depleted Water energy shows itself in us physically as well as emotionally. We display lots of nervous energy, maybe even physical ticks or twitches. Our movements become jerky and sudden, lacking fluid grace. We appear anxious or agitated. Often constant eye movement accompanies this imbalance, as though we were always surveying our surroundings for threats.

Body language appears to be quite self-protective, with arms crossed over the chest and with our backs to the wall, literally. Always feeling vulnerable and exposed, we think we must be aware of everything going on around us, so there will be no surprise attacks.

Water energy is the energy that supports our sexual vitality, so we develop trouble relating to romantic partners when we're out of balance here. A characteristic stance for this condition is to stand or sit with legs crossed to protect our sexual region.

A dark or deep blue color will appear on the skin when Water energy is out of whack, especially under the eyes and at the corners of the mouth; we take on an overall washed-out look. A chronically aching lower back indicates that the kidneys have become overtired. Swelling of the feet and ankles means that the kidneys are too weakened to do their job efficiently. The voice loses its power, lacking depth and sounding watery and halting, as though we had been weeping.

Water energy can be aggravated or excessive, but that is quite rare in our modern world. We tend much more toward depleted, weak energy, that leaves us chronically fatigued and unstable. Too much of this energy creates reckless courage, with a feeling of arrogant invincibility. We go against the crowd just for the thrill of being different. Fearless nonconformists, we enjoy the thrill of danger, of putting it all on the line, life on the edge. We grow insensitive, so only danger can create feelings of exhilaration in us. A dangerous imbalance, our judgment is often clouded, truly placing us in jeopardy.

When Water energy is excessive, we speak with a strong, almost rumbling voice, the sound mirroring all the frozen, rigid energy within. Puffy skin under the eyes and a rigid, stiff lower back and lower limbs indicate this condition.

Here's what the kidneys, bladder, and reproductive organs mean to us physically. Water energy animates the function of these organs. Of foremost concern here is the function of the adrenal glands (located just above the kidneys). If the adrenal glands are not working properly, then the body's internal alarm sounds, telling us that we can't respond quickly to a threat. The malfunction of these organs inhibits our fight-or-flight instinct. This malfunction supports our feelings of vulnerability and fear.

The adrenal function works hand in hand with the kidneys. Filtering toxins from the blood, the kidneys also balance the electrolyte level in the bloodstream, which determines the level of responsiveness of our nervous system. So again, the kidneys govern how we perceive threat and how we respond to that threat.

Water energy also governs our sexuality. According to Asian medicine, Water energy is thought of as ancestral energy, governing the creation of life. So if this energy is depleted, stagnant, or aggravated, we grow weak or rigid. Either way, we lose the ability to respond sexually. If an imbalance is allowed to continue and deepen, we begin to fear intimacy. We actually feel less; and as we weaken, we lose interest.

What should we do to keep our kidneys, adrenals, bladder, and reproductive systems strong? Choose foods that are animated by Water energy, and nourish and support this transformation with foods from the energy of potential, Metal.

The Changeable Characters of Water

The foods animated by the energy of Water are those that create strength in us, keep our sense of adventure alive, and keep our center intact and our relationships tender.

Soup resides in Water energy. Although the energies from soups come from all the energy phases, the gentle, fluid energy that is Water is the predominate character of soup.

Soup or broth corresponds with the primordial sea, where life began. When we eat soup, we are returning to our evolutionary roots, so to speak, renewing our life energies. Throughout history, soup has been an integral part of all traditional cuisines.

For whole grains, buckwheat serves us best. Grown under cold, adverse conditions, in poor soil, buckwheat has a strong, warm energy that prepares us for hard work or to rise to a challenge. It is a great grain for weakened conditions or when we're feeling chronically tired. Buckwheat isn't a grain, but a dried fruit kernel, like the seeds of a strawberry. High in amino acids, especially lysine, buckwheat makes for strong digestion. Because of its capacity to grow in adverse conditions, buckwheat is said to bring out the individualist in us.

Azuki, black beans, pinto beans, black soybeans, and kidney beans nourish our Water energy. Because of their low fat and high mineral content, as well as their adaptable, strengthening natures, these are ideal choices for maintaining the equilibrium of Water energy. These beans create a warm, dry energy in the body, making the perfect environment for Water energy to thrive.

Sea vegetables like agar, arame, dulse, hiziki, kombu, nori, and wakame give us flexible energy, and their high mineral content keeps the blood strong and pure. Rich in calcium, B vitamins, vitamin C, and iodine, sea plants can offset the effects of radiation therapy, prevent and lower high blood pressure, reduce cholesterol, improve circulation, and offset tumor growth. Use them wisely, however. Sea vegetables are mineral packed and if consumed excessively make the body tight and dry, resulting in a tendency to overeat and a craving for sweets in an attempt to balance the contracted condition that has developed.

Burdock, a root that drills deep into the soil but is balanced by expansive green tops, is a great example of the many directions of Water energy, with both expansive and contracted energy. Burdock alkalizes the blood and strengthens our sexual vitality. Burdock is a strong root that grows in a direct, straight line. If it encounters a rock in its growth path, it will split the rock. This incredible strength and focus give us a clear view of our goals.

The other vegetable choices for Water energy—mushrooms, radicchio, red cabbage, and water chestnuts—clean and add needed minerals to the blood. Of all the water vegetables, shiitake mushrooms are the most potent. Prized in Asia as the food for cleaning the blood and lowering cholesterol, these mushrooms have the ability to relax tight, frozen areas of the body. Tight lower backs respond, as do rigid neck muscles and hard calves. Rigid joints can benefit from a few shiitake mushrooms each week. But here is a caution: Be sure to use only dried shiitake mushrooms in your cooking, not the fresh ones that have become so popular these days. Shiitake mushrooms are considered to be quite expansive—and if eaten fresh they can be weakening. The dried version works deep in the body, but lets you keep your strength—a better choice, by far.

Fruits such as succulent, moist blackberries, blueberries, cranberries, grapes, and watermelon can relax the body, because their concentrated amounts of water diminish the affects of their sugar. Also, sweet, succulent, and fat-free chestnuts make the greatest creamy puddings and pie fillings.

Salt should also be considered as a support to Water energy. Umeboshi plums are made into a sour-salty pickle used as a condiment. Its balanced, centered energy neutralizes extreme foods, aids digestion, strengthens the blood, and neutralizes acidic conditions. Sea salt, miso, soy sauce, tamari, and umeboshi vinegar and paste, used in reasonable amounts, keep Water energy enlivened.

THE TREE TRANSFORMATION

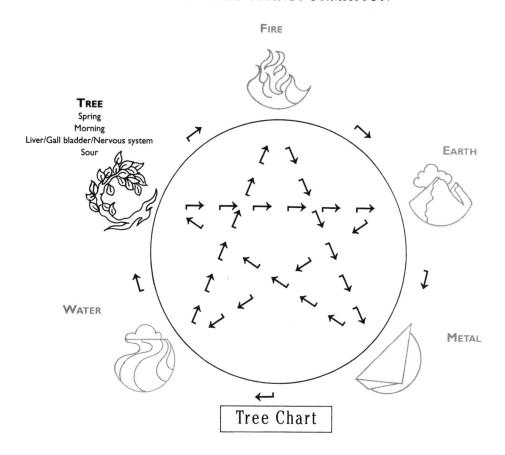

TREE
Spring
Morning
Liver/Gall bladder/Nervous system
Sour

FIRE

EARTH

METAL

WATER

Tree Chart

Energy

A strongly ascending energy, a tree branches out, while remaining rooted in the earth. Here lives inspiration and creativity. Tree energy allows us to be lighthearted and free-spirited. This upward, lifting energy gives us sprouting, fresh vitality.

Season

Spring

Time of Day

Morning

Organ Systems

Gallbladder
Liver
Nervous system

Color

Spring green

Taste
Lightly sour

Cooking Techniques
Blanching
Light pickling
Sautéing

Expression
Shouting

Emotions
Carefree
Optimistic
Patient

Grains
Barley
Oats
Rye
Wheat

Beans
Black-eyed peas
Green lentils
Peanuts
Split peas

Vegetables
Alfalfa sprouts
Artichoke
Broccoli
Green beans
Green peas

Lettuce
Parsley
Summer squash

Fruits
Granny Smith apples
Lemons
Limes
Plums
Pomegranates

Oils
Corn
Olive
Peanut
Safflower
Sesame
All other

Pickles
Olives
Sauerkraut
Sour pickles

The characteristic color for Tree energy, green illustrates the light fresh energy of spring, when all things are reaching toward the sun, growing and developing to their fullest potential. Even the animating flavor, lightly sour, makes our energy rise and move through us. Think of your body's reaction to biting into a lemon or lime. You literally suck in air and feel your energy rise and open. Sour taste, with its slightly astringent quality, opens us and relaxes any tightness in the body as stagnant energy begins to move. Early morning activates Tree energy when we go from resting in a horizontal position to an upright stance, venturing out into the sun, active and moving, facing the day with vitality.

Even the cooking techniques are light and vitalizing—sautéing; blanching; and sour pickling, made with vinegar and salt or citrus and salt to enhance the sour flavor. The organs animated by this energy phase are the liver, gallbladder, and nervous system. And because the liver supports the function of the eyes and vision, any trouble in this area can usually be related to a liver imbalance.

When in strong balance, Tree energy is symbolic of orderly growth and development. We are orderly, but not compulsive; we are patient and lighthearted. Our outlook is that life is good. As a further release of energy, the Tree phase is the seat of our ambition, the driving force that allows us to create ideas.

Our social creativity lies here as well. Passionate about our dreams, the expression of our will is seated in the Tree transformation. Balance in this energy allows us to express ourselves freely, to be uninhibited and articulate, no matter how we choose to show our creativity.

An imbalance in Tree energy can manifest itself in many ways. In our modern world, we tend to see and feel both extremes of this imbalance—deficient or stagnant, and excessive or aggravated.

Excessive or aggravated Tree energy can make us feel by turns enormously creative, yet frustrated at our inability to express ourselves. This frustration leads to irritability and anger, growing deeper and hotter the longer the imbalance remains.

Excessive Tree energy eventually causes us to feel restless, explosive, and easily angered. With rigid thinking and deep impatience, this imbalance is the perfect breeding ground for rage and aggression. The sense of order that is natural to this energy phase turns to overcontrol and pent-up feelings, leading to exploding rage, as our view of the world becomes warped. We see only chaos around us.

Interestingly, the signature of Tree energy imbalance, irritability, is not self-directed. We grow impatient and angry with those around us. We think everyone else moves too slowly; works inefficiently; and can, in no way, measure up to our standards. We are easily irritated with everyone. With a Tree energy imbalance, our internal clock puts us on an impossible schedule that we can't keep.

Physically, with this imbalance, we witness defensive and aggressive body language, especially in clenched jaws and tight neck muscles. Because the eyes are nourished by the liver function, a Tree energy imbalance makes us sensitive to light, causing us to squint to protect our sight. We are always frowning in anger, producing the furrows between the eyebrows that are characteristic of this imbalance. We find ourselves standing rigidly straight, usually with fists clenched. We lack fluidity and grace in our movements. Walking looks stiff and mechanical, with our hips, knees, elbows, and wrists tight and rigid.

Tree energy imbalance shows itself with sharp, almost violent hand gestures. The voice is loud, bordering on yelling, with an edgy quality to it. Excessive Tree energy, left unchecked, can manifest itself in any manner of angry expression, from shouting to physical violence.

More rare is Tree energy that is deficient or depleted. Without strong balanced energy here, we begin to lose our initiative. Inertia is the signature characteristic of low Tree energy. We begin to move slowly and deliberately, keeping a low profile in life, afraid to be decisive. We become followers, seeing things in only conventional ways, burying our creativity and living within the rules to avoid making a wrong move. This becomes our response to the chaos around us and our feeling of being out of control. Inhibited in expressing our feelings, we believe that if we open up, we will lose control and explode, our lives descending into disarray.

In both excessive and deficient Tree energy, headaches and tightness in the head and sides of the neck are typical. Although it may seem strange to show the same physical symptoms with opposite imbalances, in reality, it's not so difficult to understand. With excessive Tree energy, it's easy to see how the headaches and constricted neck muscles would manifest themselves. Everything about the body grows tight, with fists and teeth clenched. Even with depleted Tree energy, tightness remains. We grow paralyzed by inertia and bury our creative natures. That takes work and creates a different kind of constriction in the body—the energy is stuck and unexpressed, which also causes the head and neck to tighten as we force the body to bury energy that wants to rise and release itself.

Physically, the liver and gallbladder (supporting the nervous system) are primarily responsible for the purity of the blood. At any given time, a good portion of the blood supply is being held in the liver. The primary detox organ of the body, the liver is dealing with many toxins, both environmental and dietary. It is the job of the liver to neutralize these poisons and remove them from the blood.

The liver and gallbladder are associated with the secretion and storage of bile, a liquid used by the body to emulsify fats in the digestive process. If excess bile is produced, which isn't reabsorbed into the body, it can back up into the bloodstream. When this happens, the bile actually affects the cells of the blood, irritating the nervous system. Hence, the impatient nature that goes along with this imbalance.

Another important job of the liver is to regulate the release of sugars into the body for fuel. If this release is blocked owing to the accumulation of fat in the body, the liver becomes stressed, and we feel that we may lose control, because we can't tap into our fuel reserves. Liver and gallbladder trouble, which ultimately become nervous system dysfunction, is the direct result of overconsumption of dense, fatty foods, such as animal and dairy products. As the liver malfunctions, our emotions misfire, leading to a bad temper and aggression.

Choosing foods that animate Tree energy keeps our body's energy strong and even. Support and nourish it with foods from the Water transformation to ensure smooth sailing.

The Characters That Grow Healthy Tree Energy

Lightly sour, delicate grains animate Tree energy beautifully. Wheat, oats, rye, and barley each contain a dispersing, opening quality that can help move energy through us, keeping us vital and preventing our life force from becoming stagnant.

Along with barley, wheat is the oldest cultivated grain. The protein in wheat has a unique character among grains. When wheat is ground into flour and mixed with water, the proteins are bound to form gluten—the key substance in leavening bread. Wheat, when ground, opens up its energy. Stir in water (the energetic quality that supports Tree energy) and you create a substance that leavens bread.

Because wheat is tough and difficult to digest, we consume it mostly in a refined form. Along with the commonly used whole wheat flour and pasta, wheat is also eaten as couscous and bulgur, both cracked wheat products that cook quickly into a light grain dish.

Although there are many opinions to the contrary, flour products can be quite useful in our diet. When used wisely, flour products can relax us, particularly if we are eating mostly whole grains and vegetables, which means lots of fiber. Good-quality flour products can help us control our appetite, because they help us feel satisfied with less. Eaten in excess, flour products can make digestion sluggish and cause weight gain.

Pasta cooked with a lot of water makes the flour easier to digest and carries the energetic quality of relaxing and softening us.

And then there's seitan. Kneading wheat flour into dough and then washing the starch away creates a product known as gluten, a meaty, pliable, chewy substance that is then simmered in a savory broth, creating *seitan*, which has a meatlike texture. It adds a great richness and heartiness to stews, casseroles, sandwiches, and stir-fry dishes. Take care with seitan, however. The commercial brands are cooked in broth that can be quite salty, and if eaten in excess, it can promote overeating and sweet cravings.

Oats grow in cool climates with lots of moisture. With their soft texture, oats are able to extract the maximum amount of nutrients from the soil. For us that means that they are relaxing, strengthening, and satisfying. Usually cooked into a thick porridge, oats have a grounding energy, making us feel sturdy on our feet; they are the highest of all grains in protein and fat. They can help lower cholesterol, stabilize blood sugar, and absorb excess salt from our bodies.

Rye is not commonly used in modern cooking, but it is one of the sturdiest grains. It can flourish in poor soil, at high altitudes, and in intolerably cold climates. Used most often as flour for bread and pasta, it is strongly flavored and works best in its whole form when combined with other grains.

Rye has the uncanny ability to absorb excess water and is seen by some as a way to lose weight, because it eliminates excess liquid from the body. Mostly, though, rye is ideal for building deep strength and stamina.

Extremely adaptable, barley can grow in hot or cold temperatures, in wet or dry climates. The qualities of adaptability and flexibility are imparted to us, moving through the body to break down hardened, accumulated fat and restoring smooth organ function. Barley can loosen rigid muscles, restoring flexibility and graceful movement. Stewed with vegetables or simmered in soup, barley creates a thick, rich, creamy texture that is quite warming to the body. Cooked as a grain and tossed with vegetables, barley turns into the most delightful, cooling salad.

Barley is available in many forms, but the most common are whole barley and pearled or cracked barley. Job's tears (hato mugi) barley, which is known in Asia as "beauty pearls," is recognized for its ability to cleanse the blood that nourishes the kidneys, making for a smooth, flawless complexion.

Beans that support Tree energy include green lentils, split peas, black-eyed peas, and peanuts. All are as nutritious as any other bean, but they maintain a light quality. They cook quickly but never make us feel full and heavy. Legend has it, in fact, that these particular beans can be used to dampen ardor and thus were served in monasteries to keep thoughts pure and on matters of the spirit, not of the flesh. The thinking was (according to the legend) that the beans, enlivened by Tree energy, cause the body's energy to rise and open, rather than pool and concentrate itself in the lower part of the body, which is the natural character of most protein-dense foods. Use this bit of trivia as you will, but if you think about it, it may not be just some amusing tale passed on for generations.

The vegetables that animate Tree energy include the artichoke, broccoli, lettuce, parsley, green beans, green peas, alfalfa sprouts, and summer squash. All of these veggies have a delicate ascending nature, branching out from their anchoring roots. Their stems draw nutrients from the soil and send it out to the branching clusters of peas, pods, and leaves. This rising quality creates in us the ability to draw nutrients from the food to filter it and dispense it to the appropriate place in our bodies for use. These vegetables allow us to be flexible without losing grounding. We can open to our creativity, but have the common sense to know how to channel that energy.

Fruits for Tree energy support are lightly sour. Granny Smith apples, lemons, plums, limes, and pomegranates, with their delicate structure and tart taste, are perfect. These are fruits that raise our body's energy, making us feel light and energized.

It is interesting to note that oils are animated by Tree energy. Pressed from seeds, fruits, and nuts, these are expansive foods and fatty liquids. When oils are used to cook foods, they draw fire into the foods, opening them, so they can be digested easily. Fresh, crisp, stir-fried vegetables enliven our life force as the energy rises.

With light pickling as a cooking technique characteristic of this phase, vinegars animate Tree energy. So included here would be sauerkraut, olives, and sour pickles. Fermented in nature, they strengthen digestion (rooting our strength), but fermentation also allows our energy to rise and branch out.

THE FIRE TRANSFORMATION

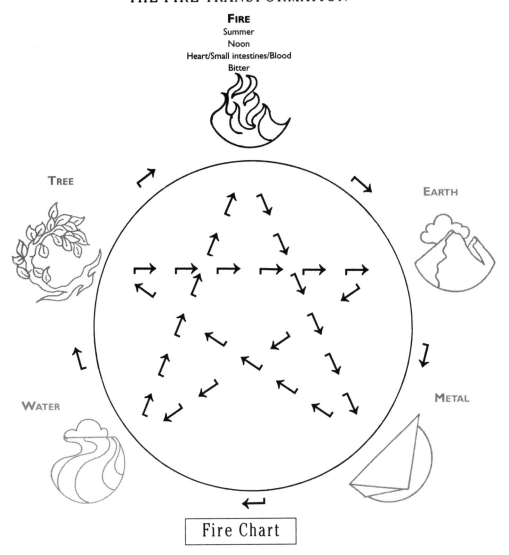

FIRE
Summer
Noon
Heart/Small intestines/Blood
Bitter

TREE

EARTH

WATER

METAL

Fire Chart

Energy

The most dramatic energy phase of all, Fire is like the sun, radiant, warm, burning to its very core to fuel its energy. Fire energy is what we use to make things happen. Joy and passion live here, with creative inspiration moving us through our lives. Fire energy is the seat of our will and expression; it is here that we articulate our feelings and act on our desires. Within the Fire transformation, we can discover who we are and what we want to be in the world.

Season
  Summer

Time of Day
  High noon

Organ Systems
  Circulatory system
  Heart
  Small intestines

Colors
  Orange
  Red

Taste
  Bitter

Cooking Techniques
  Deep-frying
  Grilling
  Roasting

Expression
  Laughter

Emotions
  Joy
  Passion

Grains
  Amaranth
  Corn
  Quinoa

Bean
  Red lentil

Vegetables
  Arugula
  Asparagus
  Belgian endive
  Broccoli rabe
  Brussels sprouts
  Chives
  Collard greens
  Dandelion greens
  Kale
  Mustard greens
  Red bell pepper
  Scallions
  Snow peas

Fruits
  Apricots
  Raspberries
  Strawberries

Nuts and Seeds
  Sesame
  Sunflower

Extreme Foods

- Bell pepper
- Chocolate
- Coffee
- Eggplant
- Potato
- Sugar
- Tomato
- Tropical foods and fruits

It is often said that the Fire transformation consumes the Tree transformation; blazes brightly; and reduces itself to ash, sinking to the Earth transformation, beginning the continuum of the transformation of energy over and over.

Under the Fire sign, the heart beats to provide blood, nutrients, and oxygen to every inch of our bodies, at the cellular level. The small intestines, also governed by Fire energy, transfers the nutrients provided by food to our blood, determining the quality of the blood nourishing the body.

As in many traditional cultures, Asian medicine notes that the heart is the place where the spirit resides. From the heart, we show our true natures.

The drama of Fire energy has many sides. At its peak during the heat of summer and at high noon, Fire energy is what we burn to make things happen—to take action. It's no surprise that the most active season and the peak time of day are enlivened by Fire energy. The joy and passion associated with the color

red and the sound of laughter are the perfect illustrations of the vitality associated with Fire energy. Bitter taste sharpens our thinking, and cooking styles like deep-frying, roasting, and grilling are vitalizing; thus Fire energy inspires us to move decisively in our lives. Bitter taste—characteristic of foods like nuts, seeds, and greens like dandelion and broccoli rabe—helps sharpen our focus. Look at the dandelion leaf, for example. Although considered more yin, or expansive, by virtue of its being a leafy green vegetable, its leaves are sharp and contracted, turning back on their stems, rather than branching out like kale. Couple that with its sharp, almost dry flavor, and you create an energy that moves quickly and demands your attention. Nuts have a similar character. Eaten raw, their flavor imparts a bitter taste, and they are quite hard to digest, making the body work to assimilate them. Lightly roast them, however, and their flavor is enhanced and their energy, more gentle in the body (because introducing the element of Fire in cooking will settle the energy toward Earth as they cook).

A strong, balanced Fire energy shows itself in our capacity to express our true selves freely and with clarity. Giving us a sharp mind and clear intellect, balanced Fire energy allows us to absorb information easily, sort through it quickly, and use it as we see fit. When we have balanced Fire energy, we have a good sense of who we are and how we want to be in the world.

When our Fire influence is strong, we

are perceived as highly charismatic, with the ability to communicate our feelings clearly and passionately, making us incredibly inspiring. Along with that, Fire energy gives us the ability to resonate with the feelings and intentions of others to bring forth a deep sense of compassion and empathy. Like physical fire, this transformation radiates energy through activity, while maintaining an internal calm and strength. So although we can align ourselves with the feelings of those around us, we never lose ourselves in the process. There always remains a strong sense of who we are and of our chosen purpose. Our deepest, most centered feelings of inner calm, along with the ability to control the rhythms of our lives, come from strong, balanced Fire energy in the body.

With all of the drama associated with the extreme nature of Fire, you can just imagine the drama when it's out of balance in our bodies. If Fire energy grows excessive or aggravated, we grow highly excitable; we talk with excessive animation, punctuated with a lot of laughter—which, in truth, is merely an attempt to cover our nervous, anxious feelings. Our lives become one big drama when this phase is overstimulated. We magnify everything—both positive and negative—by exaggerating situations, overreacting to the least disturbance. Fits of anger, crying, or even excessive joy become the norm.

Even our speech patterns and movements reflect this excessive energy. With rapid speech and thought, we move from topic to topic, seemingly without taking a breath. Our hand gestures grow wildly expressive, but nervous—they lack grace. Performers of all kinds require a high level of this energy (although in balance to maintain themselves) to fortify their ability to send energy out to large crowds of people.

Excessive Fire energy shows itself as erratic behavior: flamboyant, extravagant, but at the same time incredibly charming. People find this attractive, because we find drama so interesting. We appear quite diverse and animated in our character and may even express ourselves quite cleverly and with great humor. But we are exhausting to be with for long periods of time, because we are always on.

If Fire energy grows weak, however, a whole new set of circumstances arises. Depleted Fire energy leaves us weak, slow moving, and slow to react. Everything about us is flat and depressive. Think about the ashes left behind by burning flames. We lose our ability to experience joy or simply to feel happy. Interestingly, if Fire energy is depleted, we may not even recognize that we're depressed. We just go through life in a sort of haze, bland and expressionless.

Depleted Fire energy finds us organizing like crazy. We make lists of our lists. We organize to the point of inertia. Paperwork becomes ritual, but in reality is a mask to cover our inability to move, to act. We lose our passion for life, no longer able to initiate activity or dive into a task with enthusiasm.

When Fire energy is out of balance in the body, we may experience both extremes of the energy, as the Fire in us is overstimulated but, ultimately, burns itself out. We see this in an almost dual personality. There is the public version of us—outwardly happy, expressive, good natured, and fun loving. We do not, however, allow anyone to get too close. Our extravagant behavior is designed to attract people's attention but not to invite their intimacy. As we burn out, we become exhausted, sliding into self-pity and negative thinking. Our lives become a performance when we are around others, with no energy to reflect on our true natures when in solitude.

To maintain the balance of this dramatic energy, Fire must constantly be energized and allowed to release. We must balance the expression of ourselves with an ability to retreat into ourselves to take stock of our purpose and maintain our focus.

Fire energy animates the function of the heart and small intestines, both systems responsible for the working of the circulatory system. Of the many jobs of these systems, two serve us best for illustration. First, the temperature of the body is maintained and controlled by the circulatory system, adapting and altering to make us comfortable in any environment. Second, the heart adapts its rhythms to accommodate any situation. It is the pressure caused by the beating heart that drives blood through the body, carrying nutrients where they are needed for function and action. The healthy heart can increase and decrease blood pressure to create heightened response or induce a relaxed feeling.

An excess of Fire energy shows itself in a red complexion, tension in the throat, and a speaking pattern that rises as we grow more excitable. Expansive hand gestures reveal excessive energy that is seeking release. Depleted Fire energy manifests itself as a lack of expression and inability to act or even participate in life, seeking anonymity in what little we do.

So how do we maintain the balance of an energy phase that contains within itself extreme activity, but also serves as the seat of our true natures, the calm, center of our being? Choosing foods that animate Fire energy keeps the blazes stoked. Draw foods from Tree energy to nourish and support a constant burning of energy. And to keep the blaze under control, use some foods from Water energy because it is water that can keep a burning fire under control.

Sizzling Fire Characteristics

When thinking about foods animated by Fire energy, think in terms of expansion, drama, and high vitality.

Whole grains have the reputation of creating a stable, calm energy in us, with enduring stamina as their gift. Grains contain within them the capacity to increase our potential.

With an ability to reproduce without much help—or interference—from humanity, as well as their versatile and adaptable natures, whole cereal grains make us shine brightly. The grains belonging to this energy phase create high vitality in us, while keeping our Fire energy on a constant simmer.

Corn, the epitome of summer sunshine, is the perfect Fire energy grain. Although corn has a tremendous crop yield, it requires human intervention to reproduce itself, which means it creates in us a great sense of cooperation with others, making us more social. Sound strange? Consider this. Most whole grains require no help from humans to reproduce and grow to maturity. They have independent natures. That fosters independent thinking in us. Why? The food we eat has its own character, just as we have our characters. When we eat food, our character merges with it, creating the people that we are. Now the modern view of nutrition is that when we eat food, we take nutrients only. Really, though, we take on the character of the food as well. So it's not such a leap of logic to say that eating a food like corn—a grain that requires cooperation with humanity to re-create itself—fosters characteristics of cooperation in us. Growing high on stalks, seemingly reaching toward the sun, corn is infused with the vital energy of Fire and summer. In turn, this vitality becomes a part of us.

And then there's popcorn. From a primitive variety of corn, the kernels burst upon heating. With a large endosperm and high starch content, the internal moisture converts to steam under extreme heat, causing the endosperm to explode. A great vitalizing snack, popcorn gives us a lot of energy.

Quinoa (*keen-wah*) has earned the reputation of the new power grain. A relative newcomer to our cuisine, quinoa, in fact, has been around since the time of the Incas. Thought by many to be the ancestor of corn, these tiny, ivory-colored grains contain a higher concentration of protein than any other grain, as well as the perfect balance of amino acids needed by our bodies for strength and growth.

Quinoa thrives despite dry conditions; in fact, it grows in places that other grains would never survive. This ability to thrive under adversity makes quinoa very strengthening for us—and satisfying. It cooks quickly and has a splendid, nutty flavor. Being a whole grain, it gives us all the endurance we need from our grains.

Amaranth, considered to be sort of a sister grain to quinoa by virtue of its nutty flavor, quick cooking, and ancient ancestry, is another splendid whole grain, full of sunny, vitalizing energy. These tiny, tiny golden grains cook up to a silky texture. Intensively cultivated by the Aztecs, amaranth held religious importance for that culture; a portion of the harvest was offered in tribute to the gods. After the Spanish conquest of Mexico, the Aztecs were forbidden to grow amaranth, putting an end to its use for centuries. Only recently has amaranth made a comeback, because, like quinoa, it packs a nutritional punch. Resistant to drought, with an ability to grow in a variety of conditions, amaranth strengthens us and gives us a flexible attitude.

Of all the bean choices available to us, the most reflective of Fire's sunny nature are red lentils. These jewel-like, flat beans originated in the western Mediterranean and central Asia. Needing lots of moisture, well-drained soil, and temperate weather, red lentils are high in minerals, especially potassium, folic acid, and iron. When cooked, they are richly creamy and deep yellow in color—perfect for satisfying soups and flavorful dips and spreads. Their versatility, rich texture, peppery taste, and strong mineral content make for lots of vitality.

As for the vegetables that are animated by Fire energy—asparagus, arugula, red bell peppers, bok choy, broccoli rabe, Brussels sprouts, collard greens, kale, dandelion greens, Belgian endive, mustard greens, snow peas, scallions, and chives—are all expansive and lively. The tender shoots and stems of asparagus, scallions, chives, and bok choy hold the plant erect and have a cooling effect on our circulatory system, supporting the movement of energy through the body. The more compact, layered structure of both Brussels sprouts and Belgian endive are the perfect illustration of growth expanding in an outward direction from the core of the vegetable.

And then there are the dark leafy green veggies—broccoli rabe, dandelion greens, collards, kale, and mustard greens. You can never get enough of the nutrients that fill these lovely leafies. Yet, as important as calcium, folic acid, magnesium, zinc, potassium, and vitamins C and D are to our health, it is equally if not more important to eat greens for their vitalizing and softening natures.

The leaves of a plant are the most electrifying part. They transform the energy of light into chemical fuel for our use. Light, as we know, electrically enlivens what absorbs it. One such process, known as photosynthesis, allows the leaves to absorb light and transform it into life-giving fuel. Photosynthesis is essentially an energy-storing process, complemented by the respiration of the leaves, a releasing of the stored energy. Leaves' green color comes from the chemical chlorophyll that, with the aid of light, will turn carbon dioxide and water into sugars, which the leaves will store for use as fuel.

The veins of a leaf draw moisture and nutrients to every inch of the leaf (just like our circulatory system), and if the environment becomes too dry, they shut down and store moisture for the plant's survival. We spend billions of dollars on creams and lotions to help our skin retain its moisture, when we could simply eat kale, drawing all the moisture we need to our skin, keeping it supple and smooth.

With the leaves of the plant taking in and releasing energy, you might say that they act as the plants' respiratory system. Energetically, they embody feelings of lightness and flexibility. They stretch upward, extending their limbs toward the light to absorb as much energy as possible. They open our energy to all possibilities. They encourage the pulse of life in us; they oxygenate the body, feeding our cells to produce hemoglobin, making our blood strong and us vital.

All the vegetables from Fire energy embody the characteristic bitter taste that sharpens our focus and allows us to see our way clearly to our goals.

Fruits enlivened by Fire energy are, like corn, the picture of summer: raspberries, strawberries, and apricots are at their peak during this season and animate us with sweet warmth. The wiry stems and branches of the berries pull concentrated amounts of nourishment into the fruit, resulting in their signature tart flavors. Highly perishable, berries are best consumed at their peak, soon after picking, to get the full benefit of their concentrated, potent energy.

The nuts and seeds associated with Fire energy—almonds and sesame and sunflower seeds—with their high fat content and potential to push entire plants and flowers high toward the sun make them vitalizing, energizing, warming, and strengthening, incredible sources of fuel.

With Fire energy's capacity for extremes, of course, extreme foods reside here as well. Dramatically stimulating foods like coffee, chocolate, tobacco, alcohol, drugs (recreational and prescribed), and the nightshades—potatoes, tomatoes, eggplant, and peppers—and almost all tropical foods are enlivened by Fire energy. They have extremely explosive natures that deeply affect our equilibrium, depending on our conditions, desires, and environment. This is not to say that use of these foods will have you reeling (although depending on your health, they may not serve you as well other foods), but I prefer to use them sparingly and in small amounts in my cooking. Their strong natures and highly acidic qualities can throw us into an unbalanced state more quickly and dramatically than our less-stimulating food choices.

Personally, I use extreme foods like those enlivened by Fire energy very specifically. By that I mean I use them with thought. For instance, if the weather is particularly hot and humid, using summer tomatoes or red bell peppers as a garnish or part of a sauce lightens my energy and helps me feel better in the heavy, stagnant weather. By the same token, during the winter, food is cooked for longer periods of time, with more fire, salt, and oil. So now and then, to refresh my body and prevent stagnation, I might add some orange juice to a dressing or use fresh orange or lemon slices in a pressed vegetable salad. Thinking about what you are cooking and creating with understanding allows you to make choices based on your needs and desires and helps you achieve the results you want.

THE ESSENTIAL PANTRY

WHAT YOU WANT to create is a stress-free kitchen that includes the basics you need day to day to put together healthy, delicious meals without a lot of fuss. When your pantry and refrigerator are stocked, you can walk in the door and put a meal together simply and quickly.

The first step I recommend is a "spring clean-up" of your kitchen. Starting with the nonfood items, throw out or give away stuff that you haven't used in more than a year; chances are you'll never use it. (Unless, of course, it a great big wonderful wok that you've been afraid to use up until now!) You need to get rid of the clutter and simplify your kitchen and your life. A good sharp knife is worth a dozen electric gizmos that are often more trouble than they are worth. I am not against high tech in the kitchen, but the closer you are to the food—whether you're slicing and dicing or frying or mashing—the more energy you can impart to the food you are preparing. You may even want to buy some new things—like a large wok if you don't already have one. You can probably use what you have until you determine what you really do need. But you will want to organize your pots and pans, cutlery, and dishes for the most efficient use of your time and energies. There's nothing more draining or frustrating than constantly searching for what you need.

The good news is that whole natural cuisine requires very few fancy kitchen "toys." But what you do have should be the best. My list of essentials for making the recipes in this book is pretty basic.

KITCHEN ESSENTIALS

You will need a great wooden cutting board, and not one the size of a postage stamp; get a comfortable size, with room to spread out a bit. To go with your board, buy a wonderful knife. Carbon steel blades are great. They may stain with use, but they stay really sharp. These are the workhorses of knives. If you cook a lot, their substance will make you more efficient. Stainless steel blades keep their lovely shine, maintain their edge well, and are a bit lighter, less hefty than carbon steel. And then there's my personal favorite, the amazing ceramic blade knife. Light as a feather, with the ability to split hairs, this knife feels like an extension on the end of my arm. The only drawback I can report is that the blade is delicate. It can take on any kitchen chore; it will slice and dice with the best of them—but if you drop it, it can break. Whatever you choose, take good care of your knife. Keep it clean, store it in a safe place—for it and others—and keep it sharp. For carbon or stainless knives, you will need a steel for quick touch-ups in between sharpening and you will need a stone for serious sharpening. I like a stone with both a medium and a fine surface for sharpening and then refining the blade. I recommend sharpening about once a month, with touch-ups on the steel two or three times a week. (Ceramic knives don't usually need sharpening for several years.) The sharper the blade, the less likely you are to have an accident. A dull blade can slip and cause you to get cut. Sharp blades are efficient and accurate.

Next, you'll need good-quality pots and pans. Choose enamel cookware, ceramic-covered cast iron, stainless steel cookware, or good old-fashioned cast iron cookware. I like to have some of each around, in various sizes and styles, since they all have, shall we say, their specialties. Enamel cookware is perfect for stews and beans. Cast iron cooks evenly and holds heat well, making it perfect in colder weather. Stainless steel is the best for everyday, all-around great cooking. I also have a few pieces of clay cookware—they provide incredibly even heat and are great for beans, stews, and for meals that go from oven to table.

You'll need a large soup pot or Dutch oven, one-, two-, and three-quart saucepans, a small and large sauté pan, a deep skillet, a wok, some heavy pots for stewing, and a pressure cooker. In my opinion, no kitchen should be without a pressure cooker; these efficient pots are indispensable. They cook foods at a higher temperature than boiling, so they make food more digestible, especially whole grains and beans; they lose very little nutrition to steam—everything stays in the pot—and they make food deliciously tender and sweet. And before you panic, the modern versions of this pot are safe—no more chickpeas or tomatoes on the ceiling as the lid explodes. Today's pressure cookers have so many safety features that you can enjoy the benefits of this style of cooking without the stress of worrying about it blowing up.

Your other essential tools are small—but vital. They include: a vegetable brush for cleaning vegetables, a colander, a few fine-mesh strainers, a variety of wooden spoons (I am obsessed with pretty wooden spoons, scouring craft shows for them), a ginger grater, a box grater, a vegetable peeler, a zester, spatulas, whisks, a bamboo steamer, mixing bowls, a food mill, a chinois (a very fine metal conical sieve for pureeing), a suribachi (ceramic grinding bowl) and pestle, and measuring implements.

If you like, you can include a food processor, electric blender, and a heavy-duty mixer or hand mixer; these come in handy now and then. Make your kitchen a place you want to be, filled with whatever you love to have around you. Pottery bowls, crystal, beautiful wooden spoons, gadgets, plants, windowsill herb gardens—this is the environment where you create the life you want—make it the space you want.

CLEANING OUT OLD INGREDIENTS

Once you've purged and reorganized the non-food items in your kitchen, you're ready to tackle the ingredients. This is a good opportunity to get rid of the old dust-collectors: spices that are more than a year old, boxes or jars of unidentified matter that could be fine bread crumbs or whole wheat flour. If you ask, "What is it?" I recommend tossing it. And at the back of the refrigerator there's probably something that looks like a forgotten science experiment. Get rid of it. In the freezer, there's all that stuff that's covered with an icy protective coating. If it ever had any nutritional value it's long since been lost in the ice age. Finally, I'll let you decide which items have stood the test of time that you really want to keep, but I encourage you to decide based on what these will contribute to the life you want.

SHOPPING

Let's go shopping. The truth is that you can now do most of your shopping in any supermarket. A wide range of fresh produce, oils, and other condiments—even dried grains and beans are readily available. I do advise, however, that you venture into a local natural food store. Or develop a relationship with one of the many mail-order companies that will ship natural products to your home. This is part of an adventure that will introduce you to a whole new world of foods—new ingredients, exotic veggies, and a wide variety of tastes and textures. You will want to start with the kinds of superior, organic products that these outlets can provide. (For the purposes of this section, I am excluding fresh produce. For more on vegetables see the introduction to the vegetable recipes on page 182.)

With each of the following recommendations, I list the essential character of the food in relation to the Five Transformations of Energy. You will immediately see how valuable each of these can be in achieving balance.

GRAINS

You'll need to stock a variety of whole grains (preferably organic, which is where the natural food store comes in handy), which will give you a range of interesting taste choices. But, more important, they will provide the elements to balance your eating and keep your energy moving smoothly through your body.

Essential Grains

Rice (Metal)

Start with one or two pounds each of short, medium, and basmati brown rice. These varieties will create the foundation of your whole-grain pantry with their balanced energy and nutritional value. (See the discussion of Metal transformation beginning on page 24 for more about how grains contribute to this essential element. Also see the introduction to the grains recipes on page 117.)

Yellow Millet (Earth)

A staple grain in Asia, millet is high in protein and contains more amino acids than most other grains. The only grain to counteract stomach acids, millet is the perfect Earth-enlivened grain. A light and airy grain that cooks easily into creamy stews, soups, and cereal dishes, millet creates a warm and dry energy in the body, making it the perfect comfort food.

Whole and Hato Mugi Barley (Tree)

Said to be the oldest cultivated grain, Tree energy enlivens these two strains of cereal. Creating a warm and damp condition, barley is quite adaptable and changeable. Cooked with root vegetables into a stew, barley is warming to the body. Boiled lightly with diced summer vegetables, barley creates a lovely cooling salad. While hato mugi is an Asian strain of barley, with particularly strong cleansing properties, most of our common barley, while delicious, goes to feed cattle and make beer.

Quinoa (Fire)

Pronounced *keen-wah*, this ancient grain is one of the finest sources of complete protein in the vegetable kingdom. Believed to be the predecessor of corn, quinoa has a superior nutritional profile, high in lysine and other amino acids, with a warm and dry effect on the body. Strongly flavored, quinoa cooks quickly and partners well with just about any other ingredient, although it goes particularly well with corn.

Wild Rice (Fire)

A long-grain marsh grass indigenous to the northern lake states and Canada, wild rice isn't a true cereal grain. Creating a cool and damp energy in the body, wild rice partners well with brown rice, as its lighter energy is a natural complement to the heartiness of the brown rice.

Dried Sweet Corn (Fire)

For the bright, shiny energy of summer all year long, dried sweet corn is pure perfection. This freeze-dried version of fresh summer corn maintains the sweet taste and vitality that is the nature of corn, but drying it does more than preserve it. By removing the moisture, the corn will have a more warming energy in the body, making it ideal for use in cooler weather.

Supplemental Grains

Couscous (Tree)

Arabic for semolina, couscous is the hard heart of durum wheat that has been ground into small granules, not unlike pasta. Quick cooking and easy to digest, couscous is the perfect instant food. Great in salads to keep us cool in warm weather, couscous is also the perfect addition to any soup for just a bit of heartiness. Like other wheat products, couscous adds moisture to the body.

Dried Pasta (Tree)

A simple combination of flour, water, and salt, pasta is a deliciously light way to enjoy wheat. Easy to digest and very versatile, there are many varieties of pasta, whole grain and refined. I use both in my cooking. Whole-grain pastas are hearty and more substantial and are perfect in cool or cold weather. Semolina pasta, like the delicious Italian versions available to us, while more refined, are great for lighter meals and are even easier on digestion.

Japanese Noodles (Water and Tree)

Different from Western pasta, there are many varieties of Japanese noodles: whole-wheat udon and somen, buckwheat soba, mugwort soba, wild yam udon, and lotus root soba. Adding herbs and vegetables reputed to have certain healing properties makes Asian noodles more than just a dish of pasta. During the drying process, Japanese noodles are rolled in salt to prevent sticking, which is why they have the honor of two energy phases enlivening them.

Polished Rice (Metal)

Polished rice is brown rice that has had the bran and germ removed, leaving only the starch for consumption. Not very nutritious, white rice is a simple carbohydrate with most of its nutrients lost in the polishing. It has its uses, although I use it only occasionally. It's a great accompaniment to heavy dense proteins, like fish, as it's easy to digest. It's nice as an occasional, lighter grain dish in hot weather. It's also great with more oily foods, like tempura; it helps the body soak up the oil and digest it a little better.

BEANS

Dried beans are essential sources of protein and, more important, provide stamina. While canned beans are certainly convenient, they have been cooked at a high heat and have sat in those cans for quite a while. They're not the best source of vitality. The protein and vitamins and other stuff in the canned beans are intact, but the sun, earth, air, and water energies so essential to us are long departed. (For more about beans see the introduction to the beans chapter on page 155.)

Red Azuki (Water)

These little jewels are essential to your healthy pantry. High in minerals like potassium and low in fat, these Asian beans are particularly beneficial to the kidneys, which is why azuki beans give us the strength to meet life's challenges. The kidneys are the seat of our strength and these little beans are the best choice for keeping them strong. Available in Asian markets and natural foods stores, azuki beans cook relatively quickly and are considered to be the most important of the beans we choose for their restorative powers.

Chickpeas (Earth)

Also called garbanzo beans, these round beige beans have a mild flavor. But don't let them fool you. They're a powerhouse of energy. Hard, with lots of energy, these beans are higher in fat than other beans, making them ideal in stews or in dips and spreads, like humus.

Black Soybeans (Water)

A higher mineral content than their yellow soybean sisters is evident in their rich black color. Rich in protein and phytoestrogens, black soybeans are a bit easier to digest than the yellow; their richer minerals make the fat and protein easier on the digestive system.

OTHER DRIED FOODS

Dried varieties of popular fresh ingredients provide the strength that is essential to vitality without the risk of spoilage. These items can be stored in glass jars, plastic containers, or bags to maintain freshness.

Dried Daikon (Metal)

A deep cleansing, concentrated form of the fresh variety, this spicy root goes deep into the body to dissolve accumulated fat and protein that can make the body feel sluggish.

Dried Sea Vegetables (Water)

Like their fresh counterparts, dried sea vegetables provide a variety of concentrated minerals that are essential to healthy blood and smooth organ function. The most commonly used varieties include:

Kombu: High in glutamic acid, which helps the body break down and assimilate fat and protein, this sea plant is most often used in cooking grains and beans.

Wakame: More delicate than kombu and milder in flavor, this sea plant is most often used in soups and salads as a gentle source of minerals.

Nori: A great source of calcium—and so easy to use. Take it from the package and wrap it around some rice or noodles or shred it over soup or on a salad for minerals and a distinctive flavor all its own.

Hiziki: The greatest source of calcium on the planet, not to mention iron, folic acid, and vitamin C, this strongly flavored sea vegetable makes a most distinctive side dish.

Delicious when sautéed and combined with sweet vegetables like carrots and onions, hiziki is a good source of minerals and other nutrients.

Arame: From a large-leaf sea plant, arame is finely shredded and pre-boiled before drying to make it tender. Mild in taste, arame is a great source of protein and minerals like potassium and calcium.

Other sea plants such as agar flakes, dulse, sea palm, and Irish moss are delicious and interesting. Agar is a flavorless sea plant used to gel desserts and aspics; dulse is great in soups and delicate salads and is high in potassium; sea palm and Irish moss are more exotic and fun to experiment with now and again.

Dried Shiitake Mushrooms (Water)

These dried mushrooms provide an intense flavor, but have a gentle, relaxing, cleansing energy. Prized in Asia for their restorative powers, shiitake mushrooms are reputed to aid in lowering blood pressure, reducing cholesterol, and cleaning accumulated fat from the veins and arteries.

Dried Tofu (Metal)

A good source of concentrated protein and calcium, dried tofu maintains the relaxing quality of fresh tofu but is not quite as cooling. With the moisture removed, the proteins and energy of tofu are concentrated and the texture is heartier, making it great in long-cooked stews and casseroles.

CONDIMENTS

Oils (Metal)

For cooking or salads, use extra-virgin olive oil or light and toasted sesame oil. Corn oil is best for baking. All add richness and vitality to your cooking. Be sure to choose the very best quality oil you can—cold-pressed, unfiltered, and organic wherever possible.

Vinegars (Tree)

Brown rice and sweet brown rice vinegars are the least acidic and cause fewer digestive problems than the fruitier versions such as red wine, raspberry, and other vinegars based on fermented fruits. If you do choose a fruit vinegar, stay with a good-quality balsamic, which is aged in wooden kegs and can help strengthen digestion. Its delicate, sweet flavor also helps the body to relax. Umeboshi vinegar, while slightly acidic, will not affect the body dramatically and can benefit digestion.

Dried Herbs (Fire)

I like to keep a few dried herbs in the pantry—usually dried from my own garden or window box, which is always your best bet for herbs. If you are purchasing them, how- ever, go to a natural food store, where you can be assured that they have not been irradi- ated. Buy the amount that you might use in a six-month period. After that, dried herbs lose their flavor and their vitality.

Let your foods' natural characters and flavors create the taste of the dish. Don't over- power the food with the flavor of herbs or their extreme Fire nature. Using herbs now and then to add a sparkling vitality to a meal or to create a lighter energy when you feel sluggish is okay. The overuse of herbs can leave you feeling nervous and jittery. I tend to stay with milder herbs like basil, oregano, thyme, and rosemary, avoiding the stronger flavors of other varieties. The milder the herb's flavor, the less extreme the effect on us, so broad-leaf herbs like basil, and more con- tracted leaf structures like rosemary, will lift your energy but not aggravate your nervous system. Stronger herbs are best used with dense proteins, like those in animal foods. They help the body to digest the heavy pro- teins and fats more easily.

And then there's the dried versus fresh question. I almost always prefer fresh herbs to dried, with the exception being dishes in which the herbs need to cook for a long time. Dried herbs will hold their flavor in longer cooking, while the delicate flavor of fresh will not. Fresh herbs are my first choice because, well, they're fresh and seasonal and at their peak of not only flavor but vitality.

Spices

As with herbs, I play it safe with spices, using them sparingly when I am looking for strong energy. Spices, as opposed to herbs, are the seeds or fruits or stems of plants, with concentrated flavor and strong energy. Relying heavily on spices can mask the true nature and flavor of whatever you're cooking and even leave you irritable.

Powdered ginger (Metal): Used mostly in baking, powdered ginger has a stronger flavor than its fresh counterpart; it has a deeply warming energy, but can taste bitter if you use too much.

Cinnamon and Nutmeg (Fire): Commonly used in fruit desserts and pie fillings, these spices can have a strong effect on us, as they generate a great deal of internal heat from their Fire nature. But, if you tend to have cold feet and hands, these spices are for you, and they balance the simple sugars of fruit quite nicely with their hot personalities.

Salts (Water)

A variety of good-quality salts are essential to a healthy diet. Enlivened by Water energy, salt pulls the moisture in foods to the surface and helps our bodies to hold the liquid it keeps. Keep in mind that salt, while used lightly to maintain good health, is important for maintaining strong blood.

Soy Sauce: For full-bodied flavor, this liquid condiment is composed of pressing soybeans, cracked wheat, and salt for at least one year. Fermented salts help the body digest food more efficiently as they encourage the production of digestive enzymes.

Sea salt: The unrefined white variety can be used sparingly to aid in digestion.

Miso: The barley and brown rice kinds are ideal for flavoring soups and sauces and making digestion strong, with their high concentration of friendly bacteria that promotes the production of digestive enzymes in the intestines, making for strong, efficient digestion. The best misos are those aged for at least eighteen months.

Mirin (Tree)

A sweet, sherrylike cooking wine, it adds delicate sweetness to any dish. Made from rice, it is less acidic than sherry.

Prepared Stone-Ground Mustard (Fire)

Mustard adds spicy taste and vitality to cooking. It is best to buy your mustards from a natural foods store. The quality of the salts, spices, and vinegars will be superior to those used to make standard commercial brands, which makes for better flavor and, of course, better energy.

Black and Green Olives (Fire) and Capers (Tree)

These are all wonderful little luxuries to keep on hand for when the spirit moves you . . . and your meals need a bit of variety and sparkle.

SWEETENERS

Brown rice syrup is the best for producing light, flavorful pastries and cakes. For the best results in your desserts, however, use a brand of brown rice syrup that has been traditionally aged with koji (a cultured rice) and not enzymes. While enzymes are a natural form of fermentation and the products are still of good quality, the enzymes may liquify your thickeners, resulting in runny puddings, or break down baking powder, making cakes heavy.

Malt (barley, wheat, or rye): Malted grain sweeteners are made by simply cooking the sprouted grains. The most common varieties include barley, wheat, and rye malt, each with strong flavors not unlike molasses. I love these sweeteners in spice cakes, nut breads, and cookies, as well as in sweet bean stews.

Dried fruit: Choose organic dried raisins, apricots, and cherries. Their concentrated flavors add zest to any baked good. Organic fruits contain no pesticides or other additives—that's good.

TEAS (Metal or Tree or Fire)

To go with my delicious baked products or as the finale to any meal or as an afternoon de-stressor, I keep a variety of teas in my pantry. Kukicha (Metal), a Japanese twig tea, has an earthy flavor and is high in calcium. Roasted barley tea (Tree) will refresh and cool the body in warm weather. For lighter energy, I choose herbal teas. Lemon, orange, and cranberry teas relax and cool the body, making them ideal after a hearty meal or in warmer weather.

EXTREME FOODS

E XTREME FOODS, LIKE extreme sports, tax the body and the mind, driving them to the edge of our limits, and sometimes beyond. Although both may provide immediate thrills, living life constantly on the edge is not on the path to longevity and well-being that most of us seek. The irony is that if you engage in extreme sports, you have to sacrifice extreme foods to achieve peak performance!

Now that you've committed to a healthy lifestyle and stocked your pantry with the best-quality foods you can find, it's important to recognize those things that could sabotage your new lease on life.

When I was diagnosed with cancer back in 1983, I read *The Cancer Prevention Diet* by Michio Kushi, who was later to become my teacher. He wrote that we create our conditions of illness by what we choose to eat. Of course, there are other influences from our lifestyles that promote disease; but primarily, our food choices are at the core of it all. My first reaction? Yeah, right. But in spite of my cynicism, I found his words to be utterly compelling.

Perhaps I was looking for validation of what I was doing to regain my health. Because I had chosen nutrition as the way to help me recover, I took what he said at face value and simply ate what were considered appropriate foods for my condition. At the time, I had no idea why these foods were better for me than others, just that a Japanese philosopher said so in his book. I didn't care why; because I had no better ideas, I thought I'd give him the benefit of the doubt. Once I had regained my health, everything changed. I had cured myself with my diet changes, and I wanted to know why. I began to study food intensively. I had cooked all my life, and I loved to discover how food worked in recipes. I was fascinated by the creative energies released in me when I was in the kitchen. And I was especially gratified to see how happy and contented people were when they were eating together. Yet the more I studied, the more I acknowledged that I had no clue about food—about the *experience* of food in the body. Throughout this period of study and cooking and experimenting, I felt by turns overwhelmed and humbled. But I eventually accepted a few truths that have served me well. I have learned that, like it or not, we create our lives—our health, our crises, our joys, our day-to-day adventures—everything. There are no accidents and we are never victims. We may *unconsciously* create our situation, but we create it nevertheless. And only we, along with divine inspiration, can change it and create the life we want. It all starts with the one thing in life over which we have complete control: the food we eat.

We can choose from the three basic groups of food energies: extremely contracting (yang), relatively balanced, and extremely expansive (yin). Obviously, a diet chosen primarily from the balanced category will create the best environment for a healthy body.

What are these extreme foods that don't serve us? I'm not going to hold forth on cholesterol, fat grams, sodium, and all the nutritional information we either know or can read about in any newspaper or magazine. My purpose is to show how we *experience* these foods in our bodies, how we choose them to create the people we are. It's time to see food differently and have a new relationship with it. The extreme foods are many and varied, but here I focus on those that I believe are the most damaging. By eliminating or reducing the consumption of these foods, you will enjoy immediate and long-term benefits that are nothing short of miraculous.

ABOUT MEAT

My father was a butcher. He brought home only the best cuts of beef, pork, veal, and chicken. And my mother, who was an amazing cook, turned the meat into splendid meals. Yet, when I was a kid, getting me to eat meat was a daily challenge for my parents. From a very young age, I had trouble with it. I just didn't like the smell, the texture, or the taste. Still, I ate my fair share of it, to be sure.

When I entered high school, I signed up for an extra-curricular class in pottery and my life was changed, not only by the creative process of the art but by the instructor. An outspoken vegetarian, he spent a lot of effort trying to educate us about not eating meat. During this same time, my father was offered the opportunity to make a bit of extra money by working for a few days in a slaughter-house. He jumped at the chance for the extra cash, because he and my mother struggled to provide for four growing children. He left early on a Saturday morning, but to our sur-prise, he was home by noon. As we ran to greet him, we realized something was wrong. My father was, and still is, a tall, strapping, healthy specimen of a man, with a body that is used to hard work. As we met him, his shoulders were slumped, and he was ghostly pale. He walked past us with barely a word, very unlike my dad, who was, and still is, per-petually delighted to see his children. He went directly to my mother in the kitchen, where we found him sitting at the table, sob-bing as though his heart would break.

"I couldn't do it," he said to my mother. "I looked into their eyes, and I just couldn't do it. I couldn't kill them. You can see their fear. You can actually feel it through the whole place."

For several months, we were an experi-mental vegetarian family, with my mother joking that she would write a cookbook called *365 Things to Do with Broccoli*. It didn't last. Before long the shock wore off my father, and the meat was back on the table. But I didn't forget so easily. The thought of eating meat was unbearable. So when I was four-teen years old, I became a vegetarian, and I have never looked back. Although lots of things have changed in my life, my opinion that the human body doesn't need, or thrive on, meat hasn't.

Since studying macrobiotic cooking, I have discovered a lot of things about food. One of the beautiful things about macrobi-otics is that the choices you make are based on understanding the *energy* of the food you are eating, and determining how that choice serves you. It's not about morality and senti-ment. It's about functioning at our optimum levels, so that we can fit easily and harmo-niously into the environment, so that we can work together in peace and live happier lives, actually benefiting the environment by our presence.

And meat just doesn't fit the bill for us. I *know* that meat has been a food choice throughout the world for ages. Animal foods have been used as part of the human diet in most cultures, in varying proportions. And I know that there has never been a traditional society that was totally vegetarian.

Yet, as humans, we simply aren't built to

consume great quantities of meat. The structure of the intestines, stomach, teeth, and even our skin is not designed to process and discharge meat without the body having to work incredibly hard. We don't need meat in our diet as human beings . . . not for strength or energy or vitality. In fact, we get just the opposite when we eat it.

Meat is incredibly dense, composed of three basic ingredients: protein, water, and fat, in varying amounts, depending on the animal. These proteins and fats are different from one animal to another and behave differently in us. Each animal has a unique makeup and this character is infused into every part of the animal, even into the quality of its protein and fat.

Meat's structure is composed of long, thin cells that make up muscle tissue. Muscle tissue fibers are bound together by thin, but tough, sheets of connective tissue that hold these fibers together in bundles. The protein of meat is "protein of movement," meaning that when it gets the appropriate message from the animal's nervous system, the protein can propel the organism into action. When we eat meat, we are consuming tough fibers designed for movement, so we have to work quite hard to digest it. As a result, eating meat takes our strength. When we eat a densely caloric food, our intestines must draw energy from just about everywhere in the body to process it. That kind of effort, especially on a regular basis, keeps our bodies in high gear all the time. It simply wears us out.

When we eat meat, we create a sort of internal friction as our intestines expand and contract, working to digest. In fact, all of our organ functions move into overdrive. We produce a lot of heat, thereby producing a lot of energy, but we can use only so much fuel. The body seeks release of excess energy, just as it seeks release in other ways. As heat builds internally, the body grows irritated and aggravated. Think about how you feel when the weather is hot and humid. It's the same feeling, only inside your body. This energy can discharge in a variety of ways. Many people argue that it gives us strength. Remember that red meat was served to warriors. To create what? The ability to discuss reasonably and passively around a table? Meat creates irritability, excessive aggression, and quick tempers. And these traits come with the organic, free-range, old-time farm meat that's being touted as better for us. But in commercially produced meat you also get the "benefit" of antibiotics, growth hormones, pesticides, and herbicides from the environment and animal feed.

Meat makes our muscles bulky and tight, contracting the body, leaving little room for flexibility. Our bodies grow tired from overwork. Our nervous systems are irritated because our livers are in overdrive, trying to accommodate the excessive nutrition and energy. We seek more and more intense stimulation in the form of stimulants, hot spices, and sugar to open and relax the body. A layer of saturated fat builds up under the skin, desensitizing the skin to stimulation, causing us to require more and more intensity in our lives. Thus it's harder for us to feel things when we eat meat.

DO WE NEED A CHICKEN IN EVERY POT?

Chickens have very different eating and digestive patterns than humans do. Because chickens have no teeth, food passes through the gizzard, where it is ground for digestion. In humans, that translates to difficulty in digesting the meat of chicken, because its digestive process creates a tough, fibrous flesh. Because most mass-produced chickens are raised in complete confinement, with inferior feed as their only source of food, they suffer malnutrition to some degree, resulting in fragile brittle bones. If chicken is a regular part of our diet, these deficiencies are passed on to us.

THE INCREDIBLE EGG

Eggs are the seeds of their species—birds, reptiles, or fish. Eggs symbolize the potential of an entire living, breathing creature. So in an egg, the character of a species is greatly concentrated.

Although humans eat lots of different eggs, chicken eggs are, without question, the egg of choice in our culture. Considered to be one of the most versatile foods around, eggs have the unique ability to bind ingredients together, like in puddings, custards, and sauces. They have an even more uncanny ability to expand and remain bound, like in meringues or cakes. Their shells are composed mostly of calcium carbonate and a bit of protein. The yolk is composed of water, fat, protein, iron, cholesterol, lecithin, and vitamin A. Egg whites are composed mostly of water and albumin (protein). They have lots of energy in them. So, what's the problem?

Eggs, by nature of their concentrated energy, cause the human body to contract. They give the body a very concentrated form of heat as the digestive organs labor to break them down during digestion to assimilate them. Because they are one of the most concentrated forms of animal energy, eggs cause extreme reactions in us, like sweet cravings, the desire for hot spices, and deep thirst—all attempts by the body to release and balance this intense contracting energy. The strong binding nature of eggs as well as their ability to leaven cause the intestines to expand and contract with such intensity that digestion is greatly compromised.

Here's an interesting parting thought on eggs for women. Traditionally seen as a symbol of fertility, eggs are heavy and, in fact, sink in a woman's body, affecting the lower organ systems. The twenty-one-day gestation period of chicken eggs can alter our own twenty-eight-day cycle, throwing our natural clock into an imbalance, causing irregular menstruation and aggravated symptoms of premenstrual syndrome (PMS).

AND THEN THERE'S MILK

Milk has been seen as the salvation of human nutrition and considered by many to be the perfect food, with its high calcium and protein content. Many nutritionists and increasing numbers of consumers, however, are questioning the wisdom and safety of this food. The bad news is that the excessive consumption of dairy products has created human beings with deficient immune function; weak constitutions; brittle bones; and rampant reproductive disorders, such as cancer. John McDougall, M.D.—author and nutrition expert—sees dairy products as the leading cause of allergies and has linked them with no less than forty-five diseases. Frank Oski, M.D.—author of *Don't Drink Your Milk*—concurs, stating that milk so alters the human body that he would like to see it placed on an official hazardous food list. Finally, Martha Cottrell, M.D., notes major concerns in regard to dairy consumption, immune function, and degenerative disease in her book *AIDS, Macrobiotics and Natural Immunity*.

Mother's milk is our first food. It is the food that introduces us to the world outside of the womb. Although it creates the bond between mother and child, it also prepares us for life away from her. It creates and nourishes us, imprinting the patterns that make us human. Milk nourishes the young of most species. When the young consume milk from the same species, it imparts to them all of the characteristics and behavior patterns of that species. And that's the key—to nourish the young of that species. To use the milk of one species to nourish another creates a tangled, confused identity crisis, to say the least.

Human beings are creatures of intuition, intelligence, and creativity, with great capacity to think freely, and to act on those thoughts. We are the only species (on earth, anyway) that can create whatever it is that we envision, from bridges to technology to war. Drinking human mother's milk as our first food reinforces our human patterns, giving us the opportunity to be the best human we can be.

Much of the current thinking about milk is based on the fact that it contains all the vital nutrients essential to life. And that's true. Any mother creates the perfect food for her babies. What's left out of this equation is the misguided notion that milk for cows, goats, rabbits, cats, or even humans is the perfect food for any species other than its own.

One can argue that humanity has used animal milk for centuries and that, of all species, humans have great capacity to consume anything. Both of these facts are true.

There are even circumstances in life when the milk from another species can be used to effect a change in a condition. Milk is often used in many folk remedies to help alleviate pain or relax the body after trauma. But we consume dairy foods, especially cow's milk, *excessively* and long into adulthood. In fact, humans are the only species with a lifelong habit of consuming milk.

How did we become so dependent on the milk of cows? One viable theory holds that cow's milk, with forty-five grams of lactose per quart, is the closest of any animal milk to human, which has seventy-five grams of lactose per quart. (Lactose is a disaccharide present in the milk of all mammals— although it is energetically different in each animal.) Human infants seemed to thrive on it and took easily to the flavor. Also cow's milk was readily accessible to us. So cow's milk was considered the most reasonable substitute for human milk. Yet the key to understanding why dairy products can eventually prove more harmful than beneficial lies in understanding the role of *lactase* in the digestive process.

Lactase is an enzyme contained in the small intestines that breaks down the lactose in mother's milk. Lactase, which appears in an embryo's intestines during the last trimester, remains active in the small intestines until the baby is about a year old. Then it begins to wane, although it can remain relatively active up to about four years. With the dwindling production of lactase, the ability to digest lactose also dwindles. If the amount of lactose present in the intestines is more than what the lactase can digest, the lactose accumulates in the large intestines, undigested, where it ferments in the natural heat of the body, causing various chemical reactions with the bacteria that reside there. Eventually, the lactose turns into carbon dioxide and lactic acid, which together cause water retention in body tissue.

In the digestive system, the large intestines work together with the lungs to regulate intake and elimination of waste in the body. The large intestines take in solid food and through fermentation process what is needed and eliminate the rest. The lungs take in oxygen and eliminate carbon dioxide. If the large intestines begin to overload the lungs with excessive carbon dioxide from the fermenting lactose, it is harder to get proper oxygen to the brain (and the rest of the body), resulting in high levels of lactic acid in the blood, lethargy, and mental exhaustion.

Casein (sodium caseinate), the protein in milk, is really tough to digest. A very sticky protein, casein mostly remains undigested in the body, accumulating in soft tissue, causing sluggish circulation and inhibited digestion. Because it's soft and dense, casein is not the best protein for building and strengthening muscle tissue—which, in case you forgot, is one of the main reasons we need protein in our bodies. Casein also has the unique ability to bind, so much so that it's an ingredient in some plastic and glue products. As this protein passes through a body incapable of digesting it (which is most of the time), it pulls together, eventually forming fatty cysts and tumors.

The fat in dairy products is even more problematic than the protein. Saturated fats, the fat from dairy foods, accumulate in the body, causing hardened, bulky muscles, slowing metabolism, and inhibiting oxygen from getting to body tissues. With the inefficient use of oxygen and the degeneration of tissue, we become lethargic and depressed.

Fat-free dairy foods aren't the answer, though. Skim milk (fat-free) and low-fat milk are all by-products of whole milk. All we did was remove the fat. It really doesn't improve the milk or its effect on us—it still contains both casein and lactose, just with less fat. It actually concentrates the protein . . . which leads us to calcium.

Milk is loaded with calcium. But just because dairy has calcium doesn't mean we can use the mineral efficiently. The calcium in dairy products is bonded to casein, and seeing how difficult it is to digest casein is a clear indicator to the usability of dairy calcium.

The calcium in dairy foods, although abundant, is relatively unavailable to us. In fact, we can use only about 10 percent of it, leaving the rest undigested in the body, because without magnesium or phosphorus, we can't assimilate calcium. Neither of these elements is in dairy foods.

Did you know that most of the world's peoples don't rely on dairy foods for their calcium? Or that Americans take in twice the amount of dairy foods as most of the world? Protein-rich diets, like those of people consuming great quantities of dairy foods, produce a greater excretion of urea from the kidneys, depleting the body of essential nutrients like calcium, magnesium, and potassium. It is interesting to note that the incidence of osteoporosis is significantly higher among people who consume great quantities of animal protein. In contrast, populations existing on low-protein diets, even with marginal calcium intake, often have a lower incidence of osteoporosis.

Poor digestion of casein and lactose and the intake of high concentrated protein from fat-free dairy foods cause the blood to become highly acidic. And remember that the body will have balance, with or without our cooperation. What the body relies on to counter an overly acidic condition is serum calcium, the form of calcium that dissolves in the blood to be available for metabolism. The use of dairy for calcium not only causes the body to accumulate unusable calcium but makes the body require more calcium. And as we eat more dairy products, the cycle continues. Better to choose vegetables and beans that are rich in calcium that is usable: dark leafy greens, soy products, and sea plants. And by reducing the amount of animal protein in your diet, your need for calcium is also reduced, because you excrete less in the digestive process. You can get all the calcium you need from the food you eat, if you choose wisely. And supplements? For certain conditions, they may be appropriate; but in my opinion, they are the last resort for getting calcium.

Fermented dairy products are another story . . . and it's not a fairy tale. Dairy products that are cultured, like yogurt and buttermilk, are lactose-free (mostly), because the lactose converts to simple sugar and is used up in the fermenting process. Although the lactose is eliminated as a problem, the fermentation creates another challenge to the digestive system. Taking fermented animal foods and placing them in a hot, wet environment like the intestines causes them to become even more acidic. And the *Lactobacillus bulgaricus* in yogurt that is said to support digestion by inhibiting the production of harmful microbes can't survive the heat of the intestines and so does us no good.

In the production of cheese, enzymes are introduced to coagulate the casein; whey is pressed out; and fat, protein, and lactose are broken into simple molecules by bacteria, resulting in a very concentrated form of dairy protein and fat. The production of most cheese relies heavily on various molds and bacteria. Cheese causes the body to become acidic, resulting in damp (congested) intestines, fluid retention, kidney stones, pale skin, and wrinkles.

Agitating cream until fat granules form and bond makes butter. This dense substance is about 80 percent fat. Although butter is high in short-chain fatty acids, these are not fatty acids the human body needs, and they can even inhibit the metabolism of essential fatty acids. Neither does butter contain sufficient nutrients needed for metabolism, making it taxing on the body.

Just as butter remains stable under heat during cooking, so it is hard to break down in the heat of our intestines, as we attempt to digest it. Instead of *stable* fat, perhaps we should think of butter as accumulating fat.

Finally, my personal favorite—at least it was when I was growing up—ice cream. The effects of the dense protein and fats of dairy food are, in essence, concentrated in ice cream. Combining them with sugar and freezing temperatures make ice cream as indigestible as a dairy food can get. Anything that is freezing cold will cause organ function to slow, grow sluggish, and accumulate fat, especially in the intestines. As congestion builds in the digestive tract, it is more difficult to oxygenate the brain, and we begin to feel dull. Think about the times in your life when ice cream has tasted the best to you. It's often when we need a comfort food. This frozen sweet is great for numbing body function and for paralyzing us emotionally.

Although dairy foods are an ingrained part of our culinary culture, they are not the health-promoting foods that advertising would have us believe. In the final analysis, you can feel the effect dairy food is having on your body only by giving it up and experiencing the difference in your health.

ABOUT SUGAR

I had a powerful sweet tooth growing up. I saw most meals as the means to an end—dessert! I didn't appreciate what a dramatic effect sugar was having on my life until years into my macrobiotic practice when I realized that I was enslaved to sugar. I still enjoy good-quality desserts, but now I eat sweet things out of joy and enjoyment, not because I can't go two hours without more sugar.

Eating a diet high in sugar will take a toll on your body, your emotions, and your ability to function. First, sugar is one of the main reasons we are so overweight. We all love to blame fat, which, of course, is a factor. But with everybody eating everything in low-fat and no-fat form, why are we still gaining and gaining? The answer is simple. Refined sugar is dense with calories and virtually nutrient free. Eating sugar introduces a lot of calories into the body that take a lot of work to burn off. So if we eat fat-free snacks that are laced with sugar, we get fat.

Glucose is the fuel on which the body operates and is the sugar that is an important energy source. Simple sugar, including refined white sugar, brown sugar, maple syrup, honey, cane juice, molasses, corn syrup, sucrose, and fructose pose major health concerns for us, the very least of which is tooth decay. *Depleting* is the word I would use when talking about sugar's effect on our health. It depletes our bodies of B vitamins; takes calcium from our bones and teeth; inhibits the absorption of nutrients, including protein, calcium, and other minerals; and interferes with the production of friendly intestinal bacteria.

Naturally occurring complex sugars—like the kind in whole grains, beans, and vegetables—end up as glucose just like everything else, but not until essential nutrients and fiber have been extracted and used by the body. Simple sugars bypass the nutrient-gathering step and move right to glucose, actually leaving us malnourished. The more sugar we eat, the hungrier we are and the more often we need to eat.

The benefits of eliminating simple sugars from your diet go well beyond physical well-being. Your emotions and moods will also dramatically improve. The brain relies on glucose from the blood for energy to think, but simple sugars cause fluctuating glucose levels and thus erratic delivery of fuel to the brain—excessive and then depleted; the result is unpredictable emotional behavior.

Giving up sugar makes eating a greater pleasure. Everything you eat tastes better. Once your body stops working so hard to balance itself from the ravages of sugar's extremes, your taste buds become resensitized to all the subtleties of flavors and textures. Your body comes alive to the sensations of the more balanced flavors and energy of vegetables and grains. And finally you gain control over when to eat something sweet.

Are we doomed to a grim regime of foods that taste like they're good for us? Are we to never enjoy a dessert again? The answer is, emphatically, no! The best choice for sweeteners are those that contain maltose. These are sweeteners that are as close to whole foods as you can get. Delicate in flavor and not nearly as concentrated as simple sugars, sweeteners like brown rice syrup and malts (such as barley, wheat, rye, and oat) are easy to find in natural foods stores and easy to work with in recipes. At least half the nutrients in grain-based sweeteners are the same as those found in whole grains. As a result, they break down slowly in the stomach and intestines, so they don't affect blood sugars as dramatically. We avoid the roller coaster of energy and mood swings that comes with simple sugars.

FOOD ADDITIVES

As far back as recorded history—and perhaps before then—humankind has tried to preserve food to prevent spoilage, by drying or salting or using herbs and spices. In many cases, the herbs and spices were used simply to camouflage spoiled foods. Today, the bulk of commercially produced food is laced with chemicals, preservatives, and other additives. Although these chemical compounds preserve food, the least of their effect is that they provide us with no nutrition at all.

We are consuming compounds that may be at home in a test tube in a chemistry class but have no place in our bodies. There are nearly three thousand chemical additives that are approved by the Food and Drug Administration (FDA) as safe for use in food. Safe? You decide.

Additives and chemical preservatives affect the very nature of the foods they invade. No one really knows the far-reaching effects of chemicals in foods. Most likely we won't know that for generations to come. We do know some of the immediate effects: allergies, lethargy, mental confusion, headaches, nervous anxiety, and fatigue. The body has no idea how to assimilate the added chemical compounds; but in its infinite wisdom, it tries to isolate the foreign substances in one place in the body. This can aid in the formation of—in the worst cases—cancer and environmental sensitivity owing to immune system suppression.

Now, I don't live in a dream world. I know that the chances of living additive-free are slim to none, but we can control how much we take into our bodies. As challenging as it may be, read labels to avoid additives!

And then there's biotechnology—the manipulation of the genetic patterns of plants to preserve them, improve their appearance, and make them uniform and bug resistant. In its infancy, this terrifying twist on agriculture should have us shaking in our boots. The genetic engineering of food violates the very soul of nature and has all the makings of a nightmare. A little detail that the monolithic chemical companies behind this technology are leaving out of the marketing of this area of agribusiness is that organic farming will become obsolete, with hybrid plants producing seeds with no natural way to battle strains of resistant pests that will ultimately be the result. Plus no one has a clue how they would ever clean up the mess from a genetic accident, such as might produce a dangerous virus.

Food additives are far removed from nature and are designed to have such an extreme effect on foods' characters that there is no way that they won't have an extreme effect on us. Do we think that rampant cancer is accidental? Do we ever wonder why people are developing degenerative diseases at younger and younger ages?

Maybe the solution lies in strict labeling. For every additive, pesticide, herbicide, irradiation process, or genetically engineered seed, there should be a warning label. With the vertical integration of farming, conventional food would become as expensive as its organic counterpart, owing to the added cost of printing labels. But at least we'd know what we were eating.

What's the answer? Organic food, of course. With certified organic foods you can be sure that you are eating the very best quality that farmers and manufacturers can produce and that the food was cultivated under natural conditions. You can be sure that the food was produced with methods that support and sustain the planet and do not perpetuate the processes of pollution and resource stripping that is so out of control in commercial food processing. And you can be sure that the food you consume helps you build your health, not compromise it.

THE JAVA JIVE

We've all heard countless times that we should limit our intake of caffeine. It can contribute to high blood pressure, irregular heartbeat, and ulcers; and at the very least, it can leave us with frayed nerves, anxiety, and panic attacks. We have even recently heard about the link between caffeine and osteoporosis, especially in women. We know that caffeine is at best energizing and at worst extremely addictive. We know when we've tried to give it up, we are plagued with strong withdrawal symptoms, from fatigue to headaches to the sweats. And because caffeine is found in so many foods, from coffee to chocolate to a wide variety of sodas and teas, flavored ice creams and yogurt, we surely get our fair share each day.

Reaching peak concentration in the bloodstream roughly an hour after ingestion, this powerful chemical affects the body for four to six hours before it wears off. That means the body stays in high gear for a long time with no rest. That kind of strain is incredibly depleting, leaving the organs and nervous system exhausted and in need of a boost of energy.

When caffeine becomes a regular ingredient in our diets, we have more difficulty keeping our focus. While it appears that we have lots of energy and can even seem more alert, the truth is that our body is overstimulated: Our nerves are on edge, our heart is pumping furiously, and our entire being is in a flight mode ready to jump out of our skins. That kind of energy leaves little room for us to go deep inside where we tap into our creative focus, where we can find our calm center.

On top of that, caffeine is hard on the kidneys and adrenal glands, causing them to work at peak performance constantly, making it difficult for us to rest and rejuvenate ourselves. That's one of the reasons why giving up caffeine leaves us so exhausted; our kidneys, the seat of our vitality, have been totally beaten up.

TROPICAL FRUITS

You've got to love the tropics—the warm sea, bright sunshine, perpetually warm weather, balmy breezes. And tropical foods, we love them, especially the fruit: grapefruit, oranges, papaya, mangoes, bananas, figs, kiwi fruit, and passion fruit. They're sweet, succulent, and juicy. And they're jam-packed with vitamin C. What could be inappropriate or extreme about these delicious foods? Well, nothing, if you live in the tropics, which most of us do not.

Here's how it works in nature. Each region of the planet creates food to support the life that exists in that environment. The tropical regions of the world are located in a band that wraps around the globe along the equator, creating either hot and wet climates or hot and dry climates, but always hot. Nature, in her infinite wisdom, designed foods for these regions that are sweet, juicy, and acidic, so that the body will remain cool and damp to balance the heat of the surrounding environment. That's great news for anyone living in tropical regions. Nature has provided foods to keep the body cool.

If we live, however, in more temperate regions, as most of the world does, tropical foods may not serve us quite as well. Most tropical fruits are wrapped in a thick, outer skin designed to protect the fragile, sweet fruit inside. These tough, inedible skins were created by nature because the fruit doesn't adapt well to dramatic climate changes. We've all heard of entire orange and grapefruit groves being lost to freak cold snaps in

Florida. At those times, even the tough skins can't protect the fruit.

And what does that mean to us? Regular consumption of tropical foods, especially fruit, creates a cold, damp energy in our bodies, making our blood a bit more acidic than normal. Tropical foods keep our internal air-conditioner on high year-round, and we became uncomfortable as the weather naturally turns colder. We become more like the fruit, losing our ability to adapt to weather changes. And so we either gripe about the weather or we retire somewhere warm, where our bodies will not need to change with the weather.

We need these foods for vitamin C, right? Interestingly, the vitamin C in many tropical fruits is most concentrated in the peel, which we don't eat, rather than in the fruit and juice. In addition, these fruits contain no minerals needed by the body, are as high as 60 percent sugar, and are incredibly acidic—all of which exhaust the kidneys, deplete the blood of minerals, and keep us cold all winter long. Eat tropical foods on occasional hot summer days when your body really needs to be refreshed—that's a job they do beautifully.

THE DEADLY NIGHTSHADES

The deadly nightshade family includes some of the most common varieties of fruits and vegetables: tomatoes, potatoes, peppers, and eggplant. Nightshade, from the word *nihtscada,* meaning "shadow of night," actually refers to the narcotic qualities that are reputedly possessed by the flowering plants of this family. Considered poisonous, even today, by many cultures, nightshades contain quite concentrated amounts of naturally occurring toxins. The most common of these are glycoalkaloids, which weaken red blood cells; alkamines, which contribute to nervous disorders; and solanine, a poison that has been linked to skin disorders.

With their cool, damp natures, these extreme plants can make the body so cold inside that we begin to crave animal foods and strong, heat-producing spices as the only way to reignite our fires.

Nightshades are as extreme as vegetables can get, creating radical energetic qualities in us. Although small quantities of these powerful plants can benefit some conditions, nightshades generally cause physical and mental weakness; pale, wrinkled, or sallow skin; poor circulation; stiff joints; tight muscles; insomnia; and cravings for animal foods.

THE SPICE WORLD

Condiments, seasonings, and flavorings are added to foods to enhance and support the taste and, in many cases, support the energetic qualities of food. There are lots of choices: oils, vinegars, fresh and dried herbs, mild spices, nuts and seeds, and various forms of salts. Used in small amounts, as supporting players, these ingredients add sparkle to our food, creating a dance of energies in us. With strong, dispersing qualities, spices have the reputation of stimulating and opening our energy. By studying the inherent qualities of each, we can decide which of these powerful condiments are appropriate for us and which are too intense. With mildly stimulating condiments like mustard, ginger, and horseradish, all of which enliven the body, animate circulation, and strengthen organ function, we can create delicious spicy flavor without an extreme reaction in the body. Other spices should be used sparingly, with great attention paid to how you feel the day after consuming them. You might be surprised at your lack of focus and irritability. Let's take a look at just a few of the more common flavorings so you get an idea of their power.

Cinnamon

Cinnamon is a lovely spice that makes apple pie, apple pie. It's the little sparkle that makes rice pudding special. Cinnamon is the bark of a tree that grows sixty feet high. It is incredibly stimulating, and it's warm and spicy with a splendid aroma and earthy flavor.

For some people, cinnamon can be quite helpful in stimulating sluggish energy. A pinch here and there in cooking, on occa-

sion, can open your energy and warm a cold body. The problems come when too much cinnamon is used too often or when the body is delicate. It can overstimulate and irritate the kidneys, bladder, and reproductive organs, causing increased symptoms of PMS, frequent urination, and—in some sensitive people—insomnia.

Garlic

Garlic is a member of the onion family, which includes onions, leeks, shallots, chives, and scallions, and is more potent than any of its spicy relatives. The tight bulb of cloves, which wrap around each other in a cluster, each protected in its own paper-thin sheath, joins at a strong root base. One of the first foods cultivated, garlic has always been mysterious and exotic. It has many faces.

On one hand, garlic is considered one of the earliest, if not the oldest, antibiotics known. It has the reputation for reducing high cholesterol, purifying the blood, increasing oxygen absorption, detoxifying the intestinal bacteria of meats and other animal products, and having strong healing powers.

Its sheer power is what concerns me the most. Strongly stimulating, garlic can animate us to the point of anger. Reputed to have a hot temperament, garlic doesn't necessarily increase our internal body temperature. Rather, garlic has an irritating effect on the nervous system, causing us to have quick tempers.

On yet another hand, garlic is a great condiment for those of us who choose to eat animal food. It has an uncanny ability to cleanse the body of harmful bacteria from meat and other animal fats. For vegetarians, it can be a bit too stimulating, causing us to see our lives as only high drama, with everything blown out of proportion.

And finally, garlic has this miraculous reputation for being a powerful antibiotic. And while natural, garlic can have the same effect on the intestines as chemical antibiotics, weakening digestion. So take care with this powerful condiment.

Pepper

Black and white pepper are probably the most commonly used spices in the world. Black pepper is made from peppercorns that have been ripened and blackened in the sun; white pepper is made from peppercorns that have been soaked.

Pepper has a strong, dispersing nature. When used in heavy foods, like animal products, pepper creates deep warmth and aids in digestion. In lighter cooking, pepper stimulates the blood. Pepper can also cause the release of deep body heat, leaving us feeling cold and tired.

All in all, spices are powerful tools that can create changes in us and so must be used wisely in cooking. Remember that spices have the ability to disperse and move things, to stimulate, to release. The few examples discussed above simply illustrate the strong effects of these powerful foods. Used in excess, strong ingredients can cause dramatic reactions in the body. Used wisely, they can add a sparkling, enlivening energy to our cooking that can't be beat.

It's easy to see that we are what we eat and that eating a balanced diet can keep us on an even keel. A diet that is rich in extreme foods can create an overworked, overstimulated body and erratic behavior. An extreme diet inhibits our ability to function effectively. We lose focus and are anxious, irritated, or lethargic. In any kind of extreme state, we can no longer see our way clear to making sound decisions. We swing from extreme to extreme in a constant state of imbalance. We become enslaved by our food, no longer in control of our bodies or our emotional responses. The lessons I hope you learn from this book include the all-important aspect of taking control of the things you can, including what you eat. Making wise choices and avoiding extreme foods sets you on a course to attain the life you want. It's worth thinking about the next time you sit down to that burger, chili fries, and diet soda or milk shake.

Menus for the Life You Want

WE LIVE IN a world of convenience and processed foods, take-away meals and meals that you slip into the microwave for a minute or two. Adopting a truly healthy eating plan requires thought and planning, so that we can easily incorporate it into our lives. Remember this: Although it may require some thought, it isn't rocket science; it's cooking simple, whole ingredients to create healthy, delicious meals.

When I first decided to take my health into my own hands there were far fewer options for eating healthfully than there are today. Ingredients were more difficult to find, restaurants weren't serving anything remotely like what I wanted, and even take-out was limited to the steamed vegetables from the local Chinese place. So I cooked . . . and I cooked. Piecing together whatever information I could from books, knowledgeable friends, and the helpful folks at the local health food store, I wrote out my menu plans each week so that I could shop accordingly. But writing out the menus also helped me to balance my meals. Were there two protein dishes in the same meal? Too many carrots? Did I forget the sea veggies? Even though it was at first difficult and inconvenient, I was motivated by the killer disease that was threatening me.

As I reflect on it all now, I realize what a gift it was to be recovering at that time. I cooked, because I had no choice but to prepare my own food. And my food was, in effect, my medicine. The result was that not only did I recover my health, but I came to understand the power of food in my life—and how ignorant I had been of this power.

Today we live in a world that makes eating well much easier. More and more restaurants offer some variety of whole foods choices. We have more opportunities to eat out or pick up take-away meals from natural foods deli counters. There are even fast-food versions of "healthy" foods in the frozen food section of every supermarket (many of which don't hold up too well under scrutiny). And, of course, there are an infinite variety of no-fat, low-fat prepared foods that claim to be the key to health and happiness. Yes, we have more choices than ever before, but I still believe that we must learn to cook and understand that what we do in the kitchen has an incredible affect not only on how we feel but on who we are in the world. With more opportunities to eat out or hire a home chef to cook our meals or pick up take-away meals from natural foods counters, we run a risk. We run a risk of giving our destiny to any chef who claims to know how to cook a pot of rice. He or she is in charge of who we are and what we feel and how we behave. That

may sound dramatic, but the truth is that whoever is cooking is in charge of the people we become. The more opportunities afforded us for eating out, the less need for us to cook. I love it that whole, natural foods are more available to more people, and I am not, on any level, opposed to eating out. I love the social aspect of restaurant dining, but I think we must be vigilant. We must learn to cook and understand why what we do in the kitchen does what it does to us.

So eat out and enjoy, but do it wisely and don't stray far from your own pots and pans too often if you want to really take charge of your life.

The following sample menus are just that—samples. They have been devised to show you how you can combine the energetic qualities of foods to create specific results and to enhance overall well-being. To look better, to have more vitality, to feel refreshed or less stressed, each menu addresses a physical or emotional condition with which all of us can identify. Choose the one that best fits you, adding, subtracting, or substituting dishes as fits your needs, creating your own Personal New-trition Profile.

The real secret of a great meal is a gentle blending of the five flavors—sweet, pungent (spicy), salty, sour, and bitter—in a meal. Weaving these flavors together is what makes the difference between a so-so meal and a deeply satisfying feast, even one composed of the simplest ingredients.

EATING WITH ALL THE SENSES

We eat with our eyes as much as with our mouths and stomachs. If food isn't a delight to the eye, we won't be attracted to it. Beige, although a stylish color for interiors, doesn't make much of an impression on the plate, even though it might be good for you. Picture this: creamy golden squash soup; brown rice, dotted with parsley and minced black olives; stir-fried tofu with carrots, mushrooms, and orange peel; and steamed watercress with a garnish of roasted red pepper ribbons. This is as balanced and as beautiful a meal as you could hope for—and made so much more delicious, as a result of its eye appeal.

Whole, natural foods are quite sensual, quite diverse. There's crunchy, creamy, smooth, coarse. In our modern diet, so many refined foods simply turn to mush in the mouth (except meat, which we need to chew and chew and chew . . .). In natural cooking, the high fiber content of the basic ingredients helps create a diversity of textures that keep the mouth active and the diner interested. Chewy whole grains combined with creamy soups and cooked beans with crisply steamed greens add to the variety we need to keep dining exciting.

As you look over the various themes I've laid out and see how the various energy phases come together to create the balance that you need, know that you can play with them and still get the results you want. Substi-tuting various dishes from the same energy phase will alter the energy slightly, but you still have lots of room to create personalized meals. Looking for vitality, but aren't crazy about quinoa? Use corn or amaranth, instead. Want to relax, but can't get used to millet just yet? Stew some sweet winter squash.

One final tip: Create ambiance for your meals. The presentation of your food, whether you are eating alone or entertaining family or friends, should be an enhancement of your

THE ART OF CHEWING

My Japanese teacher, Michio Kushi, used to say, as he pointed to his belly, "No teeth here." And then, pointing to his mouth, "Teeth here."

Chewing is where digestion begins. Chewing helps release all the flavors of the food you're eating, which makes all your food very satisfying. Mechanically, chewing helps break down food, releasing gastric juices and stimulating the release of saliva. Food needs to be chewed until it is liquid in form. The stomach has no idea what to do with solid food. Solids pass through the intestines, undigested, and leave us feeling bloated and puffy. Nutrients will pass through us, with no benefit to our body. So chew, chew, chew.

efforts. Garnishes can be both colorful and healthy complements to any dish. Set the table with thoughtfulness for you and your guests. Sit down and enjoy your meal in a contented and relaxed atmosphere. The rewards will be many. You'll eat more slowly. The food will taste better. The company, even if it's only your own, will be more congenial. And, practically speaking, sitting down to a well-set table makes for better digestion. The best benefit, however, is that you are giving yourself and your loved ones a gift beyond measure.

BEAUTY FROM THE INSIDE OUT

Choosing foods that are heavy, dense, or fatty overtax the body in some way, can leave us looking as tired as we probably feel or as tight as the body has become. Lines, creases, blemishes, puffiness, and poor skin tone (either flushed or pale) are all the result of overworking the body in some way, and whatever organ is currently paying the price of our excesses leaves signs on our face. If we continue to overwork the body, we start to look old before our time, reflecting the fact that our organs are doing the same.

Eating foods that create clean, strong blood results in optimally working organs, leaving us with firm, supple skin that's free of blemishes, lines, spots, and dots; with hair that's lustrous; and with nails that are strong and flexible.

In this menu, you'll notice that all Five Transformations of Energy play an important role, with a bit of extra focus on water energy. Although our goal is to keep all of the energy phases supporting and nourishing each other, for our true beauty to shine, our kidney function must remain strong and efficient, so that the blood that nourishes the rest of our organs is strong and clean, making function smooth, allowing us to put our best face forward.

Azuki Bean Vegetable Soup (Water) (page 104)
Hato Mugi Risotto (Tree) (page 135)
Arame with Dried Daikon and Ginger (Water) (page 216)
Sweet Nishime Squash (Earth) (page 193)
Steamed Greens Medley (Fire) (page 209)
Ginger-Poached Pears (Metal) (page 219)

GENTLEMEN, START YOUR ENGINES

The world we live in is incredibly hard on everyone, but the toll on men's health seems to be especially acute. This may be owing to a combination of generally high stress levels and the diets that men stereotypically choose: "manly" foods like meat, shellfish, eggs, and fatty foods. Operating under the misconception that these kinds of foods make them feel big and strong, they are, instead, wearing themselves down and out, in more ways than one. Choosing a diet high in dense animal protein and fat can block a man's energy flow. As men grow more tired, interest in romance and sex also diminish. Their bodies are working too hard to digest their food, so there isn't any energy to spare, especially energy that will get expended and released. They become more concerned with holding their energy in, as they try to hold on to their lives.

Choosing from the more strengthening of the plant foods and preparing them in hearty, vitalizing ways keep our men centered and focused on their goals, leaving them with some energy to spend on romantic pursuits.

So why will this particular menu keep our men big and strong? The energy phases in this combination of dishes come from Earth for grounded, centered strength and Fire for vitality. The strong focus on Water energy allows for flexibility, an adaptable nature, and strong kidneys, which enliven sexual vitality and strength.

Tempura Vegetables over Soba Noodles in Broth (Water) (page 140)
Azuki Relish (Water) (page 161)
Burdock Kinpira (Water) (page 187)
Harvest Salad (Earth) (page 185)
Red and Green Medley (Fire) (page 208)

I'M TIRED OF BEING TIRED

What we choose to eat is largely responsible for how we feel each day. If we eat food that is highly processed and devoid of nutritional value, we'll be tired. If we eat calorie-dense foods (like meat, dairy, eggs, and shellfish), poor-quality or excessive salt, refined simple sugar, caffeine, and alcohol, we'll feel and look tired because our body has to work so hard to process these foods.

Bringing together the energies given here keeps your feet on the ground but gives you energy to burn. The dish from Earth energy keeps you centered, and the strong Water influence keeps your blood strong (through efficient kidney function), so that Tree energy is supported, allowing you to reach for the stars. And with the vitality of Fire to top it all off, you won't tire out before reaching your goals.

Hearty Lentil Soup with Fried Tofu and Herbs (Tree) (page 95)
Kasha with Noodles (Water) (page 120)
Sweet Root Vegetable Stew (Earth) (page 186)
Sesame Hiziki Salad (Water) (page 214)
Warm Escarole and Shiitake Salad (Fire) (page 210)
Mustard Pickled Sweet Vegetables (Tree) (page 207)

THE DE-STRESSOR

We live in a world that seems to move faster every day. I wonder what will be on the horizon when we grow so pressed that instant e-mail isn't quick enough for us. As the pressure builds and our loads seem heavier, we find ourselves wondering how much more we can take before we surrender, waving the white flag and giving up completely. Sometimes, we just want to get off.

Overcome with stress, we can't sleep or eat well. We're cranky and rushed, making mistakes, overlooking details, and causing accidents . . . and then we live filled with regret. Every single thing in life seems overwhelming and much too much to take. Well, we can't take the stress out of our lives, but we can cook in such a manner that we manage stress with grace and style. We remain calm and strong, with a clear mind and sharp focus. The key is to create food that relaxes the body but provides incredible energy to face the world. You don't want to relax so much that you go through life like a zombie.

Combining Earth energy with Metal energy—remembering that Earth nourishes Metal—we create a menu that settles us down, allowing us to find our center. Just calming ourselves, however, won't help us manage stress. Nourishing the strengthening character of Metal gives us the fortitude to face life's challenges fully, and the centering energy of Earth keeps us clearheaded and calm.

Sweet Winter Squash Bisque (Earth) (page 94)
Millet with Sweet Vegetables and Corn (Earth) (page 132)
Dried Tofu and Winter Squash Stew (Metal) (page 175)
Sweet Onion Tart (Metal) (page 202)
Spicy Asian Coleslaw (Earth) (page 195)
The Best Rice Pudding (Metal) (page 223)

I'VE GOT TO GET IT TOGETHER

We lose focus and grow indecisive when we take in too many foods that weaken us with internal expansion.

Eating refined and simple sugars, including too much fruit, can cause us to grow weak, easily swayed or manipulated. Simple, refined sugars can also give us too much energy, making us feel jittery and nervous, unable to focus on any one thing through to completion. Chemical sweeteners and soft, sweet dairy foods like yogurt, ice cream, and frozen yogurt paralyze the will, making it difficult to be decisive in our lives.

On the surface, caffeine appears to make us feel sharper, with more focus. It creates great expansion, which can seem to open us up to creative thinking. But that's only the short-term effect. Over time, as we require more and more caffeine to get our juices going, we get scattered, filled with nervous energy—and we can't seem to get it together anymore.

When a candy bar or a cup of coffee beckons, choose foods that gather energy into our bodies, nourishing us with their freshness and vitality. Consider the character of the food: Rooted veggies ground us (Metal); sharp, spicy flavors help us keep (or gain) our focus (Fire); and lightly cooked foods (Tree) or light soups (Water) keep us flexible and easy to get along with. And cooking with high heat (Fire) or stewing (Earth) gathers our strength.

In this menu, we combine all our resources to gather our energy and sharpen our focus. The centering energy of Earth gets our feet on the ground and nourishes the strength of Metal to give us fortitude. Metal energy nourishes Water for flexibility and strong blood, and Water energy nourishes Tree energy to sharpen our focus and lift our spirits. We *can* get it together. Add a bit of garnish from Fire energy to this menu and you will be a force to be reckoned with.

Winter Vegetable Soup with Mochi
Croutons (Earth) (page 109)
Crostini with Lentil Pâté (Tree) (page
157)
Candied Sweet Potatoes and Parsnips
with Bitter Greens (Earth) (page 191)
Spicy Cucumber Ribbon Salad (Metal)
(page 198)

Marinated Kombu Salad (Water) (page
214)

FOR THE JOCK IN ALL OF US

A mostly plant-based diet is the greatest fuel an athlete can hope for—and truly enough for the weekend warriors that make up most of the population. We do need to choose carefully, however, to nourish the athlete hiding inside all of us.

Now I will concede that an athlete looking to build muscle might need a bit of animal protein to achieve that goal, although I have seen many people meet their goals without it. The good news is that fish will do the trick in most cases. Any other animal food makes us look bulky and thick, instead of defined and lean.

Whole grains and beans provide not only protein but also the staying power that is the signature of complex carbohydrates. The best choices are quinoa and amaranth, which are very high in protein and provide great Fire energy for training. Millet, mochi, and sweet rice stick to your ribs and provide lots of staying power plus Earth and Metal energies for endurance. Noodles, especially whole-grain types, are easy to digest, making them a good source of quick energy. Athletic pursuits can be hard on the kidneys, so keep them strong with red azuki beans and black soybeans from Water energy.

All veggies help keep you hydrated and relaxed while you work out; but root veggies give you the most strength, and delicate leafy greens keep your body flexible and supple.

Don't underestimate the power of good-quality vegetable fat. It provides you with quick-burning fuel that can buffer you from muscle loss when you're working out intensely. And finally, nuts and seeds are little powerhouses of nutrients and vitality that really add to your staying power in the gym, on the track, or on the yoga mat.

Earth energy is calming, so we add just a bit to this menu to ground you, in the form of a dessert with nuts. Deeply nourishing to Metal energy, which in turn nourishes Water, this menu keeps your body strong, lean, and flexible.

The vitality of Fire rounds out the energies here, so you'll have energy to burn while you leap tall buildings in a single bound.

Spicy Kidney Bean Soup (Water) (page 96)

Minted Quinoa with Crunchy Pine Nuts (Fire) (page 134)

Herb-Scented Roasted Daikon (Metal) (page 186)

Roasted Vegetable Terrine (Metal) (page 206)

Stir-Fried Cauliflower and Mustard Greens in Lemon-Sesame Sauce (Fire) (page 208)

Pecan Squares (Earth) (page 231)

PLAYING WELL WITH OTHERS

Life can be quite challenging at times, and if our bodies aren't working optimally, with the energy of life moving smoothly through us, especially the liver and gallbladder (which in turn regulate the nervous system), we may find ourselves, at the very least, easily irritated. It's important in the world we live in that we keep our livers relaxed and soft, so that we can maintain our compassion and our patience with those around us.

Dense animal protein, eggs, dairy (especially hard, salty cheese), and shellfish make the liver hard and tight—and you hard and tight as well. Foods like caffeine and alcohol leave the liver and gallbladder bloated and flaccid, and you lose your compassion, growing complacent and unmotivated.

Choosing foods that support and nourish the liver and gallbladder in their vital functions, as well as cushion the nervous system against irritation, ensures that you face life's challenges with balance and confidence. Of course, a plant-based diet is your best choice. A lightly sour taste is the signature flavor of the liver, because sour taste enlivens it through Tree energy, which governs liver function, keeping it fresh and clean, helping it hold up under stress. So foods with a delicate sour flavor help you keep your cool.

Whole grains like wheat, barley, and oats are all great choices for insulating you against the world. They lift your energy while keeping you grounded, in typical Tree fashion. They also have the unique ability to relax the body, so you aren't so irritable.

Look at the energy of vegetables that support the liver—broccoli, lettuce, green beans, fresh peas, and parsley. They have a gentle, rising energy and yet remain relaxed. Add to them the zesty sparkle of lemon and you can take on the world . . . and get along with everybody around you in the process.

Choose from all the five energy phases, placing the emphasis on a specific need, but don't ignore the other four in your zeal to support your liver. For instance, keep in mind that Water energy nourishes Tree energy, so it would be wise to include that in your menu.

All Five Transformations of Energy play a role in this menu, because keeping the nourishing flow of energy from one phase to the next on an even keel keeps you on track. With two dishes from the Tree phase, however, we lend a bit of extra support to the liver, so you can keep your cool.

> Spicy Kidney Bean Soup (Water) (page 96)
> Toasted Barley Salad with Braised Portobello Mushrooms (Tree) (page 136)
> Winter Vegetable Salad (Metal) (page 188)
> Spicy Asian Coleslaw (Earth) (page 195)

> Spicy Sautéed Collard Greens (Fire) (page 213)
> Lemon Gingerbread Trifles (Tree) (page 222)

GETTING OFF THE ROLLER COASTER

Do you wish that you were on a more even keel instead of feeling fine one minute and ready to kill—yourself or someone else—the next? While it's true that life is unpredictable, it doesn't have to be such a drama.

Our moods are regulated by organ function. If our bodies are working smoothly, with things clicking along, our moods will be even and stable. To get off the roller coaster and get your feet planted firmly on the ground, give up simple sugar! Not only does this include white sugar, brown sugar, artificial sweeteners, and low-calorie sweeteners but also honey, raw sugar, organic cane juice, maple syrup, molasses, and fruit juice concentrates. Simple sugars, even those in their natural state, have an extreme effect on our blood chemistry and our emotional state.

The brain, like the rest of the body, relies on glucose for fuel. Now, many foods break down into glucose, but if you are loading up on sugar all the time (besides what you're getting from your real food), the brain can't focus, can't think straight, can't remain stable. Your moods are wildly out of control, with ups and downs, nervous energy and manic thought—followed by a crash into the depths of depression and exhaustion. So we take in more sugar, get a lift, and keep the cycle going.

Using grain sweeteners and some cooked fruit will satisfy your sweet tooth, without shifting your moods to the extreme.

But sugar's not the only culprit in the mood-swing department. Animal protein can make us feel tired and heavy or aggressive and irritable, depending on our own condition. That kind of dense food makes the body work very hard and creates a lot of internal "friction," as the body struggles to digest it.

Caffeine, alcohol, and other stimulating foods, like hot spices, when used in excess, can irritate the nervous system, and our moods reflect that.

The energy phases that give us our foundation, as it were, are Earth and Metal; the other phases support, nourish, and keep things lively and light.

Ironically, the flavor of food that relaxes and centers us is sweet. The problems arise when we choose that taste from inappropriate sources, such as simple sugars. Sweet taste should leave us feeling satisfied, relaxed, and centered. Metal comes into the picture with a spicy, pungent flavor that keeps us rooted, instead of overstimulated.

Whole grains, especially millet and brown rice, fill the bill on all counts. Nothing gives us quite as much stamina and endurance. Nothing is quite as grounding. And nothing is as nourishing. Cooked with sweet vegetables, these grains provide us with the most delicious energy.

Squash, parsnips, onions, and green cabbage are a few of the sweet-tasting vegetables available for making us feel stable. And for real grounding, go for the sweet root vegetables, like carrots and daikon. And don't forget lovely dark leafy greens to promote a flexible attitude.

You can see from the combination of dishes in this menu the creation of a grounded center from Earth energy, rooted endurance from Metal energy, focused direction from Tree energy, and a bit of lively sparkle from Fire energy. A menu like this will keep your moods as smooth as silk.

Chilled Cucumber Bisque (Metal)
(page 103)
Lentil Pilaf with Sweet Vegetables
(Tree) (page 158)
Vegetable Hotpot with Biscuit Topping
(Earth) (page 200)
Butternut Squash and Leek Pie (Earth)
(page 203)
Lemony Baby Carrots with Caraway
(Metal) (page 190)
Steamed Greens Medley (Fire) (page
209)
Spiced Pecan Baked Apples (Earth)
(page 220)

OH, THOSE HOT FLASHES

During menopause, it's important to make food choices that are stable, so that we're nourished with an energy that counters the extreme changes occurring in us.

As you might guess by now, animal protein will not serve you so well during this time of your life. Not only is it heavy and dense, it produces a lot of internal heat as the body labors to digest it, so hot flashes only intensify if you eat animal foods. So to keep cool minimize (or eliminate) meat, poultry, eggs, and dairy foods, especially salty cheese. Even fish might be too strong, depending on your condition.

Another concern for perimenopausal women is bone strength. After menopause, you begin to lose bone density, so it's important that you take care of your skeleton during menopause, with proper diet and exercise. Avoid simple sugars and dairy foods, as they both leach calcium and other minerals from the body. You might also want to avoid veggies such as spinach and chard that are high in oxalic acid, which can inhibit the body's ability to absorb and use calcium.

And the mood swings? Once again, sugar is the enemy, upsetting our blood chemistry, immediately and dramatically. Caffeine and alcohol also overstimulate the nervous system and overwork the liver, making our moods unstable.

Choose foods that keep you cool, calm, and collected in the face of the uncertainty of perimenopause. Barley, corn, quinoa, wild rice, basmati rice, and wheat work really well during hot-flash time.

Soyfoods are a great friend to you during perimenopause, for many reasons. Not only will they help regulate your haywire hormones, but they come from the soybean, which by nature is cooling and strengthening to the body. Tofu, tempeh, black soybeans, soy milk, soy sauce, and miso serve you very well in life, but especially during perimenopause.

On to the vegetables—again, you want to relax, cool, and refresh the body, while staying strong. Dark leafy greens—kale, collards, watercress, mustard greens, Chinese cabbage, bok choy, escarole, broccoli rabe, and broccoli—are incredibly valuable for staying relaxed, cool, and refreshed. That these greens are high in calcium, iron, and folic acid is an important feature; but to me, the flexibility and moisture you get from them are of more value during menopause.

Daikon and dried shiitake mushrooms also help us stay relaxed and fresh, preventing stagnation, so energy moves smoothly, instead of intensely and erratically, through the body.

Strengthening vegetable stews and vitalizing sautéed veggie dishes keep you grounded and give you energy—but not manic mood swings. In fact, you probably couldn't eat too many vegetables at this time of life; they keep the body moist and fresh and light. And don't forget sea vegetables; they're high in minerals and keep the blood strong.

One last thing—don't ignore oil and desserts during menopause. Sautéing, even occasionally frying, foods keeps the body moist and flexible. And desserts keep you relaxed and happy; just stay away from simple sugar.

This menu, with its grounded center coming from Earth energy, which supports and nourishes Metal energy, gives us the fortitude we need during these challenging years to keep the body calmly strong. The cool flexibility of Tree energy comes into play to soften and open the body, so it can smoothly release excess energy.

Daikon-Shiitake Consommé (Metal) (page 104)

Hato Mugi Risotto (Tree) (page 135)

Pickled Cucumber and Baked Tofu Salad (Metal) (page 198)

Candied Sweet Potatoes and Parsnips with Bitter Greens (Earth) (page 191)

Braised Cabbage with Sesame-Ginger Sauce (Earth) (page 197)

Dried Cherry and Sweet Pear Pie (Metal) (page 246)

Your Personal New-trition Profile

After looking over these sample menus you should begin to understand how to use the Five Transformations of Energy to create the life you want. I think of it as your Personal New-trition Profile—and the good news is that you get to create it for yourself. No self-proclaimed expert is telling you what's best for you. *You're* the expert here: only *you* know what you need. Develop your understanding of the natural character of the foods you choose, determine how to apply the Five Transformations of Energy to your own life, tune in to your intuition—and follow its lead. You make your choices, plan your menus, and then cook according to your personal needs and lifestyle.

By studying these sample menu plans, you can start to understand how the energy of food can be used in your own life. Need energy? Fire energy to the rescue, supported by grounded Tree energy and tempered by the sweet taste of Earth energy. Feeling edgy? Settle yourself with calming Earth energy, the grounded centeredness of Metal energy, but keep your spirits high with the vitality of Fire energy. Rigid? Inflexible? Choose from Water energy for adaptability, Metal energy for support, with a bit of Tree energy to keep your feet on the ground. Need focus for that important meeting? Tree energy will keep you centered and your eye on your goal, with Metal energy for strength, with the charisma of Fire energy so you can communicate your ideas with clarity and charm. See how easy this is? Simply find the dishes from each energy phase (all dishes for each energy transformation are listed under separate headings in the Index), finding the one that appeals to you on all levels—taste, texture, color, and time needed to prepare it. Pick and choose from the Five transformations of Energy to put together daily menus that help you balance your life, maintain (or regain) your health, and create the energy you need for the adventure we know as life. You'll see that you really can cook your way to the life you want.

RECIPE SECTION

SENSATIONAL SOUPS

IN MACROBIOTIC, WHOLE foods cooking, soup is prepared according to the principles of balance. As the first course of a meal, soup introduces food to the body. It sets the tone and creates the appetite for the rest of the meal. The taste, texture, flavor, fragrance, and ingredients should all complement the other dishes served. If a meal is light and simple, then a creamy, rich, hearty soup is appropriate. If the meal is rich and substantial, a lighter soup, a clear broth, a simple vegetable soup, or consommé will work toward achieving balance.

In a similar manner, ingredients, cutting techniques, and cooking styles are altered seasonally. Cool or cold weather makes hearty soups and stews, thick with grains and beans, laden with chunky root vegetables, a natural choice. Warm, humid, or hot weather calls for lighter, fresher soups when light leafy greens, shiitake mushrooms, delicately sliced vegetables, all mildly seasoned, have the most appeal.

In the typical whole foods kitchen, soup is made daily, using only the freshest vegetables, grains, and beans to ensure the best flavor and the most vitality. The quality of energy you get from soup depends on the quality of ingredients used.

Although I use stock on occasion—for a special soup or to achieve a particular richness in a recipe—I do not make it a habit. From an energy viewpoint, making stock creates a soup that has been cooked twice: once during stock making and again during soup making. Soup should retain a light energy, so it can do its job of relaxing the digestive tract. Stock creates a soup that is heavier and hotter in the body, inhibiting digestion. Fresh water makes a light, fresh soup. When you choose to make stock, however, use the same rule as for soup—add only the freshest ingredients.

Soup seasoning varies. Commonly, miso is used to create a rich, full-bodied flavor as well as to improve digestion. A dark puree made from soybeans, sea salt, and barley or rice, miso is combined with koji, a cultured rice that stimulates fermentation. The resulting miso is aged in wooden kegs for one or more years. A staple in Asian cooking, miso has become more and more familiar in Western cooking. Miso has long been prized in Asia for containing living enzymes that strengthen digestion; improve the quality of the blood; and provide a nutritious balance of complex carbohydrates, essential oils, protein, vitamins, and minerals. Asian legend tells us that miso was given to humanity by the gods to ensure health and happiness. True or not, miso lends a sweet, subtle flavor to soups (and sauces and pickles). Available in a variety of flavors, miso is a bit salty and should be used lightly as a seasoning, usually ¼ to ½ teaspoon per cup of soup. Excessive miso will create a counterbalancing craving for sweet taste and liquids, so use it moderately for the best health.

Clear soups are traditionally made from a light broth, using kombu, shiitake mushrooms, or other vegetables. Mild in flavor and made with simple ingredients, like a few vegetables or cubes of tofu, clear soup is a perfect starter for a heavy meal.

Dashi, a tamari or soy sauce stock, is the basis for a full-bodied soup. Usually laced through with delicately cut vegetables, tiny cubes of tofu, and maybe some sea vegetables, this delicious type of broth is often served with cooked noodles in it.

The variety of soups to be made are limited only by what you can imagine. Grain soups, bean stews, vegetable soups, noodles in broth, and simple consommé broth are just the beginning. Varying the grains, beans, vegetables, cutting techniques, and cooking styles—from simmering to sautéing to pressure cooking—come together with your choice of ingredients to create all kinds of delicious soups. So go for it. Read the recipes, study the techniques, and master the basics; then, just do it. Make soup—better yet, create soup. You'll wonder how you lived before you regularly had soup in your life.

Orange-Scented Sweet Potato Soup

This is a sophisticated soup for special occasions. Sweet potatoes are a bit expansive and can cause the blood to become acidic, so it's best to use them infrequently. Serving a soup this sweet and delicate at an autumn feast, however, can lend an energy to the meal that is unparalleled. The combination of ingredients, along with the sautéed vegetables, creates a soup that relaxes and brings out people's social nature—a great starter for a dinner party.

2 pounds garnet yams or sweet potatoes,
    peeled and cut into 1-inch chunks
2 to 3 teaspoons corn oil
Soy sauce
1 sweet onion, finely diced
2 teaspoons minced fresh ginger
Pinch sea salt
Finely grated zest of 1 orange
4 cups spring or filtered water
2½ teaspoons sweet white miso
1 to 2 tablespoons brown rice syrup
1 cup fresh orange juice
About ¼ cup minced flat-leaf parsley, for
    garnish

Preheat oven to 400F (205C).

In a large bowl, toss sweet potato pieces with 1 to 2 teaspoons of oil and lightly season with soy sauce, taking care to coat pieces well. Spread evenly on an ungreased baking sheet. Bake sweet potatoes, uncovered, about 30 minutes, until very tender and browned on edges.

Heat the remaining 1 teaspoon of corn oil in a soup pot over medium heat. Add onion, ginger, and salt; sauté 2 to 3 minutes. Add orange zest and cook, stirring, until onion is soft, about 3 minutes. Add roasted sweet potatoes; cook, stirring gently, for 2 minutes. Add water, cover, and bring to a boil. Reduce heat to low, and simmer, covered, for 20 minutes.

Puree soup in batches in a food mill or a food processor fitted with the metal blade. Return soup to the pot over low heat, and bring to a simmer. Remove a small amount of liquid, and use to dissolve miso. Add miso mixture, rice syrup, and orange juice to the pot, and simmer, uncovered, for 3 to 4 minutes to activate enzymes in miso. Serve hot, garnished with parsley.

Makes 5 or 6 servings

Sweet Winter Squash Bisque

There is nothing quite like winter squash for delicate sweetness and relaxing energy. Growing close to the ground, winter squash has the ability to stabilize blood sugar and relax the body's middle organs—the spleen, pancreas, and stomach—which can improve digestion and create a calm, centered feeling in us. This bisque helps you face life's little roadblocks fully in control. The best squash for this soup is butternut, buttercup, or kabocha, each tremendously sweet. Serve with a scallion garnish for a great starter course.

*3 cups plus 3 tablespoons spring or fil-
tered water*
1 small onion, finely diced
Sea salt
5 cups cubed winter squash
1 to 2 parsnips, chopped
1 to 2 cups plain rice or soy milk

2 to 3 tablespoons mirin
*1 to 2 scallions, thinly sliced on the diago-
nal, for garnish*

Heat 3 tablespoons of water in a soup pot over medium heat. Add onion and a pinch of salt, and sauté 2 minutes. Add squash, parsnips, remaining 3 cups water, rice milk, mirin, and a light sprinkling of salt. Bring to a boil over medium heat, covered. Reduce heat to low and simmer for 20 minutes. Season lightly with salt to taste (remember that the soup should taste sweet, so go lightly), and simmer, covered, until squash is quite soft, about 15 minutes.

Puree soup in batches in a food mill or a food processor fitted with the metal blade. Return soup to the pot and warm over low heat for 2 to 3 minutes, to develop flavors. Serve hot, garnished with scallions.

Makes 5 or 6 servings

Hearty Lentil Soup with Fried Tofu and Herbs

Bean soups are brilliant. A great source of protein, beans provide us with tremendous endurance and stamina. Put that together with the relaxing energy of soup, and you have the winning combination of a clear head and incredible staying power. This soup combines the peppery taste of lentils with the richness of fried tofu—and to ensure that the energy doesn't get too heavy, we've added the uplifting energy of herbs.

1-inch piece kombu

1 cup dried green or brown lentils, sorted and rinsed

5 to 6 cups spring or filtered water

½ teaspoon each dried rosemary and thyme

Safflower oil, for frying

4 ounces tofu, cut into ¼-inch cubes

1 small onion, finely diced

1 to 2 stalks celery, finely diced

1 carrot, finely diced

½ cup corn kernels

1 tablespoon barley miso

About ¼ cup minced flat-leaf parsley, for garnish

Place kombu in a soup pot, and add lentils. Add water, and bring to a boil, uncovered, over medium heat. Boil for 5 minutes. Add herbs; cover, reduce heat to low, and simmer 20 minutes.

Meanwhile, heat about ¼-inch of oil in a saucepan over medium-high heat. Add tofu and fry until golden brown, 2 to 3 minutes, turning to brown evenly. Drain on paper towels. Set aside.

Add onion, celery, carrot, and corn to soup. Do not stir; keeping veggies on top ensures maintenance of color. Cover and simmer until vegetables are soft, about 15 minutes. Stir in tofu cubes. Remove a small amount of liquid, and use to dissolve miso. Stir miso mixture gently into the pot, and simmer, uncovered, for 3 to 4 minutes to activate enzymes in miso. Serve hot, garnished with parsley.

Makes 6 or 7 servings

Spicy Kidney Bean Soup

Beans, especially larger beans, have lots of protein and give us lots of stamina, but they can also be quite heavy and create a sinking energy in us. When I use those beans, I like to sauté the vegetables to infuse them with the vitality of high fire and add some hot chili to balance the sinking with the spice's splendid, upward rush of energy.

Short on time? Use a can of organic beans instead of cooking your own.

1-inch piece kombu

½ cup dried kidney beans, sorted, rinsed, and soaked 6 to 8 hours

8½ to 10 cups spring or filtered water

2 to 3 teaspoons extra-virgin olive oil

1 small leek, split lengthwise, rinsed well, and thinly sliced

Soy sauce

1 to 2 stalks celery, cut into large dice

1 carrot, cut into large dice

1 cup cubed winter squash (if organic, do not peel)

4 to 6 dried shiitake mushrooms, soaked until tender, thinly sliced

1 tablespoon chili powder or 1 to 2 small dried chilies, seeded and diced

1 cup pearled barley, rinsed well

1 roasted red bell pepper, finely diced, for garnish (recipe follows)

Place kombu in a small saucepan. Drain kidney beans and pour over kombu. Add about 1½ cups of water. Bring to a boil, and cook, uncovered, over high heat 5 minutes. Cover, reduce heat to low, and simmer until beans are tender but not quite done, about 45 minutes. (You may also pressure cook beans 15 minutes.)

Heat olive oil in a soup pot over medium heat. Add leek and a dash of soy sauce; sauté until limp, about 2 minutes. Add celery and another dash of soy sauce; sauté 1 minute. Add carrot, squash, and another dash of soy sauce; sauté, stirring occasionally, until just shiny with oil, about 2 minutes. Finally, stir in mushrooms and chili powder.

Top vegetables with barley, beans with their liquid, and 6 to 8 cups water. Bring to a

---

TO ROAST A BELL PEPPER

Place a clean whole bell pepper over an open flame, and roast until skin is totally charred. Transfer to a paper sack, and seal shut. Allow pepper to steam 10 minutes. Then simply slip black skin off with your fingers. Quickly dip pepper in cold water to rinse off residue. You may also roast peppers by splitting them lengthwise—leaving seeds in—and placing them on a baking sheet, cut side down. Broil until skin turns black. The flavor is better when roasted over an open flame.

---

boil, covered, over high heat. Reduce heat to low, and simmer until vegetables and beans are quite soft and barley is creamy, 25 to 30 minutes. Season lightly with soy sauce, and simmer 7 to 10 minutes more. Serve hot, garnished with a light sprinkling of roasted red pepper.

Makes 8 to 10 servings

Creamy White Bean Soup with Escarole

This wonderfully creamy soup is most satisfying and relaxing. White beans have a cooling energy in the body, helping us de-stress, and are a great source of protein. Swirling the soup through with hearty leafy greens prevents the soup from being too heavy; they add a light, fresh vitality, lots of calcium and iron, and a contrasting taste to the mild character of the dish. All this and delicious, too.

1-inch piece kombu
1 cup dried cannellini beans, sorted,
    rinsed, and soaked 4 to 6 hours
5 to 6 cups spring or filtered water
1 teaspoon extra-virgin olive oil
1 sweet onion, finely diced

Sea salt
1 to 2 stalks celery, finely diced
2 parsnips, finely diced
1 tablespoon sweet white miso
3 cups finely diced escarole

Place kombu in a soup pot. Drain beans, and pour over kombu. Add water, and bring to a boil, uncovered, over high heat. Boil 5 minutes. Cover, reduce heat to low, and simmer until soft, about 1 hour.

Meanwhile, heat oil in a skillet over medium heat. Add onion and a pinch of salt; sauté until limp. Add celery and another pinch of salt; sauté 1 to 2 minutes. Add parsnips and another pinch of salt; sauté, stirring occasionally, until shiny with oil, about 5 minutes. Add 1 tablespoon of water, cover, and steam over medium heat for 10 minutes.

Transfer beans, reserving liquid in soup pot, to a food processor fitted with the metal blade, and puree until smooth. (A food mill doesn't work well here for creaminess.) Return beans to the pot over low heat. Remove a small amount of liquid, and use to dissolve miso. Stir miso mixture, sautéed vegetables, and escarole into the pot; simmer 3 to 4 minutes to activate enzymes in miso. Serve hot.

Makes 7 to 8 servings

Sparkling Carrot Soup

A definite party soup, this one. Sparkling water (or beer if you're feeling a bit daring) adds a bit of zip that is the loveliest contrast to the sweet flavor of the carrots. And the energy . . . you just can't imagine. You have the strength of root vegetables, the calm centeredness of winter squash, and the zesty light energy of sparkling water. Fabulous!

1 sweet onion, cut into large dice

1 to 2 cups cubed winter squash

1 pound carrots, cut into large dice

2 ripe pears, peeled and cut into large dice

2 cups plain rice or soy milk

1 cup spring or filtered water

1 bay leaf

Sea salt

1 cup sparkling water or beer

¼ cup minced parsley, for garnish

Layer onion, squash, carrots, and pears in a soup pot in the order listed. Add rice milk, spring water, and bay leaf. Cover, and bring to a boil over medium heat. Reduce heat to low, season lightly with salt, and simmer until vegetables are quite soft, about 30 minutes. Season lightly with salt to taste. Put soup, in batches, through a food mill to create a silky texture and a calm energy. Return soup to pot. Stir in sparkling water, and simmer over low heat for 5 to 7 minutes. Serve hot, garnished with parsley.

Makes 5 to 6 servings

Vegetable Soup with Pesto

Now I'll admit, I could eat basil pesto on anything, but served on top of rich vegetable soup, it makes for a most splendid starter course. The light, fresh energy of the herb is a perfect complement to this hearty bean and veggie soup—the basil's lightness prevents the soup from becoming heavy, sinking in the body.

The pesto may be prepared in advance, but cover it tightly or it will discolor.

Pesto

1 cup packed fresh basil leaves

¼ cup extra-virgin olive oil

1 to 2 teaspoons white miso

4 to 5 tablespoons lightly toasted pine nuts

1 teaspoon umeboshi vinegar

1 teaspoon brown rice syrup

Soup

1 small sweet onion, diced

1 small leek, split lengthwise, rinsed well, and diced

1 to 2 turnips, diced

2 carrots, diced

1 to 2 yellow summer squash, diced

1 cup cooked cannellini or other white beans

5 cups spring or filtered water

1 bay leaf

2½ teaspoons white miso

1 cup fresh green beans, trimmed and sliced on the diagonal into ½-inch pieces

Prepare the pesto: Blanch basil in boiling water for 30 seconds and drain well. This will help pesto hold its green color. Combine all ingredients in a food processor fitted with the metal blade, and pulse to create a coarse paste. Set aside.

Prepare the soup: Layer onion, leek, turnips, carrots, and squash in a soup pot in the order listed. Top with beans, and add water and bay leaf. Cover, and bring to a boil over medium heat. Reduce heat to low, and simmer until vegetables are quite soft, about 15 minutes.

Put soup, in batches, through a food mill to create a silky texture and a calm energy. Return soup to pot over medium heat. Remove a small amount of liquid, and use to dissolve miso. Stir miso mixture and green beans into soup, and simmer for 3 to 4 minutes, taking care not to boil, as it will destroy enzymes in miso that aid digestion. Serve soup with a dollop of pesto in each bowl.

Makes 6 to 8 servings

Sweet Pumpkin Soup with Cloves

Soup doesn't come sweeter than this one. The combination of carrots, onion, and pumpkin creates soup that is almost too sweet. The splendid, savory flavor of cloves adds just the right complement of taste. This soup creates warmth and vitality from sautéing the vegetables, deep strength from the rooted carrots, and pleasant relaxation from the winter squash and onion—the perfect cool-weather soup.

2 tablespoons corn oil

1 sweet onion, diced

Sea salt

2 to 3 carrots, diced

1 to 2 stalks celery, diced

5 cups cooked, pureed pumpkin or winter squash

3 cups spring or filtered water

3 cups plain rice or soy milk

5 to 6 whole cloves

2 tablespoons brown rice syrup

About ¼ cup minced flat-leaf parsley, for garnish

Heat oil in a soup pot over medium heat. Add onion and a pinch of salt; sauté until limp. Add carrots and a pinch of salt; sauté, stirring, until shiny with oil, about 2 minutes. Add celery and a pinch of salt; stir to mix. Add pumpkin, water, and rice milk. Wrap cloves in a small piece of cheesecloth, tie into a small bundle, and add to soup. Add rice syrup; cover, and bring to a boil. Reduce heat to low, and simmer, covered, until carrots are very soft, about 25 minutes. Season to taste with salt, and simmer, covered, 7 to 10 minutes more.

Puree soup, in batches, in a food mill or a food processor fitted with the metal blade. Return soup to the pot, and cook over low heat until hot. Serve hot, garnished with parsley.

Makes 8 to 10 servings

Spiced Apple Soup

This sweet-and-savory fruit-and-vegetable soup has a hint of spicy flavor that will warm your bones on a chilly night. A great starter course, this soup can make you feel relaxed, but the spicy taste brings out your social nature.

1 tablespoon corn oil

1 sweet onion, diced

1 to 2 cloves garlic, minced

Sea salt

3 McIntosh apples, peeled and diced

3 Granny Smith apples, peeled and diced

¾ teaspoon chili powder

Grated zest of 1 lemon

4 cups spring or filtered water

¼ cup mirin

½ cup Arborio rice (do not rinse)

About ¼ cup minced flat-leaf parsley, for garnish

Heat oil in a soup pot over medium heat. Add onion, garlic, and a pinch of salt; sauté until onion is limp, about 3 minutes. Add apples, chili powder, and lemon zest. Add a pinch of salt, and cook, stirring, until apples are shiny with oil, about 2 minutes. Add water, mirin, and rice; cover and bring to a boil over medium heat. Reduce heat to low and simmer until apples are very soft, about 25 minutes.

Puree soup in batches in a food processor fitted with the metal blade until smooth. (A food mill will not give you the desired texture in this instance.) Return soup to the pot over medium heat, and season lightly with salt. Simmer 5 minutes more to develop flavors. Serve hot, garnished with parsley.

Makes 5 or 6 servings

Tuscan Bread Soup

This splendid soup is more than just a starter—it's practically a meal in itself. It's a thick, rich stew laden with vegetables and beans, delicately seasoned; perfection in a bowl. The hearty nature of this soup makes it ideal in cool weather, when you need to keep your internal fires blazing. Use any veggies you like to create many variations of this winning recipe.

1-inch piece kombu

1 cup dried white navy beans, sorted, rinsed, and soaked 4 to 6 hours

10 to 11 cups spring or filtered water

1 tablespoon extra-virgin olive oil

1 sweet onion, diced

1 small leek, split lengthwise, rinsed well, and diced

Sea salt

Generous pinch dried basil

2 to 3 carrots, diced

1 cup diced winter squash

2 to 3 small turnips, diced

1 to 2 stalks celery, diced

¼ to ½ small green head cabbage, diced

3 to 4 teaspoons white miso

1 to 2 yellow summer squash, diced

1 bunch dark leafy greens, such as kale or broccoli rabe, thinly sliced

About 9 slices whole-grain sourdough bread

About ¼ cup minced flat-leaf parsley, for garnish

Place kombu on the bottom of a heavy pot. Top with beans and 3 cups of water. Bring to a boil, uncovered, over high heat. Boil for 5 minutes. Cover, reduce heat to low, and simmer until just tender, about 45 minutes. Transfer beans and remaining cooking liquid to a bowl and mash until about half-broken. Set aside.

Heat oil in a soup pot over medium heat. Add onion, leek, and a pinch of salt; sauté for 1 minute. Add basil; sauté until onion is limp, 1 minute. Add carrots, winter squash, turnips, and a pinch of salt; sauté 1 minute. Add celery, cabbage, and a pinch of salt; sauté until cabbage is limp. Add 6 to 8 cups of water and the mashed beans; cover, and bring to a boil. Reduce heat to low, and simmer until vegetables are tender and beans are quite soft, about 45 minutes.

Remove a small amount of liquid, and use to dissolve miso. Stir miso mixture, summer squash, and greens into the pot. Simmer, uncovered, for 3 to 4 minutes to activate enzymes of miso.

To assemble soup, place a layer of bread slices on the bottom of a soup tureen. Ladle a generous amount of soup over bread. Repeat with another layer of bread and then soup.

Continue layering until tureen is full. Make sure the top layer is bread. Cover tureen, and allow soup to stand 5 to 7 minutes before serving. Ladle soup and bread into individual serving bowls. Garnish with parsley.

Makes 8 to 10 servings

Chilled Cucumber Bisque

The intense heat of summer requires keeping the body cool and refreshed. Reaching for icy cold drinks and frozen snacks only make us feel warmer, because the message that gets sent to the brain when we eat these things is that it's winter. Our internal body temperature rises to keep us warm, making us perspire and feel thirsty. Some of the most effective body coolers are cucumbers and tofu; both are cool by nature and light and moist in color and texture. Lightly chilled, this simple summer bisque helps you keep your cool.

1 teaspoon corn oil
4 to 5 large cucumbers, peeled, seeded, and diced
Sea salt
1 pound silken tofu, crumbled
2 cups plain rice or soy milk
1 tablespoon brown rice syrup
¼ cup minced dill

Heat oil in a large saucepan over medium heat. Add cucumbers and a pinch of salt; sauté 1 to 2 minutes. Add tofu and rice milk. Stir in rice syrup, and season lightly with salt. Cover and bring to a boil. Reduce heat to low, and simmer for 5 to 7 minutes.

Puree soup in batches in a food processor fitted with the metal blade until smooth. Transfer soup to a heat-resistant bowl, and allow to stand, uncovered, 10 minutes. (This allows the soup's energy to settle down after being pureed; a food mill will not effectively puree this bisque.) Cover and chill thoroughly. Swirl dill through the soup just before serving.

Makes 5 or 6 servings

Daikon-Shiitake Consommé

The combination of shiitake and daikon can be instrumental in aiding the body in the breakdown of excess protein and fat that may have accumulated in various organs. Also effective as a blood cleanser, this consommé is the perfect starter to a hearty meal. Light and fresh, this thin soup relaxes the body and aids in the digestion of rich feasts.

4 to 5 cups spring or filtered water

3-inch piece kombu, soaked and diced

2 to 3 dried shiitake mushrooms, soaked
   until tender, thinly sliced

8 to 10 (¼-inch-thick) fresh daikon rounds

Soy sauce

1 to 2 scallions, thinly sliced on the diago-
   nal, for garnish

Place water and kombu in a saucepan over medium heat; cover and bring to a boil. Add mushrooms. With the tip of a sharp knife, score each daikon round and add to soup; cover, and simmer until mushrooms and daikon are tender, about 10 minutes. Lightly season with soy sauce; simmer for 5 minutes more. Serve hot, garnished with scallions.

Makes 4 or 5 servings

Azuki Bean Vegetable Soup

Azuki beans are prized in Asia for their ability to restore the strength of the kidneys. Eating them can reduce puffiness and discoloration in the skin, especially around the eyes. These low-fat beans are high in potassium and, combined with sweet vegetables, can relax the middle organs of the body and restore smooth kidney function. Add to that the vitalizing energy of corn and you have delicious energy in a bowl.

1-inch piece kombu

1 cup azuki beans, sorted, rinsed, and
   soaked 6 to 8 hours

7 to 8 cups spring or filtered water

1 sweet onion, diced

¼ head green cabbage, diced

1 cup diced winter squash

1 to 2 stalks celery, diced

1 cup fresh or frozen corn kernels

*3 to 4 teaspoons barley miso (¼ to ½ tea-
spoon per cup of liquid)*

*2 to 3 scallions, thinly sliced on the diago-
nal, for garnish*

Place kombu on the bottom of a heavy soup pot. Top with drained beans. Add water, and bring to a boil, uncovered, over high heat. Boil 5 minutes. Cover, reduce heat to low, and simmer until beans are still firm but beginning to soften, 35 to 40 minutes. Add vegetables, and bring mixture back to a boil over high heat. Reduce heat to low, and simmer, covered, until beans and vegetables are soft, about 40 minutes.

Remove a small amount of liquid, and use to dissolve miso. Stir miso mixture gently into soup, and simmer 3 to 4 minutes to activate enzymes in miso. Serve hot, garnished with scallions.

Makes 8 to 10 servings

Squash and Sweet Corn Chowder

A calming, sweet starter course, this creamy, rich bisque is laced through with sweet corn. The perfect soup to transition from the intense heat of summer to the brisk, chilly days of autumn. Warming winter squash will relax your middle organs, while the sunny yellow corn keeps the memories of summer alive.

1 small leek, diced and rinsed well

3 cups cubed butternut squash

3 cups spring or filtered water

3 cups rice or soy milk

2½ teaspoons sweet white miso

1½ cups fresh or frozen corn kernels

*About ¼ cup minced flat-leaf parsley, for
garnish*

Layer leek and then squash in a soup pot. Add water; cover, and bring to a boil over medium heat. Add rice milk; cover, and reduce heat to low. Simmer until squash is quite soft, about 35 minutes.

Puree soup, in batches, in a food mill or press through a Chinois (fine strainer) for a silky texture. Return soup to the pot over low heat, and bring to a simmer. Remove a small amount of liquid, and use to dissolve miso. Stir miso mixture and corn gently into pot, and simmer 3 to 4 minutes to activate enzymes in miso. Serve hot, garnished with parsley.

Makes 6 to 7 servings

Chickpea-Vegetable Soup

This is great summer soup. Replete with summer veggies, fresh herbs, and the rich flavor of chickpeas, this starter course will have you dreaming of Mediterranean beaches. This light soup packs lots of vitality with the sunny disposition of the veggies and the endurance of the beans.

1 tablespoon extra-virgin olive oil
1 sweet onion, cut into thin half-moon slices
Sea salt
1 to 2 carrots, diced
1 cup sliced button mushrooms
1 to 2 yellow summer squash, diced
1 to 2 small zucchini, diced
1 cup fresh corn kernels
1 cup cooked chickpeas
4 to 5 cups spring or filtered water
2 teaspoons white miso
1 to 2 stalks celery, diced
4 or 5 basil leaves, minced
2 to 3 sprigs rosemary, leaves removed and minced
About ¼ cup minced flat-leaf parsley, for garnish

Heat oil in a soup pot over medium heat. Add onion and a pinch of salt; sauté for 1 minute. Add carrots and a pinch of salt; sauté until shiny with oil. Add mushrooms and a pinch of salt; sauté until limp and releasing juices. Add summer squash, zucchini, corn, and a pinch of salt; sauté for 1 minute. Top with chickpeas, and add water. Cover, and bring to a boil. Reduce heat to low, and simmer until vegetables are tender, about 15 minutes.

Remove a small amount of liquid, and use to dissolve miso. Stir miso mixture, celery, basil, and rosemary gently into soup. Simmer, uncovered, 3 to 4 minutes to activate enzymes in miso. Serve hot, garnished with parsley.

Makes 6 to 8 servings

Pasta e Fagioli

There's nothing like Italian bean soup. Maybe it's because it's my heritage, but in my opinion, no one does bean soup better. This one was a religious experience in my house—at least for my father—my mother made it every Friday. I can still see him sitting at the head of the table, with a heel of Italian bread and his big bowl of soup. I don't think he realized the vitality he was getting from this seemingly simple soup. The combination of beans and light, fresh, sautéed vegetables create the perfect balance of energy and endurance.

2 to 3 teaspoons extra-virgin olive oil

1 sweet onion, diced

1 to 2 stalks celery, diced

Generous pinch each of dried basil and rosemary

Sea salt

1 cup dried cannellini beans, sorted, rinsed, and soaked 6 to 8 hours

6 cups spring or filtered water

1-inch piece wakame, soaked until soft, diced

2 cups small cauliflower florets

2 small zucchini, diced

1½ cups cooked pasta, such as small shells, orzo, acine, or elbows

1 cup diced dark leafy greens, such as kale, collards, or broccoli rabe

About ¼ cup minced flat-leaf parsley, for garnish

Heat oil in a soup pot over medium heat. Add onion, celery, herbs, and a pinch of salt; sauté until onion is limp. Add beans, water, and wakame. Cover, and bring to a boil. Reduce heat to low, and simmer until beans are still firm, but beginning to soften, 35 to 40 minutes. Add cauliflower and zucchini; cover, and simmer until beans are soft, about 40 minutes.

Season lightly with salt, and stir in pasta and greens; simmer for 5 minutes. Serve hot, garnished with parsley.

Makes 6 to 8 servings

Summer Vegetable Soup with Quinoa Salad

This is a great summer dish—a light soup and grain meal all in one bowl. Summer vegetables have lots of moisture and keep us cool, especially when served as soup. A scoop of quinoa salad makes this the perfect summer soup, because quinoa is a whole grain that grows in a hot climate, so it cools us down. Plus it cooks quickly, so you won't create lots of heat in the summer. The best part is that this soup is splendidly pretty on a summer table.

Soup

    2 teaspoons corn oil
    1 small leek, split lengthwise, rinsed well,
        and thinly sliced
    Sea salt
    2 to 3 carrots, diced
    2 to 3 yellow summer squash, diced
    4 to 5 cups spring or filtered water
    2½ teaspoons white miso
    1 to 2 scallions, thinly sliced on the diago-
        nal, for garnish

Quinoa Salad

    1 cup quinoa, rinsed well
    2 cups spring or filtered water
    Pinch sea salt
    2 scallions, diced
    ½ cup fresh or frozen corn kernels
    1 roasted red bell pepper (page 96), diced
    1 teaspoon umeboshi vinegar
    1 teaspoon balsamic vinegar

To prepare the soup: Heat oil in a soup pot over medium heat. Add leek and a pinch of salt; sauté until limp, about 1 minute. Add carrots and a pinch of salt; sauté 1 minute. Add squash, and stir until combined. Add water; cover, and bring to a boil. Reduce heat to low, and simmer, covered, until vegetables are quite soft, 15 to 20 minutes.

Put soup, in batches, through a food mill to create a smooth, silky texture. Return soup to pot, and simmer over low heat. Remove a small amount of liquid, and use to dissolve miso. Stir miso mixture into soup; simmer for 3 to 4 minutes to activate enzymes in miso.

While the soup cooks make the salad: Add quinoa and water to a saucepan; loosely cover. Bring to a boil over medium heat. Add salt; cover, and simmer until all liquid has been absorbed into grain and quinoa has opened up. Remove from heat, and stir in scallions, corn, bell pepper, and vinegars.

To serve, place a scoop of quinoa salad in the center of individual soup bowls. Ladle soup around the salad, and garnish with the scallions.

Makes 6 to 8 servings

Winter Vegetable Soup with Mochi Croutons

When the cold winds of winter seem to blow right through you, there is nothing quite like a hearty bowl of soup to warm your shivering bones. Winter vegetables and grain come together in this hearty soup to create warmth in the middle organs of the body, giving you strength, stamina, a calm mind, and a warm body.

Don't make the croutons too far in advance of serving time, or they will get oily and mushy. You want them crispy and fresh.

Soup

1-inch piece kombu, soaked until tender and diced
1 onion, cut into large dice
2 cups diced green cabbage
2 cups cubed winter squash
1 cup rolled oats
6 to 7 cups spring or filtered water
2 to 3 teaspoons barely miso

Mochi Croutons

Light sesame oil
24 (½-inch) mochi cubes

To Serve

3 to 4 scallions, thinly sliced on the diagonal, for garnish

Make the soup: Layer kombu and other vegetables in a soup pot in the order listed. Top with oats, and add water. Cover, and bring to a boil over medium heat. Reduce heat to low, and simmer, covered, until vegetables are soft and oats are very creamy, about 40 minutes. Remove a small amount of liquid, and use to dissolve miso. Stir miso mixture gently into soup, and simmer, uncovered, 3 to 4 minutes to activate the enzymes in miso.

Make the croutons: Just before serving, heat enough sesame oil to generously cover the bottom of a heavy skillet over medium heat. Add mochi, and fry until golden brown on all sides, turning as it browns. Drain well on paper towels.

To serve: garnish with scallions and several mochi croutons, and serve hot.

Makes 6 to 8 servings

Creamy Mushroom Soup

Creamy soups are like comfort in a bowl. Laden with relaxing mushrooms, this soup helps you manage the little stresses of daily life that can sometimes be overwhelming. Add to that the vitality of sweet, sautéed onions and you create a calm but invigorating dish.

2 teaspoons extra-virgin olive oil

2 sweet onions, diced

Sea salt

5 to 6 dried shiitake mushrooms, soaked
    until tender, thinly sliced

3 cups thinly sliced button mushrooms

6 cups plain rice or soy milk

2 teaspoons white miso

2 to 3 scallions, thinly sliced on the diago-
    nal, for garnish

Heat oil in a soup pot over medium heat. Add onions and a pinch of salt; sauté until limp, about 5 minutes. Add shiitake mushrooms and a pinch of salt; sauté 1 minute. Add button mushrooms and a pinch of salt; sauté until mushrooms begin to release their juices. Add rice milk, cover, and bring to a boil over medium heat. Reduce heat to low, and simmer for 30 minutes to develop flavors.

Remove a small amount of liquid, and use to dissolve miso. Stir miso mixture gently into soup, and simmer, uncovered, for 3 to 4 minutes to activate enzymes in miso. Serve hot, garnished with scallions.

Makes 6 to 8 servings

Black Bean-Squash Soup

A unique soup, quite dramatic to serve, with its rich, black color and splendidly sweet flavor. This kind of soup is quite nice when you need a bit of stamina in your life. Bean soups are great endurance builders and combined with roasted sweet onions and butternut squash, they create tremendous strength in your middle organs and digestive system. A great starter to an autumn or winter meal.

1 sweet onion, cut into thin half-moon slices

1 medium butternut squash, peeled,
*   seeded, cut into 1-inch pieces*

About 2 teaspoons soy sauce

About 3 tablespoons extra-virgin olive oil

3 cups plain rice or soy milk

¼ cup mirin

3 cups spring or filtered water

4 cups cooked black turtle beans

3 teaspoons brown rice miso

2 tablespoons balsamic vinegar

About ¼ cup minced flat-leaf parsley, for
*   garnish*

Preheat oven to 375F (175C).

Toss onion and squash with soy sauce and oil in a large baking pan, taking care to coat vegetables well. Bake, uncovered, about 45 minutes, until vegetables are soft and lightly browned.

Transfer vegetables to a soup pot and add rice milk and mirin. Cover and bring to a boil over medium heat. Reduce heat to low, and simmer 15 minutes to develop flavors. Put soup, in batches, through a food mill to create a smooth bisque texture. Return soup to pot, and stir in water.

Place beans in a food processor fitted with the steel blade, and puree until smooth. Swirl beans into soup. Simmer soup, covered, for 5 minutes. Remove a small amount of liquid, and use to dissolve miso. Stir miso mixture into the soup, and simmer, uncovered for 3 to 4 minutes to activate enzymes in miso. Just before serving, stir in vinegar. Serve hot, garnished with parsley.

Makes 6 to 8 servings

Creamy Millet Chowder

I love millet—from its sunny yellow color to its creamy, comforting texture. And millet soup? It doesn't get better . . . creamy and naturally rich, nutty, and sweet. Laced through with succulent vegetables, this millet soup is more than just delicious. Its warming character and sweet vegetables relax the body, keep us warm in cool weather, and enable us to face life with a calm, centered attitude.

1 sweet onion, diced

¼ head green cabbage, diced

1-inch piece wakame, soaked until tender, diced

½ cup yellow millet, rinsed well

5 to 6 cups spring or filtered water

2 teaspoons barley miso

½ cup fresh or frozen corn kernels

1 cup diced dark leafy greens, such as kale or collards

1 to 2 scallions, thinly sliced on the diagonal, for garnish

Layer onion, cabbage, wakame, and millet in a soup pot. Add water, cover, and bring to a boil. Reduce heat to low, and simmer until vegetables are soft and millet is creamy, about 25 minutes.

Remove a small amount of liquid, and use to dissolve miso. Stir miso mixture, corn, and greens into the pot, and simmer for 3 to 4 minutes, uncovered, to activate enzymes in miso. Serve hot, garnished with scallions.

Makes 6 to 8 servings

Cream of Rutabaga Soup

An elegant starter course, this soup has a rich, creamy color and delicately sweet taste. The perfect holiday soup, it is great for keeping you warm; plus all the root veggies come together to give you great rooted strength and clear thinking.

1 to 2 teaspoons extra-virgin olive oil

1 sweet onion, diced

Sea salt

6 small rutabaga, diced

3 parsnips, diced

2 Granny Smith apples, peeled and diced

2 cups plain rice or soy milk

3 cups spring or filtered water

About ¼ cup minced flat-leaf parsley, for garnish

1 roasted red bell pepper (page 96), diced, for garnish

Heat oil in a soup pot over medium heat. Add onion and a pinch of salt; sauté until limp, about 2 minutes. Add rutabaga, parsnips, and a pinch of salt; sauté 1 to 2 minutes. Add apples and rice milk, cover, and bring to a boil. Add water, season lightly with salt, cover, and return to a boil. Reduce heat to low, and simmer until vegetables are very soft, about 40 minutes.

Put soup, in batches, through a food mill to create a smooth, silky texture. Return soup to the pot, and lightly season to taste with salt; the soup should taste sweet. Simmer for 5 to 7 minutes to develop flavors. Serve hot, garnished with parsley and bell pepper.

Makes 6 to 8 servings

Gingered Vegetable Broth with Noodles

A great snack or light lunch, this soup has everything—savory broth, lots of vegetables, and a bit of tofu, all atop hearty udon noodles. This splendid meal in a bowl is a real pick-me-up, with the vitality of vegetables, the minerals of sea vegetables, the relaxed endurance of tofu, and the comforting nourishment of pasta. Perfection.

4 cups spring or filtered water

10 to 12 thin half-moon carrot slices

10 to 12 thin half-moon fresh daikon slices

4 dried shiitake mushrooms, soaked until tender, thinly sliced

1 cup tiny cauliflower florets

Soy sauce

1-inch piece fresh ginger, grated and juice extracted (page 188)

4 ounces cooked udon noodles

2 to 3 scallions, thinly sliced on the diagonal, for garnish

1 sheet toasted nori, shredded, for garnish

Place water and vegetables in a soup pot; cover, and bring to a boil over medium heat. Reduce heat to low, and simmer until vegetables are tender, about 10 minutes. Season lightly with soy sauce, and simmer 5 minutes more.

To serve, divide the noodles into individual bowls, and ladle soup over top. Garnish with scallions and nori.

Makes 5 or 6 servings

Lemony Leek Soup

A light springtime soup. The strong sprouting energy of leeks come together with the delicately sour flavor of lemon to cleanse various organ systems, particularly the liver, giving you great patience and less irritability. On top of that, these two strong energies unite to get our stagnant, winter bodies blooming right along with the flowers.

> 2 to 3 leeks, split lengthwise, rinsed well,
>   and thinly sliced
> 1 to 2 carrots, diced
> 1 cup button mushrooms, thinly sliced
> Grated zest of 1 lemon
> 1 cup pearled barley, rinsed well
> 5 to 6 cups spring or filtered water
> 2 teaspoons white miso
> Juice of 1 to 2 lemons
> 1 to 2 scallions, thinly sliced on the diago-
>   nal, for garnish

Layer leeks, carrot, mushrooms, lemon zest, and barley in a soup pot. Add water; cover, and bring to a boil over medium heat. Reduce heat to low, and simmer until barley is creamy and vegetables are soft, about 25 minutes.

Remove a small amount of liquid, and use to dissolve miso. Stir miso mixture and lemon juice to taste into soup. Simmer for 3 to 4 minutes, uncovered, to activate enzymes in miso. Serve hot, garnished with scallions.

Makes 6 to 8 servings

Sweet Rice and Corn Chowder

Creamy grain chowders are the greatest comfort food I can imagine. Rich, without being fatty; nourishing and relaxing and comforting, without being draining. Add the enduring stamina of whole grain, the strength of pressure cooking, and the sunny vitality of corn, and you have created a soup that will give you great staying power.

> ⅔ cup sweet brown rice, rinsed well
> 1 cup dried sweet corn (see Note)
> 1 sweet onion, diced
> 1 to 2 cups diced winter squash
> 7 to 8 cups spring or filtered water
> 1 tablespoon barley miso
> 6 to 8 fresh chives, minced, for garnish

Combine rice, corn, onion, squash, and water in a pressure cooker. Cover loosely, and bring to a boil. Seal lid, and bring to high pressure. Reduce heat to low, and simmer for 45 minutes. Remove from heat, and allow pressure to reduce naturally.

Open pressure cooker, and return to low heat. Remove a small amount of liquid, and use to dissolve miso. Stir miso mixture into the pot, and simmer for 3 to 4 minutes, uncovered, to activate enzymes in miso. Serve hot, garnished with chives.

Makes 7 or 8 servings

Note

You may use fresh or frozen corn if dried sweet corn is unavailable.

Hot and Sour Soup

This is a variation on a classic Chinese favorite. Gone are the shredded pork bits and chicken stock, but the vitalizing energy remains. Richly flavored and spicy with chili oil, this soup stimulates your appetite and makes for great digestion. Using a bit of vinegar adds sparkle and aids the body in assimilating the oil in the sautéed veggies and seitan.

¼ pound seitan, shredded

½ teaspoon soy sauce, plus additional to taste

1 teaspoon mirin

2 teaspoons arrowroot

2 teaspoons sesame oil

1 to 2 teaspoons chili-flavored sesame oil

1 small onion, cut into very thin half-moon slices

4 dried shiitake mushrooms, soaked until tender, thinly sliced

3 to 4 button mushrooms, thinly sliced

4 to 5 cups spring or filtered water

1 broccoli stalk, peeled and cut into fine matchstick pieces

½ pound extra-firm tofu, cut into tiny cubes

1 tablespoon kuzu dissolved in 2 tablespoons cold water

1 to 2 tablespoons umeboshi vinegar

2 to 3 scallions, thinly sliced, for garnish

Shred seitan, and place in a medium bowl. Combine ½ teaspoon soy sauce, mirin, arrowroot, and sesame oil in a small bowl. Toss with the seitan pieces, and set aside.

Heat chili-flavored oil in a soup pot over medium heat. Add onion, and sauté until translucent, about 2 minutes. Add mushrooms, and sauté 1 to 2 minutes. Stir in seitan, and sauté briefly. Add water, cover, and bring to a boil over medium heat. Stir in broccoli and tofu cubes. Cover, and simmer 20 to 25 minutes. Season to taste with soy sauce, and simmer for 5 to 7 minutes more. Stir in dissolved kuzu until soup thickens slightly, about 3 minutes.

Remove soup from heat and season lightly with vinegar to taste. Serve hot, garnished with scallions.

Makes 4 or 5 servings

GRAINS:
THE STAFF OF LIFE

THE EDIBLE PORTION of grains is the kernel; it is a complete fruit, with a protective husk over it. In some grains—like rice, millet, oats, and barley—this outer shell is tough and must be removed to eat the seed. In the case of grains like corn and wheat, the hulls are tender and are eaten along with the fruit.

Grains contain the ability to reproduce in abundance from a single seed, making them highly productive plants. Each whole cereal grain represents both the beginning and end of the plant's life, containing within it all the potential and energy of the entire plant. Because of this unique characteristic,

grains, more than any other food, have the greatest capacity for increasing human potential, on all levels of our existence. Their ability to reproduce with very little help from us and their adaptability and versatility make grains our most valuable source of nourishment. Whole grains have the ability to finely tune the human nervous system, unifying all organ function into one smoothly operating whole.

Whole grains have constituted the principal food of humanity for tens of thousands of years. Almost every civilization before ours viewed cereals as the basis of life; produced different types of grain; and developed its own cultivation, farming, harvesting, and preparation techniques, giving rise to the great diversity and rich, ethnic differences of today's cultures and cuisines. Until modern times, cooked whole grains were eaten as the main food throughout the world.

Whole cereal grains provide us with a balanced, peaceful energy and lots of staying power. In the whole form, with the germ, bran, and endosperm intact, whole grains are a complex carbohydrate, providing long-term stamina and endurance unparalleled in other foods. This is the energy of staying power and clear-minded thinking.

In whole foods—macrobiotic—cooking, we view whole cereal grains as the cornerstone of our diet. Because grain is an essential part of our daily food, it is important, as in all cooking, to get variety. Again, don't condemn yourself to a grim existence of only short grain brown rice, as wonderful as it is. Try lots of grains: millet, barley, quinoa, amaranth, teff, Job's tears, buckwheat, oats, wheat, rye, corn, and wild rice. Then there are white rice, couscous, Arborio rice, cracked wheat, rolled oats, cornmeal, corn grits, noodles, bread, and seitan. You can try a new grain every day for a month and not repeat yourself. What a great adventure!

Cooking Grains

Cooking grains is as simple as the grain itself. There are a variety of methods used to prepare delicious grain dishes, but my favorite is pressure cooking. Relax. I can almost hear your panic—visions of exploding pots and rice all over the kitchen ceiling. Not anymore. Modern pressure cookers have lots of built-in safety features, and they are made of good-quality stainless steel. In ancient China, whole grains were cooked under pressure by cooking them in heavy cauldrons with stones on the lids. As the boiling created high pressure in the cauldron, the fire was brought down and the grains were slowly cooked. The beauty of pressure cooking is many-fold; it cooks the grain at a higher temperature than does boiling, ensuring that the grain cooks from the inside out—thoroughly—and, as a result, the grain is most digestible. Pressure cooking preserves almost all of the energy and nutrition of whole grains, because very little is lost to steam. It brings out the natural sweet, nutty flavor of grain. Pressure cooking creates great strength but a calm and peaceful mind.

You may also cook grains by boiling in a heavy pot. Using more water and cooking for a longer period of time, boiled grain has a light energy and a milder flavor than that of pressure-cooked grain. This fresh energy is the perfect way to cook grain in the warm days of summer.

Want more grain preparation ideas? Well, you can soak the grain before cooking to create a softer cereal and relaxed body. Dry roasting the grain before cooking produces an intense nutty flavor and tremendous strength. Leftover grain (there always seems to be leftover grain) can be sautéed with vegetables, rolled with nori into sushi, mixed together with lightly cooked vegetables and a dressing for a salad, made into small spheres and fried into croquettes, pressed into loaves or used as flourless pie crusts.

The possibilities are endless, and you thought eating whole grains meant a pile of rice on your plate every day for the rest of your life!

Kasha with Noodles

Kasha, or toasted buckwheat groats, is a great cool-weather grain. Grown in the harshest environment, poor soil, cold temperatures, and dry air, kasha is great at keeping us warm and strong, with lots of endurance. This simple main course is laced through with noodles and richly sautéed vegetables, making it deeply soul satisfying as well as nourishing on chilly winter nights.

2 teaspoons light sesame oil

1 sweet onion, diced

Sea salt

1 carrot, diced

1 cup diced winter squash

2 cups thinly sliced button mushrooms

2 cups spring or filtered water

1 cup kasha (toasted buckwheat groats),
   rinsed well

About 1/4 teaspoon soy sauce

3 cups cooked noodles (mini shells,
   elbows, or bow ties)
About 1/4 cup minced flat-leaf parsley

Heat oil in a deep skillet over medium heat. Add onion and a pinch of salt; sauté until limp. Add carrot, squash, and a pinch of salt; sauté for 1 to 2 minutes. Add the mushrooms and a pinch of salt; sauté until mushrooms release their juices. Season lightly with additional salt. Cover, reduce heat to low, and simmer 15 to 20 minutes.

Meanwhile, bring water to a boil in a saucepan. Stir in kasha and season lightly with soy sauce. Cover, reduce heat to low, and simmer until all the cooking liquid has been absorbed, 15 to 20 minutes.

Stir cooked vegetables, noodles, and parsley into kasha. Serve warm.

Makes 4 to 6 servings

Kasha Strudel

Here's a unique way to use this hearty grain. Wrapped in flaky phyllo pastry and dotted with sautéed vegetables, this strudel makes a great side dish or light main course. Warming and strengthening, relaxing and vitalizing, this delicious grain pastry is a splendid, cool-weather dish.

1 cup spring or filtered water

½ cup kasha (toasted buckwheat groats), rinsed well

Soy sauce

2 teaspoons extra-virgin olive oil, plus additional for brushing

5 to 6 slices fresh ginger, cut into thin matchstick pieces

1 sweet onion, diced

2 cups finely chopped kale

3 sheets phyllo pastry, thawed in the refrigerator overnight

About 4 tablespoons fresh whole wheat bread crumbs

Bring water to a boil in a medium saucepan over medium heat. Stir in kasha. Season lightly with soy sauce, cover, and reduce heat to low. Simmer until water is absorbed, about 20 minutes. Transfer to a mixing bowl, and set aside.

Heat oil in a skillet over medium heat. Add ginger, onion, and a dash of soy sauce; sauté until onion is limp, 1 to 2 minutes. Stir in kale and a dash of soy sauce; sauté until kale wilts but is still bright green. Immediately mix sautéed vegetables into cooked kasha; set aside.

Preheat oven to 375F (175C). Line a baking sheet with parchment paper.

Lay 1 phyllo sheet on a dry, flat surface. Brush lightly with olive oil and sprinkle with about 2 tablespoons bread crumbs. Top with another phyllo sheet. Brush lightly with oil and sprinkle with about 2 tablespoons bread crumbs. Place remaining phyllo sheet on top and brush lightly with oil. Spoon kasha filling along short side of dough, closest to you. Roll up, jelly-roll style, turning outer edges over filling to seal ends.

Carefully transfer strudel to prepared pan. With a sharp knife, make deep slits along the strudel, marking slices. Gently brush top and sides of strudel with olive oil. Bake for 30 to 35 minutes, until pastry is golden brown and crispy. Allow to cool for about 10 minutes (but no longer, or it becomes soggy). Cut into slices, and serve.

Makes 6 to 8 servings

Pressure-Cooked Brown and Wild Rice with Corn

This basic recipe is one of the best grain dishes you'll ever taste. The pressure cooker is important for preparing whole grains because it creates a whole grain dish so well cooked that digestion is smooth and assimilation of the nutrients is efficient. Pressure cooking also loses very little nutrition to steam, so the grain you eat contains most of its original nutrients. This combination of short grain brown rice, wild rice, and corn marries the long-term stamina of rice with the sunny energy of corn and the relaxed vitality of wild rice. It doesn't get more perfect than this.

1 cup short grain brown rice, rinsed well
½ cup wild rice, rinsed well
½ cup fresh or frozen corn kernels
2½ cups spring or filtered water
⅛ teaspoon sea salt

Place brown rice, wild rice, corn, and water in a pressure cooker. Cover loosely and bring to a boil. Add salt; seal cover, and bring to high pressure. Reduce heat to low, place pot on a flame deflector, and cook for 25 minutes. Turn off heat and leave the pot undisturbed for another 25 minutes so rice can finish cooking in the steam. Open lid carefully. Gently stir grain, and transfer to a serving bowl.

Makes 4 to 6 servings

Tangy Rice Slaw

This brown rice and veggie salad is a great warm weather dish. Dotted with fresh, colorful summer vegetables and dressed with sweet carrot vinaigrette, it is a whole grain dish that gives you endurance, without weighting you down. Fresh and vital, yet based on whole grains, this dish creates a light summer energy that will have you playing softball till dark.

Salad

1 to 2 yellow summer squash, diced

1 carrot, diced

1 small bunch watercress, rinsed well and left whole

1 cup diced daikon

1 cup finely shredded red cabbage

1 red onion, diced

2 cups cooked short grain brown rice

Carrot Vinaigrette

3 carrots, diced

Pinch sea salt

1/4 cup extra-virgin olive oil

2 teaspoons balsamic vinegar

Juice of 1 lemon

Juice of 1 orange

1 teaspoon brown rice syrup

Make the salad: Bring a pot of water to a boil over high heat. Add each vegetable separately, in the order listed, and blanch until crisp-tender, 30 to 60 seconds. When all vegetables are cooked, drain well; combine them with rice and set aside.

Make the vinaigrette: Place carrots in a small saucepan with enough water to half cover. Add salt, and bring to a boil, covered. Reduce heat to low, and simmer until carrots are quite soft, about 15 minutes. Drain, and transfer carrots and remaining ingredients to a food processor fitted with the metal blade or a blender. Puree until smooth. Slowly add a little water to thin vinaigrette to desired consistency, if needed. (I prefer it a bit on the thicker side, so it will cling to the salad and not run to the bottom of the bowl.)

To serve, pour desired amount of vinaigrette over salad, and stir gently until combined. Leftover vinaigrette will keep, refrigerated, for about a week.

Makes 4 to 6 servings

Wild About Rice Salad

This splendid rice dish will definitely dispel any myths about whole foods being boring. Brown basmati and wild rices are combined with nuts, seeds, dried fruit, and fresh vegetables, all coated in a rich mustard dressing, to create a special-occasion grain dish.

With the endurance of whole grain, the intense vitality of nuts, and the relaxing freshness and sweet taste of veggies and dried fruit, this salad packs a lot of energy. Colorful and varied, it is a symphony of tastes and textures—and a sure bet that you'll be wild about rice!

Salad

1 cup brown basmati rice, rinsed well

½ cup wild rice, rinsed well

1¾ cups spring or filtered water

⅛ teaspoon sea salt

½ cup dried currants

½ cup unsweetened dried cranberries

¼ cup coarsely minced pecans, lightly pan toasted (page 131)

¼ cup coarsely minced almonds, lightly pan toasted (page 131)

2 to 3 fresh scallions, minced

1 to 2 stalks celery, minced

1 carrot, grated

Sweet Mustard Dressing

½ teaspoon soy sauce

¼ cup extra-virgin olive oil

2 tablespoons balsamic vinegar

1 teaspoon umeboshi vinegar

Grated zest and juice of 1 lemon

2 teaspoons stone-ground mustard

1 teaspoon brown rice syrup

Make the salad: Place basmati rice, wild rice, and water in a pressure cooker. Cover loosely and bring to a boil. Add salt; seal cover, and bring to high pressure. Reduce heat to low, place pot on a flame deflector, and cook for 25 minutes. Turn off heat and leave pot undisturbed for another 25 minutes, so rice can finish cooking in the steam. Open lid carefully. Transfer rice to a serving bowl. Stir in dried fruit, nuts, and vegetables until well combined. Set aside.

Make the dressing: Combine soy sauce and oil in a saucepan. Warm over low heat for 1 to 2 minutes. Transfer to a bowl with remaining ingredients. Whisk until well combined. Fold dressing into rice salad, and allow to stand for 10 to 15 minutes before serving, to allow flavors to develop.

Makes about 6 servings

Mediterranean Vegetable Paella

Paella is the ultimate one-pot dish. There is nothing quite like brown rice laced through with savory vegetables and beans. Delicious? You bet. But the best news is that the energy of this dish is unparalleled—the complex carbohydrates of the grain creates strength and stamina; the beans provide protein and a calm, centered attitude; and the vegetables give us vitamins, minerals, a fresh vitality, moisture, and flexibility. Easy, delicious and vitalizing . . . what could be better?

About 1 tablespoon extra-virgin olive oil

1 sweet onion, diced

1 small leek, split lengthwise, rinsed well, and diced

Sea salt

1 carrot, diced

1 roasted red bell pepper (page 96), diced

½ cup white navy beans, sorted and rinsed well

1 cup brown basmati rice, rinsed well

Generous pinch saffron threads, soaked in ¼ cup hot water

¼ cup mirin

1 to 2 bay leaves

1¼ cups spring or filtered water

10 to 12 sun-dried tomatoes, soaked until tender, diced

10 to 12 oil-cured black olives, pitted and halved

2 to 3 fresh scallions, thinly sliced on the diagonal

About ¼ cup minced flat-leaf parsley

Heat oil in a pressure cooker over medium heat. Add onion, leek, and a pinch of salt; sauté 1 to 2 minutes. Add carrot and a pinch of salt; sauté for 1 to 2 minutes. Add bell pepper; sauté, stirring occasionally, until shiny with oil.

Stir in beans and rice. Add saffron with its soaking water, mirin, and bay leaf. Finally, add water. Cover loosely and bring to a boil. Add a pinch of salt and sun-dried tomatoes. Seal lid, and bring to high pressure. Reduce heat to low, and place pot on a flame deflector. Cook for 50 minutes. Remove from heat, and allow pressure to reduce naturally. Carefully open lid. Gently stir in olives, scallions, and parsley. Transfer to a serving bowl, and serve warm.

Makes 4 to 6 servings

Tofu-Vegetable Rolls

This is a lovely light starter course or light lunch. The white sushi rice is wrapped in nori and filled with baked tofu and blanched veggies. Colorful and delicious, this dish starts the meal with a lighter energy, leaving you lots of room for the rest of the meal. Polished rice and lightly cooked vegetables and tofu create a fresh vitality, giving you a social, chatty atmosphere for your feast.

Baked Tofu

2 (¼-inch-thick) slices extra-firm tofu,
   each cut into 4 rectangles
Spring or filtered water
Soy sauce, to taste
About 2 teaspoons light sesame oil
2 teaspoons fresh ginger juice (page 188)

Sushi Rice

1½ cups sushi rice, rinsed well
1½ cups spring or filtered water
Pinch sea salt

Vegetable Filling

½ cup shredded red cabbage, blanched
About 1 tablespoon umeboshi vinegar

To Assemble

3 sheets toasted nori

About 3 tablespoons stone-ground
   mustard
3 thin cucumber spears

Make the tofu: Preheat oven to 400F (205C). Place tofu in a shallow bowl, and cover with water. Season lightly with soy sauce and sesame oil, and add ginger juice. Allow tofu to marinate 10 minutes.

Drain tofu (reserving marinade), and arrange on an ungreased baking sheet. Bake 30 to 35 minutes, uncovered, until browned. Set aside.

Make the rice: Place rice and water in a pressure cooker. Cover loosely, and bring to a boil. Add salt, seal, reduce heat to low and bring to full pressure. Place pot on a flame deflector, and cook 25 to 30 minutes. Remove from heat, and allow pressure to reduce naturally, so rice can finish cooking in the steam. Transfer rice to a bowl. Set aside to cool.

Make the filling: Meanwhile, bring a pot of water to a boil and blanch cabbage for 30 to 60 seconds, just until cabbage is limp. Drain well, and toss with a generous sprinkle of umeboshi vinegar. This gives cabbage a delicate sour taste and a beautiful pink color.

Assemble the sushi: Place 1 nori sheet, shiny side down, on a bamboo sushi mat or dish towel. Press one-third of cooked rice onto nori, spreading evenly to cover, except for 1 inch of nori on the side away from you. On edge closest to you, spread a thin layer of mustard. Lay tofu end to end to cover length of nori. Lay 1 cucumber spear next to tofu and on top of that a thin layer of cabbage.

Using the mat as a guide, roll nori around rice and filling, pressing gently as you roll, creating a filled cylinder. Moisten exposed nori with water to seal shut. Moisten the blade of a sharp knife, and slice roll into 8 equal pieces. Repeat with remaining ingredients to make 2 more rolls. Arrange pieces, cut side up, on a platter. Serve with tofu marinade on the side as a dipping sauce.

Makes 6 to 8 servings

Caramelized Corn and Shiitake Mushroom Risotto

Risotto is one of the most wonderful grain dishes known to man—rich, creamy and oh, so satisfying; this one is particularly delicious. Laced through with sweet roasted corn and herb-scented mushrooms, cooked in a savory miso stock, this is a hearty main course dish. I particularly like to serve this when I feel stressed—the creaminess of the Arborio rice along with the dispersing energy of shiitake mushrooms help relax the body, but the corn and basil prevent complacency by lifting my energy.

4 ears corn, husked

About 4 tablespoons extra-virgin olive oil

6 to 8 dried shiitake mushrooms, soaked
*   until tender, thinly sliced*

1 teaspoon dried basil

5 cups white Miso Stock (recipe follows)

1 small onion, diced

1 cup Arborio rice

¼ cup mirin

2 cups finely chopped kale

1 small bunch chives, minced, for garnish

Preheat oven to 375F (175C). Line a baking sheet with parchment paper.

Lightly brush corn with some oil, and place on one end of the prepared pan. Toss mushrooms with some oil and basil, and spread over the other half of baking sheet. Bake uncovered, turning corn occasionally, about 40 minutes, until tender and lightly browning in places and mushrooms are tender and turning golden. Cool slightly, cut kernels from cobs, and combine with mushrooms. Set aside.

Prepare Miso Stock, and keep warm over low heat. Heat 1 tablespoon of oil in a deep skillet over medium heat. Add onion, and sauté until limp, about 1 minute. Stir in rice; sauté, stirring, until coated with oil. Add mirin; cook, stirring, until absorbed into rice. Add stock, ½ cup at a time; cook, stirring, over low heat. Add more stock as it is absorbed by rice. Stir in corn and mushrooms after about 15 minutes. Rice will take about 25 minutes to cook; the final dish should be creamy, but rice should still have some resistance. Stir in kale, remove from heat, and let sit, covered, 2 minutes to cook greens. Stir well, and transfer to a serving bowl. Garnish with chives, and serve immediately.

Makes 5 or 6 servings

Miso Stock

Simmer a variety of diced vegetables in 5 to 6 cups of water 15 minutes. Strain and return stock to heat. Remove a small amount of broth, and dissolve 2 teaspoons miso in it. Stir into pot, and simmer on very low heat for duration of risotto preparation. You may also make stock ahead of time and reheat it.

❡

Spicy Rice with Lentils and Candied Onions

Combining the stamina of brown rice with the peppery vitality that you get from lentils will give you a splendid, rooted energy that allows you to lighten up and keep your options open. Add to that the fiery energy of sautéed veggies and spices and you have a very vitalizing dish.

1 tablespoon corn oil

2 to 3 sweet onions, cut into thin half-moon slices

Soy sauce

1-inch piece kombu

½ cup le Puy or black lentils, sorted and rinsed

2¾ cups spring or filtered water

1 bay leaf

2 whole allspice

1 cinnamon stick

1 cup brown basmati rice, rinsed well

Pinch sea salt

About ¼ cup minced flat-leaf parsley, for garnish

Heat oil in a skillet over medium heat. Add onions and a splash of soy sauce; sauté until quite limp and lightly browned, 15 to 20 minutes, stirring frequently.

Meanwhile, place kombu on the bottom of a heavy pot. Top with lentils, and add 1½ cups of water. Bring to a boil, uncovered. Cover, reduce heat to low, and cook until lentils are tender, about 45 minutes. Season to taste with soy sauce; simmer 5 to 7 minutes more, allowing any remaining liquid to be absorbed into lentils.

Add remaining 1¼ cups water, the bay leaf, allspice, and cinnamon to a pressure cooker. Bring to a boil over medium heat. Add rice and salt. Seal lid, and bring to high pressure. Reduce heat to low, place pot over a flame deflector, and cook for 25 minutes. Turn off heat and allow pot to stand undisturbed for another 25 minutes, so rice can finish cooking in the steam. Carefully open lid. Remove bay leaf, allspice, and cinnamon.

To serve, combine lentils with candied onions. Mound rice in the center of a platter, and surround with lentils. Garnish with parsley.

Makes 4 to 6 servings

❡

Ruby Risotto

This rich pink grain dish is a lovely main course for a warm-weather luncheon. Sweet red onions combine with the bite of radicchio and the creaminess of Arborio rice to create the perfect balance of energy and taste. The rice relaxes and centers us, while the radicchio and pickled red cabbage help with digestion and vitality. I love how nature can balance to perfection.

5 cups spring or filtered water

3-inch piece kombu

Soy sauce

2 teaspoons extra-virgin olive oil

1 small red onion, diced

1 head radicchio, shredded

1 cup Arborio rice

¼ cup mirin

¼ head red cabbage, shredded

3 tablespoons umeboshi vinegar

¼ cup minced flat-leaf parsley

Bring water and kombu to a boil in a large saucepan over medium heat. Reduce heat, and season lightly with soy sauce. Simmer 15 minutes. Stock simmers all through cooking process, so keep heat very low.

Heat oil in a deep skillet over medium heat. Add onion, and sauté, until limp, about 2 minutes. Add radicchio, and sauté until wilted, about 2 minutes. Stir in rice, and sauté, stirring, until coated with oil. Add mirin, and cook, stirring, until absorbed into rice. Add stock, ½ cup at a time, and cook, stirring, over low heat. Add more stock as it is absorbed by rice. Rice will take about 25 minutes to cook; the final dish should be creamy, but rice should still have some resistance.

Meanwhile, bring a pot of water to a boil over high heat. Add cabbage, and blanch just until slightly limp, 30 to 60 seconds. Drain, and toss with a generous splash of vinegar. Set aside to pickle and allow cabbage to turn bright pink, about 15 minutes. Drain well, and gently squeeze to remove any excess liquid.

Remove risotto from heat, and stir in parsley. Transfer risotto to a serving platter, and make a ring of pickled cabbage around rim. Serve immediately.

Makes 5 or 6 servings

Thanksgiving Rice

Holiday cooking doesn't mean that health—and taste—has to go down the tubes. You could just serve a bowl of rice—or you could serve this very special showstopper. Nutty brown rice, sweet corn, tart dried cranberries, and zesty citrus flavors all come together to create a very social energy. A great dinner party dish, it will make your guests quite cheerful and chatty.

1 cup medium grain brown rice, rinsed
      well
½ cup brown basmati rice, rinsed well
½ cup unsweetened dried cranberries,
      soaked in warm water 15 minutes and
      drained
½ cup fresh or frozen corn kernels
Grated zest and juice of 1 lime
Grated zest and juice of 1 orange
1¾ cups spring or filtered water
2 pinches sea salt
1 cup coarsely minced pecans, pan
      toasted (recipe follows)

Place rice, cranberries, corn, zests, and water in a pressure cooker over medium lid heat. Cover loosely, and bring to a boil. Add salt; seal lid, and bring to high pressure. Reduce heat to low, place pot on a flame deflector, and cook 25 minutes. Turn off heat and leave pot undisturbed 25 minutes, so rice can finish cooking in the steam.

Open pressure cooker lid carefully. Gently fold in pecans and citrus juices. Transfer to a serving bowl, and serve immediately.

Makes 5 to 6 servings

PAN-TOASTED NUTS

Heat a dry skillet over medium heat. Add nuts and pan toast, stirring, until lightly browned and fragrant. Transfer to a small bowl to cool.

Sweet Corn Fritters

These fried corn fritters are great in so many ways that I'm not sure where to begin. They'll give you so much energy, you'll be soaring. You have the sweet taste of corn, along with its sunny summer vitality. You have the strong sprouting energy of scallions for a light, fresh vitality. And you have the incredible vitality of frying—high fire, the expansion of oil. Bring all this energy together for a delicious starter course or party food.

These go especially well with a spicy dipping sauce, like soy sauce, water and wasabi, or a Chinese-style plum sauce.

½ cup whole wheat pastry flour

¼ cup yellow cornmeal

Generous pinch sea salt

½ teaspoon powdered ginger

1 teaspoon baking powder

3 to 4 ounces soft tofu, finely crumbled

Juice of ½ lemon

About ½ cup plain rice or soy milk

1 cup fresh or frozen corn kernels

4 to 5 fresh scallions, diced

About ¼ cup minced flat-leaf parsley

Safflower oil, for frying

Combine flour, cornmeal, salt, ginger, and baking powder in a medium bowl. Mix in tofu and lemon juice. Slowly add rice milk,

mixing to form a smooth, thick batter. Fold in corn, scallions, and parsley, combining well.

Add enough oil to generously coat bottom of a skillet over medium heat. Drop batter by tablespoonfuls into hot oil, and cook until fritters are golden and crispy, 3 to 4 minutes per side. Drain on paper towels. Repeat with remaining batter, keeping the cooked fritters in a warm oven. Serve warm.

Makes 6 to 8 fritters

Millet with Sweet Vegetables and Corn

We all love comfort food; it makes us feel so nurtured and satisfied. Nurturing is millet's special calling. On top of that, millet and sweet vegetables combine to create a wonderfully relaxed energy, nourishing our middle organs, the organs that govern how well we manage stress in our lives: the spleen, stomach, and pancreas. With those organs functioning well, we have compassion for humankind and remain calm in a storm.

¼ cup minced onion

¼ cup minced winter squash

¼ cup minced carrot

½ cup fresh or frozen corn kernels

1 cup yellow millet, rinsed well

4 cups spring or filtered water

Pinch sea salt

About ¼ cup pumpkin seeds, pan toasted
   (page 131), for garnish

Layer onion, squash, carrot, corn, and millet in a heavy pot. Gently add water; cover, and bring to a boil over medium heat. Add salt, cover, and reduce heat to low. Simmer until all liquid has been absorbed and millet is creamy, 25 to 30 minutes. Stir gently to combine ingredients, and transfer to a serving bowl. Garnish with pumpkin seeds, and serve immediately.

Makes 4 to 6 servings

Gingered Millet with Shiitake Mushrooms and Corn

Amazingly nourishing, this millet dish also provides large amounts of energy. The relaxed energy of millet and sweet corn come together with sautéed onions for vital-

ity, ginger for strong circulation, and shiitake mushrooms for strong, clear blood to create a dish that gives you the energy you need, with a calm, clear mind to see your way.

2 teaspoons light sesame oil

1 small onion, diced

½ teaspoon powdered ginger

4 to 5 dried shiitake mushrooms, soaked
   until tender, thinly sliced

1 ear corn, kernels removed

1 cup yellow millet, rinsed well

4 cups spring or filtered water

Pinch sea salt

About ¼ cup minced flat-leaf parsley, for
   garnish

Heat oil in a deep saucepan over medium heat. Add onion and ginger, and sauté 1 to 2 minutes, until onion is limp. Add mushrooms; sauté, stirring, until shiny with oil. Stir in corn. Stir in millet and water. Cover, and bring to a boil. Add salt, cover, reduce heat to low, and simmer until liquid is absorbed and millet is creamy, about 25 minutes. Stir gently to combine the ingredients, and transfer to a serving bowl. Garnish with the parsley, and serve immediately.

Makes 4 to 6 servings

Minted Quinoa with Crunchy Pine Nuts

Quinoa is a great grain for those active types, not that the sedentary types should ignore it. High in protein, with a nutty taste, quinoa cooks quickly but still nourishes us whole-grain style. On top of that, it comes from a warm climate, making it a great summer grain; it'll keep us cool when the weather is anything but.

1 cup quinoa

1 cup tiny cauliflower florets

2 cups spring or filtered water

About 1 teaspoon soy sauce

½ cup pine nuts, pan toasted (page 131)

2 to 3 fresh scallions, thinly sliced on the
    diagonal

About ¼ cup minced mint

Rinse quinoa very well to remove the bitter saponin that coats it. Place quinoa and cauliflower in a saucepan. Add water, cover, and bring to a boil over medium heat. Lightly season with soy sauce, cover, and reduce heat to low. Simmer until all liquid is absorbed and quinoa has opened up, about 20 minutes. Gently fold pine nuts, scallions, and mint into quinoa; transfer to a serving bowl, and serve immediately.

Makes 4 to 6 servings

Hato Mugi Risotto

This is wonderful—a creamy, rich, satisfying dish that helps the body assimilate oil, fat, and protein. It's a whole-grain dish that improves kidney function and digestion, resulting in perfect skin. Laced through with moisturizing vegetables, this barley dish is the perfect beauty treatment.

5 cups spring or filtered water

3-inch piece kombu

4 to 5 slices fresh ginger

Dash soy sauce

1 teaspoon extra-virgin olive oil

1 sweet onion, diced

Sea salt

1 carrot, diced

1 cup hato mugi barley, rinsed well

2 to 3 stalks broccoli, cut into tiny florets
    and stems peeled and diced

2 tablespoons plain rice or soy milk

Bring water, kombu, ginger, and soy sauce to a boil in a saucepan over medium heat. Reduce heat to low, and simmer 15 minutes. Stock will simmer all through cooking process, so keep heat low.

Heat oil in a skillet over medium heat. Add onion and a pinch of salt; sauté until limp, about 2 minutes. Add carrot and a pinch of salt; sauté, stirring, until shiny with oil. Add hato mugi; sauté, stirring, 1 minute. Add stock, ½ cup at a time, and cook, stirring, over low heat. Add more stock as it is absorbed by barley. Risotto will take about 30 minutes, turning creamy, but barley will still hold its shape.

Meanwhile, bring a pot of water to a boil over high heat. Add broccoli stems and florets, and blanch until crisp-tender and bright green, about 1 minute. Drain.

Stir the rice milk and broccoli into risotto. Transfer to a serving bowl, and serve immediately.

Makes 4 to 6 servings

Toasted Barley Salad with Braised Portobello Mushrooms

You have to love barley, with its lovely, light energy that opens you up to the possibilities of life. Not to mention that it helps cleanse the body of stagnant, accumulated animal protein and fat, so you look great—with perfect hair and flawless skin. Toasting the barley before cooking strengthens its energy. Adding the corn, red pepper, and braised portobello mushrooms brings in the vitality of fire energy. With this dish, you'll feel as great as you look.

1 cup hato mugi barley, rinsed well

½ cup fresh or frozen corn kernels

2 cups spring or filtered water

Soy sauce

2 teaspoons extra-virgin olive oil

1 small onion, cut into thin half-moon slices

Sea salt

1 to 2 teaspoons mirin

3 to 4 large portobello mushrooms, stemmed, brushed free of dirt, thinly sliced

1 small bunch kale, left whole

1 roasted red bell pepper (page 96), diced

2 to 3 fresh scallions, thinly sliced on the diagonal

Juice of 1 lime

Heat a dry skillet over medium heat. Toast barley until light golden, stirring constantly, about 10 minutes.

Place barley in a heavy pot with corn and water. Cover, and bring to a boil over medium heat. Add a dash of soy sauce, cover, and reduce heat to low. Simmer until the liquid has been absorbed, about 35 minutes.

Meanwhile, heat oil in a skillet over medium heat. Add onion and a pinch of salt, and sauté until limp, about 2 minutes. Add mushrooms, season lightly with soy sauce and mirin, and sauté until mushrooms are quite limp. Cover, reduce heat to low, and simmer until mushrooms release their juices and reabsorb them, and are tender and richly flavored.

Bring a small pot of water to a boil over high heat. Add kale, and blanch until just tender and bright green. Drain and slice into bite-sized pieces. Set aside.

Stir bell pepper, scallions, and lime juice into barley. To serve, spread kale over a serving platter. Mound barley mixture in center, and make a ring of mushrooms around rim of platter. Serve immediately.

Makes 6 or 7 servings

Barley-Mushroom Bake

Ilove the energy of this great winter casserole. You get warm, hearty endurance from the lentils, but because of the upward sprouting energy of the barley (which also aids the body in digestion), the casserole doesn't get too heavy. Add to that the sweetness of the onions, which relax the middle of the body, and the light, dispersing energy of mushrooms and you have a casserole that won't leave you feeling lethargic and heavy but will keep you warm and cozy in cold winter weather.

1 tablespoon light sesame oil
6 to 8 baby pearl onions, trimmed and
    peeled
Soy sauce
Mirin
1 to 2 pounds mixed mushrooms (button,
    oyster, shiitake, crimini), trimmed and
    left whole
Generous pinch dried basil
1/2 cup hato mugi barley, rinsed well
1/2 cup le Puy lentils, sorted and rinsed
    well

1-inch piece kombu
1 1/2 cups spring or filtered water
About 1/4 cup minced flat-leaf parsley, for
    garnish

Preheat oven to 350F (175C).

Heat oil in an ovenproof skillet over medium heat. And onions and a dash of soy sauce, and sauté just until onions begin to soften, 1 to 2 minutes. Season lightly with mirin, and stir. Add mushrooms, basil, and a dash of soy sauce; sauté until mushrooms begin to release juices into the pan. Spread onions and mushrooms over bottom of skillet, and top with barley and lentils. Using your fingertip, push kombu to bottom of pot (take care not to burn yourself). Add water and cover.

Bake for 45 to 60 minutes, until all liquid has been absorbed, lentils are soft, and barley is creamy. Remove from oven, and gently stir to combine ingredients. If there is too much liquid, uncover, and bake about 10 minutes more. Garnish with parsley, and serve hot.

Makes 4 to 6 servings

Layered Polenta and Herb-Scented Vegetables

Similar to a lasagne or timbale, this layered grain-and-vegetable dish brings together a symphony of tastes and energies to create a main course that is sure to please. The summer energy of corn polenta is the perfect grain for this dish. Light and delicate, polenta won't weigh you down as it holds together the richly sautéed, herb-infused vegetables. Light and hearty at the same time, this dish gives you a fresh energy supported with terrific staying power.

Polenta
5 cups spring or filtered water
Pinch sea salt
1 cup yellow corn grits
1 cup fresh corn kernels

Herb-Scented Vegetables
4 teaspoons extra-virgin olive oil
1 sweet onion, cut into thin half-moon
    slices
Soy sauce
1 pound button mushrooms, thinly sliced
1 leek, split lengthwise, rinsed well, and
    sliced into ½-inch pieces
1 to 2 zucchini, cut into large dice
1 to 2 yellow summer squash, cut into
    large dice

1 to 2 carrots, cut into large dice
1 small winter squash, cut into large dice
10 to 12 leaves fresh basil, minced
6 to 8 sprigs fresh rosemary, leaves
    stripped from branches
About ¼ cup minced flat-leaf parsley
Juice of 1 lemon

Sweet Carrot Sauce
1 sweet onion, diced
1 cup diced winter squash
5 to 6 carrots, diced
Spring or filtered water
Pinch sea salt
2 teaspoons sweet white miso

Make the polenta: Bring water and salt to a boil in a large saucepan over medium heat. Slowly add corn grits, whisking constantly to prevent lumps. Stir in corn. Return to a boil, whisking. Reduce heat to low, and simmer until center of polenta forms large bubbles, about 25 minutes, stirring frequently for a creamy texture. Transfer to a bowl, and cover to keep soft. If polenta sets, simply whisk it briskly before assembling dish.

Make the vegetables: Heat 2 teaspoons of oil in a skillet over medium heat. Add onion and a dash of soy sauce; sauté until limp, about 2 minutes. Add mushrooms and a dash of soy sauce; sauté until quite limp, 5 to 7 minutes. Transfer to a small bowl, and set aside.

Wipe out the skillet, add remaining 2

teaspoons oil, and heat over medium heat. Add leeks and a dash of soy sauce; sauté until bright green and just limp, about 1 minute. Add zucchini, yellow squash, and a dash of soy sauce; sauté, stirring, until just coated with oil. Add carrots, winter squash and a dash of soy sauce; sauté 1 to 2 minutes. Reduce heat to medium-low, and cook vegetables, stirring occasionally, until tender, about 10 minutes. Season lightly with soy sauce, and add herbs. Stir gently, and simmer 5 minutes more, stirring occasionally. Stir in lemon juice.

Make the sauce: Layer onion, squash, and carrots in a pressure cooker. Add about ¼ inch of water and the salt to the pan. Seal lid, and bring to high pressure. Reduce heat to low, and cook 20 minutes. Remove from heat, and allow pressure to reduce naturally. Put vegetables, in batches, through a food

mill, and strain to produce a thick smooth sauce. Return to pot over low heat; add water to achieve a thick, sauce-like consistency. Remove a small amount of liquid, and use to dissolve miso. Stir miso mixture gently back into the sauce, and simmer 3 to 4 minutes.

To assemble: Lightly oil a deep 13 × 9-inch baking dish. Evenly spread one-third of polenta into bottom of dish. Top with vegetable mixture. Spread another third of polenta carefully on top. Spread vegetable mixture over polenta, and top with remaining polenta. Set aside until polenta is firmly set, 40 to 45 minutes. Serve, cut into squares, on a pool of carrot sauce.

Makes 8 to 10 servings

Tempura Vegetables over Soba Noodles in Broth

Rocket fuel in a cup, this one . . . vitality in a one-dish meal. The perfect energizing dish for men, although I don't know too many women who'll turn their noses up. The combination of strengthening buckwheat noodles and the vitalizing, fiery energy of batter-fried root and sweet vegetables work within a savory, gingered broth to create a strong body and clear mind. All that and it tastes great, too!

Soba Broth

4 cups spring or filtered water

¼ cup soy sauce

2 to 3 teaspoons fresh ginger juice (page 188)

3-inch piece kombu, soaked until soft, notches cut in the piece

1 to 2 dried shiitake mushrooms, soaked until tender, stems removed

Tempura Batter

1 cup whole wheat pastry flour

Pinch sea salt

1 tablespoon kuzu, dissolved in 2 tablespoons cold water

¾ to 1 cup dark beer or sparkling water

Vegetables

1 onion, sliced into thin rings

1 carrot, cut into thin oblong slices

1 medium burdock, cut into thin oblong slices

1 small sweet potato, cut into thin oblong slices

8 button mushrooms, trimmed and left whole

2 spears broccoli, cut into small florets

2 quarts safflower oil, for frying

To Serve

8 ounces soba noodles

2 to 3 fresh scallions, thinly sliced on the diagonal, for garnish

Make the broth: Combine all ingredients in a saucepan. Bring to a boil, covered, over medium heat. Reduce heat to low, and remove kombu and mushrooms. Slice both into thin pieces, and return to broth. Simmer 15 to 20 minutes, covered, to develop flavors.

Make the tempura batter: Combine flour and salt in a medium bowl. Stir in kuzu mixture. Slowly add enough beer to form a thin, but not too thin, spoonable batter. Set batter aside 10 minutes before use. (The beer and kuzu will make the coating crispy, so they are important ingredients.)

To cook: Arrange prepared vegetables on a platter for easy access. Heat about 3 inches of oil in a deep pot over medium heat. Make sure oil is hot enough to fry; you can check the temperature by simply submerging a pair of chopsticks in the oil. If bubbles accumulate around chopsticks, oil is ready. Increase heat to high, and dip vegetables, in batches, in tempura batter and drop them gently into oil. Fry until crispy and golden brown, 1 to 2 minutes. Drain well on paper towels. Keep fried vegetables in a warm oven so they stay crisp while you continue to fry.

To serve: Bring a large pot of water to a boil over high heat. Add noodles, and cook according to package directions until tender but firm to the bite. Drain and rinse well. Mound noodles in 4 individual bowls. Ladle broth over them, and top generously with vegetable tempura. Garnish with scallions, and serve immediately.

Makes 4 servings

Italian Couscous and Vegetable Salad

There's nothing quite like a quick-cooking, light grain dish to relax the body in warm weather. Using couscous as a neutral foundation, we pull together the vitalizing energy of olives, sun-dried tomatoes, herbs, and bitter greens to create incredible energy. The staying power you get from the tempeh will have you wanting to play volleyball in the yard well after everyone else has tired out.

2 cups spring or filtered water

Sea salt

1 cup couscous

4 teaspoons extra-virgin olive oil

1 sweet onion, diced

2 to 3 tablespoons capers, drained

8 to 12 oil-cured black olives, pitted and diced

6 to 8 sun-dried tomatoes, soaked until tender, and diced

1 small bunch arugula, large stems removed and leaves sliced

About ¼ cup minced basil leaves

¼ pound tempeh

Basil sprigs, for garnish

Bring water and a pinch of salt to a boil in a saucepan over medium heat. Add couscous, cover, and turn off heat. Allow to stand, undisturbed, 5 minutes. Fluff with a fork, and set aside.

Heat 2 teaspoons of oil in a skillet over medium heat. Add onion and a pinch of salt; sauté until limp, about 2 minutes. Stir in capers, olives, and sun-dried tomatoes. Sauté until tomatoes are soft, 5 to 7 minutes. Stir in arugula and basil, and sprinkle lightly with salt. Sauté until leaves are just limp but still bright green.

In a small sauté pan, heat remaining 2 teaspoons of oil over medium heat. Crumble tempeh into pan, and sauté until golden and slightly crispy.

Stir onion mixture and tempeh into couscous. Serve hot, garnished with the basil sprigs.

Makes 4 to 6 servings

Pasta with Broccoli–Pine Nut Pesto

We're all familiar with what we consider to be the classic pesto—fresh basil, pine nuts, olive oil, and garlic—but did you know that in Italian, *pesto* simply means "paste"? In Italian cuisine, pesto is made from just about any vegetable you can imagine. This one will win you raves. Richly flavored and brightly colored, with a creamy texture, it smothers pasta with delicious taste and lots of energy. The balance is perfect: You have the calming energy of broccoli, the endurance of pasta, the unparalleled vitality of nuts, and a wonderful flavor.

> 1 to 2 pounds broccoli, cut into small florets and stems peeled and diced
>
> 1 pound whole wheat udon noodles or fettucine
>
> ½ cup pine nuts, pan toasted (page 131)
>
> ¼ cup walnut pieces, pan toasted (page 131)
>
> 3 to 4 tablespoons extra-virgin olive oil
>
> 1 tablespoon umeboshi vinegar
>
> 1 teaspoon brown rice syrup
>
> 1 tablespoon white miso
>
> 1 roasted red bell pepper (page 96), diced, for garnish

Bring a large pot of water to a boil and cook broccoli florets and stems until bright green and tender, about 3 minutes. Drain well, and set aside. In the same water, cook noodles until tender but firm to the bite, 8 to 10 minutes. Drain well, and rinse; Japanese noodles are coated with salt and require rinsing for the best flavor.

Place pine nuts and walnuts in a food processor fitted with the metal blade. Add oil, vinegar, rice syrup, and miso; puree until smooth. Add broccoli, and puree until a smooth, thick paste forms. (Add water only if pesto is too thick for your taste, but do not thin too much or it will not cling to the noodles.)

Toss pesto with hot noodles, and transfer to a serving platter. Garnish with red pepper and serve.

Makes 4 to 6 servings

Sesame Noodle Salad

Spicy sauces mixed in with mild noodles give us a lot of energy and clarity of thought. The noodles relax us, while the seasonings stimulate our thinking and inspire us to action. Simple and vitalizing—who could ask for more?

1 pound somen noodles or angel hair
   pasta
¼ cup toasted sesame oil
1-inch piece fresh ginger, minced
¼ cup sesame tahini
2 teaspoons soy sauce
1 teaspoon chili powder
1 tablespoon brown rice vinegar
6 to 8 fresh scallions, thinly sliced on the
   diagonal
3 to 4 tablespoons black sesame seeds,
   lightly pan toasted (page 131), for gar-
   nish

Bring a large pot of water to a boil over medium heat. Add noodles, and cook until tender but firm to the bite, 6 to 8 minutes. Drain, and rinse well; Japanese noodles are coated with salt and require rinsing for the best flavor.

Meanwhile, heat oil in a skillet over medium heat. Add ginger, and cook 1 to 2 minutes. Whisk in tahini, soy sauce, and chili powder. Cook over low heat 2 to 3 minutes. Remove from heat, and whisk in rice vinegar. Adjust seasoning to taste.

To serve, toss cooked noodles with sesame sauce and scallions, and transfer to a serving platter. Garnish with black sesame seeds. Serve at room temperature or chilled.

Makes 4 to 6 servings

Udon with Caramelized Leeks and Walnuts

There is nothing quite like pasta to make us happy. In fact, did you know that the combination of pasta and vegetables—without protein—is the perfect feel-good food? This combination is the best stress reliever: The calming endurance of noodles with the vitality of rich, braised vegetables gives you the calm and strength of character to face life's little adventures.

2 teaspoons extra-virgin olive oil

4 to 5 shallots, minced

Sea salt

3 leeks, split lengthwise, rinsed well, and
   cut into 1-inch slices

1 pound udon noodles or fettucine

3 to 4 tablespoons mirin

¼ cup plain rice or soy milk

6 to 8 fresh basil leaves, shredded

½ cup walnut pieces, pan toasted (page
   131)

4 to 6 basil sprigs, for garnish

Heat oil in a skillet over medium heat. Add shallots and a pinch of salt; sauté 1 to 2 minutes. Add leeks and a pinch of salt; sauté 1 to 2 minutes. Add mirin, cover, and cook over low heat, stirring occasionally to prevent sticking, until leeks are browned on the edges and quite limp, about 20 minutes.

Meanwhile, bring a large pot of water to a boil. Add udon, and cook until tender but still firm to the bite, 8 to 10 minutes. Drain, and rinse; Japanese noodles are coated with salt and require rinsing for the best flavor.

Add rice milk and shredded basil to leek mixture, and season lightly with salt. Simmer, uncovered, about 5 minutes, until rice milk is slightly reduced and mixture thickens.

To serve, toss cooked noodles with leek sauce and walnuts. Transfer to a serving platter, and garnish with basil sprigs.

Makes 4 to 6 servings

Carrot Gnocchi with Spring Vegetable Sauce

Hearty, carrot-flavored gnocchi will give you a grounded, centered energy. But just to ensure that we keep our energy from sinking and growing heavy and leaving us fatigued, we serve them smothered in a light, fresh sauce made from spring veggies; their sprouting energy makes us feel refreshed and vital.

Before you can make the gnocchi dough, you will need to prepare the rice and carrot purees.

Gnocchi

¼ cup sushi rice, unrinsed

1¾ to 2 cups spring or filtered water

1 carrot, cut into small chunks

Sea salt

1 cup whole wheat pastry flour

1 cup semolina flour

Spring Vegetable Sauce

2 teaspoons corn oil

1 sweet onion, diced

Sea salt

2 cups thinly sliced button mushrooms

1 to 2 yellow summer squash, diced

1 to 2 carrots, diced

1 cup shredded green cabbage

1 cup shelled fresh or frozen green peas

1 cup rice or soy milk

Grated zest of 1 lemon

3 to 4 fresh scallions, thinly sliced on the diagonal

To Serve

6 or 7 lemon slices, for garnish

Make the gnocchi: Cook rice with 1¼ cups of water, covered, over low heat until rice absorbs liquid and is quite creamy. Transfer to a food processor fitted with the metal blade, and puree until smooth. Spoon into a bowl, and set aside. You should have ½ cup.

Add carrot to a small saucepan. Add just enough water to cover bottom of pan. Add a pinch of salt. Cover, and cook over low heat until carrot is soft, about 15 minutes. Drain, and transfer carrot to a food processor fitted with the metal blade; puree until smooth. Spoon into a bowl, and set aside. You should have ½ cup.

Combine flours, rice puree, and ½ teaspoon salt in a medium bowl. Mix in carrot puree until evenly distributed. Slowly stir in ½ cup water. Add additional water as needed to form a workable dough that is not too stiff and not too sticky. Transfer dough to a lightly floured surface. Knead until smooth and elastic, 5 to 10 minutes. Gather into a ball, and allow to rest, covered with a damp towel, 5 minutes.

To shape gnocchi, pinch off one-quarter of dough. Roll into a 10-inch log, about ¼-

inch thick. With a sharp knife, slice log into 1-inch lengths. Roll each piece on a floured gnocchi comb or on a fork to form ridges. Place gnocchi on floured baking sheets without touching. Repeat until all dough is used. (At this point, you can cook gnocchi; freeze them in sealed plastic bags; or dry them, covered with a towel, on the baking sheets for 1 to 2 days.)

Make the sauce: Heat oil in a deep skillet over medium heat. Add onion and a pinch of salt; sauté 1 to 2 minutes. Add mushrooms and a pinch of salt; sauté until limp, about 3 minutes. Add squash, carrots, cabbage, and a pinch of salt; sauté 2 minutes. Cover, reduce heat to low, and simmer 5 to 7 minutes, until the vegetables are tender. Add peas and rice milk, season lightly with salt, and simmer; uncovered, until milk reduces, about 5 minutes. Remove from heat, and stir in lemon zest and scallions.

Cook the gnocchi: Bring a large pot of water to a boil over medium heat. Add gnocchi and boil until they rise to surface, 3 to 4 minutes. Drain, but do not rinse.

To serve: Toss cooked pasta with sauce, and transfer to a serving platter. Garnish with lemon slices, and serve immediately.

Makes 6 to 7 servings

Soba Noodles with Crispy Seitan and Vegetables

This one-dish meal combines delicious flavor with tremendous energy. Soba noodles, made from strengthening buckwheat, provide enduring stamina. The rich protein of fried seitan gives us vitality; and just so things don't get too heavy, there's loads of lightly cooked veggies for freshness. This is a great light dinner or simple lunch.

8 ounces soba noodles

1 cup fresh corn kernels

10 to 12 snow peas, trimmed and left whole

1 to 2 carrots, cut into thin matchstick pieces

2 stalks broccoli, broken into small florets and stems peeled and thinly sliced

2 to 3 dried shiitake mushrooms, soaked until tender, thinly sliced

1 ripe pear, halved, cored, and thinly sliced

Juice of 1 lemon

Soy sauce, to taste

1 teaspoon kuzu dissolved in 1 tablespoon cold water

Safflower oil, for frying

About 1 cup whole wheat pastry flour

2 tablespoons tan sesame seeds, lightly pan toasted (page 131)

8 ounces seitan, thickly sliced

2 to 3 fresh scallions, thinly sliced on the diagonal, for garnish

Bring a large pot of water to a boil over medium heat. Add noodles, and cook until tender but firm to the bite, 6 to 8 minutes. Drain, and rinse well; Japanese noodles are coated with salt and require rinsing for the best flavor.

Meanwhile, bring a small pot of water to boil over high heat. Add each vegetable separately, in the order listed, and blanch until crisp-tender, 30 to 60 seconds. (Mushrooms will take a bit longer than the other vegetables, so test them.) Drain vegetables and combine in a large bowl. Reserve 1 cup of the cooking water.

Toss pear with lemon juice; add to vegetable mixture, and toss to combine. Warm reserved cooking water over low heat. Season lightly with soy sauce, and stir in kuzu mixture; cook, stirring, until mixture thickens. Spoon mixture over vegetables, and stir well to coat.

Heat about 1 inch of oil in a deep skillet. Combine flour and sesame seeds in a shallow bowl. Coat seitan in flour mixture. Fry seitan until golden on both sides, turning to fry evenly. Drain well on paper towels.

To serve, toss cooked noodles with vegetable mixture, and arrange on a serving platter. Top with seitan and scallions. Serve immediately.

Makes 4 servings

Seitan Kinpira

The combination of burdock, the most strengthening root vegetable, and carrot, another titan of power, with protein-packed seitan creates a dish that gives you a clear mind, sharp focus, and tremendous staying power. The kuzu glaze makes strong blood, giving you a dish that keeps you going.

2 teaspoons toasted sesame oil
1 sweet onion, cut into thin half-moon slices
Sea salt
1 cup matchstick-size burdock pieces
1 cup matchstick-size carrot pieces
8 ounces seitan, thinly sliced
Spring or filtered water
Soy sauce
1 teaspoon kuzu dissolved in 1 table-
   spoon cold water
1 to 2 stalks celery, thinly sliced on the
   diagonal
About 1 tablespoon brown rice vinegar

Heat oil in a skillet over medium heat. Add onion and a pinch of salt; sauté until limp, about 2 minutes. Add burdock and a pinch of salt; sauté until shiny with oil, stirring occasionally. Spread evenly in skillet. Top with carrot and then seitan. Add enough water to just cover burdock. Cover, and simmer over medium-low heat for 5 minutes. Season lightly with soy sauce, and simmer 5 minutes. Remove cover, and stir in kuzu mixture; cook, stirring, until a clear glaze forms. Remove from heat, and stir in celery and rice vinegar to taste. Transfer to a platter, and serve immediately.

Makes about 4 servings

Herb-Scented Corn Biscuits

You know, biscuits are the stuff of dreams. Light and airy, they give us the soul-satisfying energy of flour without the heaviness we can experience from many breads and baked goods. Flour products, although delicious, can make digestion sluggish. In whole foods cooking, baked goods—breads, muffins, and crackers—are used in small quantities and kept light, like these savory biscuits, which are great with soup as a starter course.

1½ cups whole wheat pastry flour

½ cup yellow cornmeal

2 teaspoons baking powder

½ teaspoon baking soda

1 teaspoon dried basil

½ teaspoon ground dried rosemary

¼ teaspoon powdered ginger

¼ teaspoon sea salt

1 teaspoon brown rice syrup

6 tablespoon soy margarine

1 cup plain rice or soy milk

1 teaspoon umeboshi vinegar

Preheat oven to 375F (190C). Lightly oil a baking sheet or line with parchment paper.

Combine dry ingredients in a medium bowl. Using a fork or pastry cutter, cut rice syrup and margarine into flour mixture until pieces the size of small peas form. Mix rice milk and vinegar together and add to flour mixture. Mix until ingredients are just combined. If you overmix, biscuits will be tough.

Turn dough out onto a lightly floured surface, and pat into a 9-inch circle. Cut into 12 wedges with a sharp, wet knife. Transfer wedges to prepared baking sheet. Bake for 12 to 15 minutes, or until biscuits have puffed and are firm and lightly browned.

Makes 12 biscuits

Cranberry-Pecan Bread with Caraway Seeds

A variation on a traditional New England bread, this delicately sweet-and-savory bread is laced through with tart cranberries, richly toasted pecans, and savory caraway seeds. The addition of the tart fruit and seeds makes the flour more digestible and the flavor unique. I like to serve this on Thanksgiving morning with a spread of brown rice syrup laced with grated orange peel.

3 ounces dried unsweetened cranberries

½ cup fresh orange juice

2 cups whole wheat pastry flour

½ cup yellow cornmeal

2 teaspoons baking powder

¼ teaspoon sea salt

1 teaspoon caraway seeds

¼ cup corn oil

⅓ cup Eden Wheat Malt

2 teaspoons grated orange zest

About 1½ cups plain rice or soy milk

½ cup pecan pieces, lightly pan toasted (page 131)

Preheat oven to 350F (190C). Lightly oil and flour a 10-inch deep-dish pie plate.

Mix cranberries and orange juice together in a small bowl, and soak about 15 minutes, stirring occasionally. Drain, discarding any excess juice.

Mix dry ingredients in a medium bowl. Mix in the oil, malt, and orange zest. Slowly mix in rice milk to make a thick spoonable batter, but do not overmix. Fold in pecans and cranberries. Spoon batter evenly into prepared pan.

Bake about 35 minutes, or until the center of bread springs back to the touch or a toothpick inserted into center comes out clean. Cool in pan about 10 minutes, then run a sharp knife around the edge to loosen. Slice into wedges. Serve warm.

Makes 10 to 12 servings

Flaming Mushroom Volcanoes

Areal show-stopper, and so simple to make, even you will be amazed. A light starter or main course, this dish brings together lots of sparkling energy. Not only will the drama of the dish impress you but the vitality of the ingredients will make you sociable and chatty.

Mushroom Volcanoes

4 enoki mushrooms

*Brandy (orange flavored, if desired) or
    sake*

4 teaspoons extra-virgin olive oil

2 to 3 shallots, peeled, finely diced

Soy sauce

1 small carrot, finely minced

Pinch Salt

About ¼ cup minced flat-leaf parsley

2 cups spring or filtered water

1 cup couscous

*2 large portobello mushrooms, stems
    removed*

*2 large carrots, cut into thin 2 to 3-inch
    oblong pieces*

Brown rice syrup

Orange Sauce

1 cup plain rice milk

½ cup fresh orange juice

Pinch sea salt

2 tablespoons mirin

*2 teaspoons kuzu dissolved in 3 table-
    spoons cold water*

To Assemble

Finely shredded carrot, for garnish

Make the vegetables: Marinate enoki mushrooms in brandy until they are saturated, about 30 minutes.

Heat 2 teaspoons of oil in a skillet over medium heat. Add shallots and a dash of soy sauce; sauté until limp, about 3 minutes. Add minced carrot and season lightly with soy sauce; sauté 1 to 2 minutes. Remove from heat, and stir in parsley. Transfer to a small bowl, and set aside.

Bring water to a boil in a medium saucepan. Stir in couscous and a dash of soy sauce; cover, and remove from heat. Let stand 10 minutes.

Preheat oven to 400F (205C). Brush portobello mushrooms with remaining oil, place on a baking sheet, and drizzle with soy sauce. Bake, uncovered, about 20 minutes until tender.

Place carrot pieces in a saucepan. Add a pinch of salt and enough rice syrup and water, in equal amounts, to cover. Cook over low heat, uncovered, until liquid reduces and a thin glaze forms, 8 to 10 minutes. Set aside.

Make the sauce: Warm rice milk, orange juice, salt, and mirin over low heat. Stir in kuzu mixture and cook, stirring, until mixture thickens, about 3 minutes. Set aside.

To assemble: Place portobello mushrooms, top side down, on 2 salad plates. Stir sautéed vegetables into couscous, and form into 2 cone shapes to fit on mushroom caps, so they look like mountains. Press carrot pieces into couscous around the cone, forming a decorative wall. Spoon orange sauce around the mushroom bases, and sprinkle with shredded carrot. Arrange enoki mushrooms in top of the couscous cones. Just before serving, light enoki mushrooms so the "volcanoes" flame.

Makes 2 servings

TIP

To form the couscous into cones, use a lightly oiled timbale mold, make a cone out of waxed paper, or use a lightly oiled funnel.

Basic Kayu Bread

This basic bread is as easy to make as it is to digest. It's bread in its simplest form—a soft whole grain, flour, water, and salt—relying on natural fermentation for leavening. A hearty loaf, it is great served with soups or stews. Vary the soft grain to create many different loaves.

2 to 3 cups soft-cooked short-grain brown
  rice, room temperature (recipe follows)
2 to 3 cups whole wheat flour
1 teaspoon sea salt
1 to 2 cups spring or filtered water

Make the rice (see below). Mix flour and salt together in a large bowl, making an indentation for rice. Mix in an equal amount of cooked rice. With a wooden spoon, work from the outside toward the center, folding in rice. When thoroughly mixed, begin working dough with your hands. It will be a bit sticky at first but will become smooth as you mix it. If dough is too dry, slowly mix in water to create a sticky dough. Turn dough out onto a floured surface, and knead, slowly adding small amounts of flour until dough no longer sticks to your hands; has a smooth, elastic consistency; and springs back to the touch, 10 to 15 minutes.

Lightly oil a 9 × 5-inch loaf pan. Shape dough into a loaf. Place into prepared pan, and cut a slit down center of dough. Cover with a damp towel, and set in a warm place for 2 to 3 hours.

Preheat the oven to 250F (120C). Bake for 30 minutes. Increase temperature to 350F (175C), and bake for 1 to 1½ hours more, or until loaf is firm and sounds hollow when tapped. Cool in pan for 5 minutes. Loosen loaf from pan by running a sharp knife around the edges. Remove from pan, and wrap in a damp towel. Wait about 1 hour before slicing.

Makes 10 to 12 servings

SOFT-COOKED RICE

To make soft rice, cook 1 cup short-grain brown rice with 5 cups spring or filtered water and a pinch of salt in a pressure cooker at low pressure 1 hour. The rice can also be simmered over low heat in a heavy pot 1 hour and 10 minutes, or cooked in a slow cooker, for 6 to 8 hours. The resulting rice will be quite soft and creamy.

THE ESSENTIAL BEAN

RIED BEANS ARE a good source of protein and, more important, stamina. Although protein exists in all foods (except fruit), in whole foods cooking, we rely heavily on beans for protein. Beans are low in some of the essential amino acids (the components of protein), but we can get them in other foods such as grains. Beans are actually seeds in pods and are said to be some of the earliest foods to be cultivated and harvested by humans. Although beans vary in size and shape, they all share the same basic structure and energy. Their two halves are the storage reservoirs for starch and protein, the essentials needed for their growth into a plant. Within this seed lies the embryo for the root, stem, and leaves—the entire plant, which is why we feel so completely nourished by beans.

We eat beans at three stages of their development. Young beans, before full development, are eaten whole: green pod and seed. If we choose them just before full maturity, they are considered fresh shelled beans, like lima, fava, and soybeans. If beans come to their full potential, they can be dried—the most commonly used form—and stored. At this stage, they may require soaking and will need to cook longer to become tender.

With their natural immune defenses so strong, beans have been shown to actually relieve mild depression—if you feel great physically, you usually feel great emotionally. Because beans are digested slowly, they regulate blood sugar, giving us prolonged stamina.

What about that nagging problem of digestion with beans? Beans, beans, the musical fruit . . . and all that? Beans contain natural protease inhibitors, which are the source of their strong immune defenses, but these same elements can inhibit digestion. Cooking breaks down the protease inhibitors. Also, adding an alkalizing ingredient, like kombu, during cooking will help with this little inconvenience.

Storing beans is easy. Keep grains and beans in glass jars with tight lids to keep them fresh. To avoid the annoying grain moths that are sometimes an unwelcome part of storing whole, unprocessed foods, put a dry bay leaf in each jar of grains and beans: Problem solved, before it starts.

Crostini with Lentil Pâté

An earthy, peppery spread over toasted bread creates the perfect starter course in any season. The energy of this savory dish will keep you grounded, with lots of endurance and clarity of mind. The ginger promotes good circulation, which makes for incredible vitality.

2 teaspoons extra-virgin olive oil

1 small onion, finely minced

1-inch piece fresh ginger, minced

Sea salt

1 carrot, finely minced

1-inch piece kombu

1 cup green lentils, sorted and rinsed well

3 cups spring or filtered water

Soy sauce, to taste

About 1 teaspoon balsamic vinegar, or to taste

1 whole-grain baguette, thickly sliced into ½ to 1-inch slices

Heat oil in a deep pot. Add onion, ginger, and a pinch of salt; sauté until onion is limp, 2 to 3 minutes. Add carrot and a pinch of salt; sauté, stirring occasionally, until shiny with oil. Spread vegetables over the bottom of the pot and add kombu. Top with lentils and water. Bring to a boil, uncovered. Cover, reduce heat to low, and simmer until lentils are quite soft, 35 to 40 minutes. Lightly season with soy sauce, cover, and simmer 7 to 10 minutes more. If any cooking liquid remains, remove lid, and cook over medium heat until liquid is absorbed. Remove from heat, stir in vinegar, and transfer to a food processor fitted with the metal blade. Pulse until thick and smooth.

Preheat oven to 400F (205C) or preheat broiler. Arrange bread slices on an ungreased baking sheet. Bake or broil about 5 minutes, until golden and crispy.

Spread lentil pâté on toasted bread and return to oven 3 to 4 minutes to set. Serve hot.

Makes 4 to 8 servings

Lentil Pilaf with Sweet Vegetables

Humble little lentils have such deep connections to peasant food that we forget just how splendid they are. In a dish like this, when lentils are combined with nutty grains and sautéed sweet vegetables, you get a virtual symphony of flavors on your tongue. Long-enduring stamina from the beans and grains, and the calm centeredness from the sweet vegetables combine with the sautéing to give you a burst of energy, so you don't zone out.

1-inch piece kombu

1 cup bulgur

1 cup le Puy lentils, sorted and rinsed well

4 cups spring or filtered water

2 teaspoons light sesame oil

1 sweet onion, finely diced

Soy sauce

1 carrot, finely diced

¼ head green cabbage, finely diced

1 cup finely diced winter squash

Grated zest and juice of 1 lemon

About ¼ cup minced flat-leaf parsley

Place kombu on bottom of a heavy pot. Add bulgur, lentils, and water. Bring to a boil, uncovered. Reduce heat to low, cover, and simmer until lentils are tender, about 35 minutes.

Meanwhile, heat oil in a skillet over medium heat. Sauté onion with a dash of soy sauce until limp, about 2 minutes. Add carrot and a dash of soy sauce; sauté until shiny with oil. Stir in cabbage, squash, and a dash of soy sauce; sauté until cabbage wilts. Stir in lemon zest, reduce heat to medium-low, and cook, stirring occasionally, until the vegetables are tender and beginning to brown, 7 to 10 minutes.

To serve, stir sautéed vegetables, lemon juice, and parsley into lentil mixture. Serve warm.

Makes 4 to 6 servings

Lentil Waldorf Salad

Lentils add a delicious touch to a classic autumn salad. The earthy flavor of lentils is the perfect complement to the crisp apples and sweet pecans. But it isn't just another delicious salad—the lentils give us great endurance while the apples relax us, but with just enough tart flavor to give us some sparkle. The pecans are so packed with vitality that you'll be dancing in the streets.

Waldorf Salad

½-inch piece kombu

*⅔ cup le Puy or small black lentils, sorted
    and rinsed well*

1¼ cups spring or filtered water

Soy sauce, to taste

*2 to 3 Granny Smith apples, halved,
    cored, diced, and tossed in 1 teaspoon
    fresh lemon juice*

1 cup diced red onion, lightly blanched

2 stalks celery, diced

Grated zest of 1 lemon

*½ cup pecan pieces, lightly oven toasted
    (recipe follows)*

¼ teaspoon freshly grated nutmeg

Tofu Mayo

8 ounces tofu

2 tablespoons stone-ground mustard

2 tablespoons umeboshi vinegar

1 tablespoon brown rice syrup

Pinch sea salt

Juice of 1 lemon

3 tablespoons corn oil

Make the salad: Place kombu on bottom of a pot and top with lentils and water. Bring to a boil, uncovered. Reduce heat to low, cover, and simmer until lentils are tender but not too soft, about 35 minutes. Season lightly with soy sauce, and simmer 1 minute more. Drain and transfer to a small bowl to cool.

Combine lentils, apples, onion, celery, lemon zest, pecans, and nutmeg in a medium bowl.

Make the tofu mayo: Bring tofu and enough water to cover to a boil in a small saucepan over medium heat, and cook 5 minutes. Drain, and transfer to a food processor fitted with the metal blade. Add mustard, vinegar, rice syrup, salt, lemon juice, and oil. Puree until smooth and creamy. Adjust seasoning.

To serve: Gently stir ⅔ cup of the mayo into lentil mixture to coat ingredients well. Serve warm.

Makes 4 to 6 servings

OVEN-TOASTED NUTS

To oven-toast nuts, preheat oven to 250F (120C) and spread nuts on a baking sheet. Toast, stirring occasionally, until fragrant and lightly browned, 25 to 30 minutes. The flavor is best when nuts are toasted slowly at a low temperature.

Azuki Garden Salad

Azuki beans are red, jewel-like small beans that are prized in Asia for their restorative powers, particularly for strengthening kidney function and cleansing the blood. At the same time, they give us the same stamina as any other bean and are quite low in fat. In this dish, their delicately sweet taste comes together with fresh garden veggies to create a side salad that will keep you strong—with a light, fresh energy so the sinking energy of the protein won't weigh you down.

Beans

1-inch piece kombu

1 cup dried azuki beans, sorted, rinsed, soaked 3 to 4 hours, and drained

3 cups spring or filtered water

Soy sauce, to taste

2 teaspoons mirin, or to taste

Marinated Vegetables

½ cup matchstick-size carrot pieces

4 to 5 leaves of kale, rinsed, left whole

1 red onion, cut into thin rings

2 to 3 red radishes, thinly sliced

2 teaspoons light sesame oil

1-inch piece fresh ginger, grated and juice extracted (page 188)

1 teaspoon soy sauce

1 teaspoon brown rice vinegar

1 teaspoon brown rice syrup

Cook the beans: Place kombu on bottom of a heavy pot. Top with beans and water. Bring to a boil, uncovered. Cover, reduce heat to low, and simmer until beans are just tender but not too soft, about 45 minutes. Season lightly with soy sauce and mirin, and simmer 3 to 4 minutes more. Drain, and transfer beans to a bowl. Set aside.

Cook the vegetables: Bring a small pot of water to a boil over high heat. Add carrot, kale, and onion separately, in the order listed, and blanch until crisp-tender, 30 to 60 seconds. Drain and transfer to a bowl. Stir in radishes.

Whisk all liquid ingredients together in a small bowl. Add to vegetables, and toss until well coated. Set aside to marinate 15 minutes.

To serve: Arrange marinated vegetables on a platter. Mound reserved beans in center, and serve.

Makes 5 or 6 servings

Azuki Relish

Valued for their ability to strengthen kidney function, azuki beans are quite powerful. When combined, as they are in this dish, with dried, shredded daikon, shiitake mushrooms, and ginger, they can help cleanse the blood and rid the body of excess fat and protein, which cause us to feel sluggish. This flavorful sure-to-please dish helps you feel strong and vital by improving organ efficiency.

1-inch piece kombu

1 cup dried azuki beans, sorted, rinsed, soaked 3 to 4 hours, and drained

2 to 3 shiitake mushrooms, soaked until tender, thinly sliced

1/2 cup dried, shredded daikon, soaked until tender, diced

3 cups spring or filtered water

1/2 cup finely diced winter squash

Soy sauce, to taste

1-inch piece fresh ginger, grated and juice extracted (page 188)

2 to 3 scallions, thinly sliced on the diagonal, for garnish

Place kombu on the bottom of a heavy pot. Top with beans, mushrooms, daikon, and water. Bring to a boil, uncovered. Reduce heat to low, cover, and simmer until beans are just tender, about 45 minutes. Add squash and season lightly with soy sauce. Cover, and cook until squash is soft and beans are done. Gently stir in ginger juice; cook, uncovered, until any remaining liquid has been absorbed. Transfer to a serving bowl, and garnish with scallions.

Makes 5 or 6 servings

Baked Azuki Pastries

Baked beans are so strengthening, so warming, and so comforting. They give us tremendous stamina and endurance. That's the good news. But there's a tiny downside—baked beans can create a heavy, sinking energy, making us feel tired. So does that mean no more baked beans? No, we simply infuse them with the vitality of sautéed vegetables, corn, and ginger . . . and we wrap them in flaky pastry for a bit of decadence. Splendid.

2 teaspoons light sesame oil

1 small onion, finely diced

Soy sauce

1 carrot, finely diced

½ cup finely diced winter squash

½ cup fresh or frozen corn kernels

About 1 teaspoon mirin

1-inch piece fresh ginger, grated and juice
*   extracted (page 188)*

1½ cups cooked azuki beans

2 to 3 scallions, diced

6 sheets frozen phyllo dough, thawed in
*   the refrigerator*

Extra-virgin olive oil

About ½ cup whole wheat bread crumbs

Preheat oven to 375F (190C). Line a baking sheet with parchment paper.

Heat sesame oil in a deep skillet over medium heat. Add onion and a dash of soy sauce; sauté until limp, 1 to 2 minutes. Add carrot and a dash of soy sauce; sauté, stirring occasionally, until shiny with oil. Add squash, corn, and a dash of soy sauce; sauté 2 to 3 minutes more. Sprinkle lightly with mirin; sauté 1 to 2 minutes. Stir in ginger juice and beans; cook, stirring, until ingredients are combined. Remove from the heat, and stir in scallions. Set aside to cool.

Divide phyllo sheets in quarters crosswise. Place one half-sheet on a flat, dry surface; keep remaining sheets covered with a damp cloth. Brush phyllo piece lightly with olive oil, and sprinkle lightly with bread crumbs. Top with another phyllo piece, brush lightly with oil, and sprinkle with bread crumbs. Top with a third piece of phyllo, and brush with oil. Spoon one-sixth of bean filling on one corner of phyllo. Roll and tuck phyllo around the filling, folding diagonally to make a triangle. Place pastry on baking sheet. Brush lightly with olive oil. Repeat with remaining filling and phyllo dough.

Bake about 20 minutes, or until crispy and lightly golden. Serve warm.

Makes 3 to 4 servings

Sweet Black Soybeans

Black soybeans are prized in Asia for their restorative abilities, particularly for their ability to help the reproductive system. If you are prone to PMS, painful menstruation, or other tension in the body, their cooling nature calms your system, relaxes the middle organs, and helps balance your hormones. Then there's that little bit of sunshine from the corn to make you feel energized and happy.

1 cup black soybeans, sorted and rinsed

1-inch piece kombu

3 cups spring or filtered water

2 cups cubed winter squash

½ cup fresh or frozen corn kernels

3 tablespoons barley malt, or to taste

Soy sauce, to taste

Place soybeans in a kitchen towel and rub dry. Heat a dry skillet over medium heat. Add soybeans and pan toast, stirring constantly. At first skins will shrivel; then they'll puff slightly; and finally skins will split open, making beans look like they have a white line through them. As soon as 80 percent of soybeans have split open and they release a nutty fragrance, they are toasted enough.

Place kombu on the bottom of a pressure cooker. Add soybeans and water, and bring to a boil, uncovered. Boil at high heat for 5 minutes. Seal lid, and bring to full pressure. Reduce heat to low, and cook 40 minutes.

Remove from heat, and allow pressure to reduce naturally. Carefully open lid, and add squash. Cover loosely, and bring to a boil. You may need to add a bit of water. Reduce heat to low, and simmer until squash and beans are soft, about 35 minutes. Add corn, and season to taste with barley malt and soy sauce. Cook, covered, for 5 minutes. Uncover, and cook until any remaining liquid has been absorbed and barley malt has turned into a thin syrup. Stir gently, and transfer to a bowl. Serve immediately.

Makes 4 to 6 servings

Black Soybean Pâté

Even foods with restorative powers can be served in a fun way. Don't experts say that laughter is the best medicine? This dramatic-looking and rich-tasting pâté will be the center of attention on any party buffet or dinner table; few will realize that you're giving them calm strength and strong reproductive organs in the form of black soybeans, not to mention splendid circulation from the ginger. Hmmm . . .

 2 cups cooked black soybeans (see Note,
 page 167)
 1 cup cooked chickpeas (see Note, page
 167)
 ¼ cup extra-virgin olive oil
 ¼ cup sesame tahini
 1 teaspoon soy sauce
 1 teaspoon grated lemon zest
 1 to 2 tablespoons fresh lemon juice
 1 teaspoon brown rice syrup
 1-inch piece fresh ginger, grated and juice
 extracted (page 188)
 Celery and carrot sticks, whole grain
 crackers, and/or pita points

Place soybeans, chickpeas, oil, and tahini in a food processor fitted with the metal blade, and puree until smooth. Add remaining ingredients, and puree until a thick, smooth paste forms.

Spoon pâté into a deep bowl. Serve with celery and carrot sticks, crackers, and/or pita points.

Makes 8 to 10 servings

Sweet-and-Spicy Chickpeas

They might be beige and delicately flavored, but chickpeas are anything but mild mannered. Packed with protein and the natural endurance of other beans, these little beauties give you rich flavor and creamy texture, with very little fat. They could be the perfect bean. Their cooling nature is a great complement to the rich, spicy sauce, making this dish calming, satisfying, and vitalizing at the same time. The root vegetables give tremendous strength and clarity of thinking. All that in one little dish.

 1-inch piece kombu
 1 cup dried chickpeas, sorted, rinsed,
 soaked 6 to 8 hours, and drained
 3 cups spring or filtered water
 1 carrot, cut into large dice
 1 parsnip, cut into large dice
 Soy sauce, to taste

¼ cup sesame tahini

1 teaspoon white miso

1-inch piece fresh ginger, grated and juice
    extracted (page 188)

1 tablespoon brown rice syrup

1 teaspoon mirin

About ¼ cup minced flat-leaf parsley

Place kombu on the bottom of a pressure cooker. Top with chickpeas and water. Bring to a boil, uncovered. Boil for 5 minutes. Seal lid, and bring to full pressure. Reduce heat to low, and cook 1 hour.

Remove from heat, and allow pressure to reduce naturally. Carefully open lid, and add carrot and parsnip (you may need to add a bit of water, if the cooking liquid has been absorbed). Cover loosely, and cook until chickpeas and vegetables are tender. Season very lightly with soy sauce and cook, uncovered, until any remaining cooking liquid has been absorbed.

Combine tahini, miso, ginger juice, rice syrup, and mirin in a small bowl. Stir tahini mixture and parsley into chickpeas and vegetables. Spoon into a serving bowl, and serve hot or warm.

Makes 4 to 6 servings

Garden-Fresh Chickpea Salad

Fresh vegetables and beans create the perfect energy. The calm, enduring stamina of beans comes together with the light, sprouting, active energy of fresh veggies, including sprouts to help the body assimilate protein and fat. Strength and energy allow us to dance through life, with clear thinking, a flexible attitude, and vitality to burn.

Salad

1 cup fresh or frozen corn kernels

2 cups small cauliflower florets

1 to 2 yellow summer squash, split lengthwise, cut crosswise into 1/8-inch-thick half-moon slices

1 carrot, cut into large dice

1 to 2 stalks broccoli, separated into small florets with stems peeled and sliced

1 roasted red bell pepper (page 96), diced

2 to 3 scallions, cut into long, thin slices

2 cups cooked chickpeas

Sweet Mustard Dressing

1/4 cup tahini

1/4 cup stone-ground mustard

1 teaspoon umeboshi vinegar

Juice of 1 orange

1/2 teaspoon soy sauce

1 tablespoon brown rice syrup

To Assemble

About 1/4 cup fresh alfalfa or sunflower sprouts, for garnish

Make the salad: Bring a large pot of water to a boil over high heat. Add corn, cauliflower, squash, carrot, and broccoli separately, in the order listed, and blanch until crisp-tender, 30 to 60 seconds. Drain vegetables well. Mix cooked vegetables with roasted pepper, scallions, and chickpeas.

Make the dressing: Whisk all ingredients together in a small bowl. (Add a small amount of water if you want dressing to be thinner, but it should not be too thin.)

To Serve: Mix the dressing into chickpea mixture. Garnish with sprouts. Serve warm or chilled.

Makes 4 to 6 servings

Chickpeas with Pasta and Broccoli

A one-pot meal, you get it all with this dish: beans, pasta, and vegetables. Simple to make, delicious, and packed with energy, this makes the perfect lunch or light dinner. It brings together the protein-packed endurance from beans, the staying power from the complex carbs of whole-grain noodles, and the light, fresh energy of delicately cooked vegetables. Together, they create stamina with a flexible attitude and relaxed clarity. There is a bit of lemon zest to help you digest the protein in the dish.

2 teaspoons extra-virgin olive oil

1 red onion, thin half-moon slices

Soy sauce

1 to 2 yellow summer squash, split lengthwise and cut crosswise into ⅛-inch-thick half-moon slices

1 carrot, cut into fine matchstick pieces

1 small bundle asparagus, cut into 1-inch lengths

2 stalks broccoli, broken into small florets and stems peeled and sliced

1½ cups cooked chickpeas (see Note)

Grated zest of 1 lemon

Dash mirin

½ cup shredded fresh basil leaves

8 ounces whole-grain noodles, such as penne, shells, udon, soba, or somen

½ cup pine nuts, lightly pan toasted (page 131)

Basil sprigs, for garnish

Heat oil in a deep skillet over medium heat. Add onion and a dash of soy sauce; sauté until limp, 1 to 2 minutes. Add squash and a dash of soy sauce; sauté, stirring, until shiny with oil. Stir in carrot and a dash of soy sauce. Add asparagus, broccoli, chickpeas, and lemon zest, and season lightly with soy sauce and a generous dash of mirin. Cover, and cook over low heat until broccoli and asparagus are bright green and crisp-tender. Stir in shredded basil.

Meanwhile, bring a large pot of water to a boil. Add noodles, and cook according to package directions until tender but firm to the bite.

Drain pasta, and transfer to a large bowl. (Rinse if using Japanese noodles; they are coated with salt and require rinsing for the best flavor.) Stir in cooked vegetables and any remaining cooking liquid. Transfer to a serving platter, sprinkle with pine nuts, and garnish with basil. Serve immediately.

Makes 4 to 6 servings

Note

You may use organic canned beans in this recipe, although you will not get the vitality you would from cooking them yourself.

Black-Eyed Chili

This is a splendid twist on a classic, spicy bean stew. Black-eyed peas are the focus of this lightly spiced, vegetable-packed dish. The cooling energy of the black-eyed peas will nicely offset the heat of the chili powder and ginger. The corn grits bring summer fire to the pot. And the vegetables provide lots of moisture to help control the flames.

2 teaspoons extra-virgin olive oil

1 sweet onion, diced

4 slices fresh ginger, finely minced

Pinch sea salt

1 tablespoon chili powder

1½ cups cooked black-eyed peas (see Tip)

½ cup yellow corn grits

2½ cups spring or filtered water

1 carrot, diced

1 turnip, diced

½ cup fresh or frozen corn kernels

½ cup fresh or frozen green peas

Soy sauce, to taste

3 to 4 scallions, thinly sliced for garnish

Heat oil in a soup pot over medium heat. Add onion, ginger, and salt; sauté until limp, about 1 minute. Stir in chili powder. Add black-eyed peas and grits. Stir in water, cover, and bring to a boil. Reduce heat to low, and add carrot and turnip. Cover, and cook, stirring frequently, until grits are creamy and vegetables are soft, about 30 minutes. Stir in corn and peas, and season lightly with soy sauce. Simmer 5 to 7 minutes. Serve in individual bowls, garnished with scallions.

Makes 4 to 6 servings

TIP

To cook the peas, place a 1-inch piece kombu on the bottom of a pot. Add 1 cup black-eyed peas and 3 cups water. Bring to a boil, uncovered. Cover, reduce heat to low, and cook until tender, 45 to 60 minutes.

To-Fu Young

This is a healthy twist on our favorite classic Chinese take-out dish. Tofu has a cooling effect on our bodies, as well as being high in protein and calcium and low in fat. Its relaxing energy makes it a great comfort food for relieving stress. The hiziki adds dramatic flavor and lots of minerals; the shiitake mushroom gravy cleanses the blood and aids the body in digesting the protein. Sautéing brings just the right touch of vitality so you feel as young as you look.

Shiitake Mushroom Gravy

1 small onion, diced

5 to 6 dried shiitake mushrooms, soaked until tender, thinly sliced

3 cups spring or filtered water

Soy sauce, to taste

2 teaspoons kuzu dissolved in about 1 tablespoon cold water

Tofu Pancakes

1 pound extra-firm tofu, drained

1/2 cup whole wheat pastry flour

1/3 to 1/2 cup plain rice or soy milk

1 cup mung bean sprouts

1/2 cup sunflower kernels, lightly pan toasted (page 131)

6 to 8 scallions, minced

1/3 cup soaked hiziki, minced

1 cup button mushrooms, thinly sliced

1-inch piece fresh ginger, grated and juice extracted (page 188)

Light sesame oil

To Serve

Cooked whole-grain noodles or brown rice

8 to 12 snow peas, lightly blanched, for garnish

Make the gravy: Combine onion, mushrooms, and water in a saucepan over medium heat. Season with soy sauce and bring to a boil, covered. Reduce heat to low, and simmer until mushrooms and onion are tender, about 20 minutes. Stir in dissolved kuzu, stirring until gravy thickens and clears.

Make the pancakes: Meanwhile, crumble tofu as finely as you can into a medium bowl. Stir in flour and rice milk to make a thick batter. Fold in sprouts, sunflower kernels, scallions, hiziki, mushrooms, and ginger juice. The batter should be fairly stiff but spoonable. Add flour if it feels too wet or soft.

Pour enough sesame oil into a deep skillet to generously cover surface, heat on medium. Drop generous spoons of batter into the hot skillet to make 3-inch pancake rounds. Cook pancakes until golden brown, turning carefully to brown both sides. Drain on paper towels, and transfer to a baking sheet. Keep cooked pancakes in a warm oven while cooking remaining batter.

To serve: Serve pancakes on a bed of noodles. Spoon gravy over all, and garnish with snow peas.

Makes 4 to 6 servings

Lima Bean Salad

Did you ever wonder why white bean sal-ads seem to be the epitome of summer? Just picture the cool, white-colored beans dotted with bright, fresh, garden vegetables and lightly marinated in a delicately seasoned vinaigrette. You can feel the cooling energy refreshing you on the hottest days of summer.

Salad

1-inch piece kombu

1 cup dried baby lima beans, sorted,
    rinsed, soaked in lightly salted water
    4 to 5 hours, and drained

3 cups spring or filtered water

Soy sauce, to taste

1 small yellow squash, diced

1 cup fresh or frozen corn kernels

1 carrot, diced

8 to 12 snow peas, halved lengthwise

1 red onion, diced

Vinaigrette

¼ cup extra-virgin olive oil

2 tablespoons stone-ground mustard

1 teaspoon soy sauce

1 teaspoon umeboshi vinegar

1 teaspoon balsamic vinegar

1 teaspoon brown rice syrup

Juice of 1 lemon

About ¼ cup minced flat-leaf parsley

Make the salad: Place kombu on the bottom of a pot. Add beans and water. Bring to a boil, uncovered. Boil 5 minutes. Cover, and reduce heat to low. Simmer beans until tender, 45 to 60 minutes.

Season lightly with soy sauce, and simmer 5 to 7 minutes more. Drain and transfer beans to a medium bowl.

Bring a large pot of water to a boil over high heat. Add squash, corn, carrot, snow peas, and onion separately, in the order listed, and blanch until crisp-tender, 30 to 60 seconds. Drain vegetables well, and add to beans. Mix together, taking care not to break beans.

Make the vinaigrette: Whisk all ingredients, except the parsley, together in a small bowl.

Gently mix the vinaigrette and parsley into beans mixture. Allow salad to marinate at room temperature 30 minutes before serving. Serve warm or chilled.

Makes 4 to 6 servings

TIP

Soaking baby lima beans in lightly salted water prevents the skins from splitting and holds the beans together. They are the only type of beans that should be soaked with salt.

Breakfast Scramble

Breakfast is served at the time of day when the body needs gentle food, an easy wakeup, instead of the harshness of foods such as bacon and eggs, high-protein foods that jolt the system. Foods that are difficult to digest make us feel, at best, irritable, at worst, sluggish and lethargic.

But here's a great dish for those of us who want heartier morning fare. With tofu as its main ingredient, this dish will relax the body, giving us a centered energy for the day, with lots of vegetable protein for vitality and long-lasting endurance.

If you want this dish to really resemble scrambled eggs, add 1 teaspoon turmeric to the vegetable-tofu mixture, which will turn the entire dish a delicate golden yellow. I also like to add fresh herbs, in season, for extra zest.

½ cup plus 2 tablespoons spring or filtered water
1 small leek, split lengthwise, rinsed well, and thinly sliced
Sea salt
6 to 8 button mushrooms, thinly sliced
1 carrot, cut into fine matchsticks
1 pound extra-firm tofu, coarsely crumbled
Soy sauce, to taste
2 to 3 fresh scallions, thinly sliced, for garnish

Heat a dry skillet over medium heat. Add 2 tablespoons water to hot skillet, and add leek and a pinch of salt. Water-sauté leek until limp, about 1 minute. Add mushrooms and a pinch of salt; cook until mushrooms release their juices and begin to reabsorb them. Add carrot and a pinch of salt; cook 1 minute. Stir in tofu, season lightly with soy sauce, and add ½ cup water. Cover, and reduce heat to low. Simmer, stirring frequently, 3 to 5 minutes. Stir in scallions, and serve hot.

Makes 4 or 5 servings

Tofu Kabobs with Gingered Lentil Sauce

The perfect complement to the cooling nature of tofu is hot spice. For optimum health, I minimize hot spices like curry, cayenne, and cumin, because they can affect the nervous system, making you irritable (unless you eat lots of meat; then they can help clean your blood). I prefer chilies and ginger to create a deep, warming heat. This dish is high in protein and calcium from both the tofu and the lentils. So while the tofu relaxes us, the ginger stimulates circulation, leaving us vital and clear minded, and the greens make us flexible and soft.

Kabobs

1 tablespoon soy sauce

2 teaspoons toasted sesame oil

1 pound extra-firm tofu, cut into 1-inch cubes

8 to 12 button mushrooms, trimmed, brushed free of dirt, and left whole

1 to 2 red bell peppers, cut into 1-inch pieces

Gingered Lentil Sauce

1-inch piece kombu

1/2 cup red lentils, sorted and rinsed well

1 1/2 cups spring or filtered water

1 small onion, diced

1 carrot, diced

1 cup corn kernels

Soy sauce, to taste

1-inch piece fresh ginger, grated, juice extracted (page 188)

1/2 cup plain rice or soy milk

Juice of 1/2 lime

To Serve

6 to 8 kale or collard leaves, large stems removed

2 to 3 scallions, thinly sliced

Soak 4 to 6 wooden skewers in water about 15 minutes. Preheat the broiler.

Begin the kabobs: Mix soy sauce and sesame oil together in a small bowl. Arrange tofu and mushrooms in a shallow baking dish. Top with soy sauce mixture, and add enough water to cover tofu. Marinate 15 minutes.

Make the sauce: Place kombu on bottom of a pot. Add lentils and water. Bring to a boil, uncovered. Skim foam from boiling lentils, cover loosely, and cook until lentils begin to soften, about 25 minutes. Add vegetables; cover and cook until lentils are quite creamy and vegetables are tender, 20 minutes. Season lightly with soy sauce. Add ginger juice, and stir in rice milk. Cook lentils, uncovered, stirring frequently, until they thicken slightly, 5 to 10 minutes. Remove from heat, and stir in lime juice.

Finish the kabobs: Preheat the broiler. While lentils cook, drain tofu and mushrooms, reserving marinade. Push tofu, mushrooms, and bell pepper pieces alternately on skewers, making 4 to 6 kabobs. Arrange in shallow baking dish, brush lightly with marinade, and place under the broiler. Cook until tofu is browned, turning frequently and brushing with marinade to keep moist, about 4 to 5 minutes per side.

To serve: Bring a pot of water to a boil over high heat. Add greens, and cook until bright green and tender, about 2 minutes. Slice into bite-sized pieces.

Arrange cooked greens around rims of 4 to 6 wide, shallow soup bowls. Spoon lentils into centers and place a kabob on top. Sprinkle with scallions. Serve hot.

Makes 4 to 6 servings

Fried Tofu with Black Bean Sauce on Scallion Pancakes

Calm, cool tofu comes together with dramatic, spicy beans to create a centered focus, with vitality to burn. Dishes like this make you "simmer," so your energy doesn't fail you. Mounded over a scallion pancake, this simple dish is a meal on its own, served with some lightly cooked greens on the side.

Scallion Pancakes

About 1 cup whole wheat pastry flour

1/4 teaspoon sea salt

1 teaspoon baking powder

1/4 cup plus 3 tablespoons light sesame oil, plus extra for cooking

Up to 2 cups spring or filtered water

3 to 4 scallions, finely minced

Tofu

1 pound extra-firm tofu, drained

Safflower oil

Black Bean Sauce

2 teaspoons light sesame oil

1 teaspoon chili powder

1 onion, diced

Pinch sea salt

1 cup diced winter squash

1 cup fresh or frozen corn kernels

Soy sauce

2 cups cooked black turtle beans

About 1/2 cup spring or filtered water

To Serve

2 to 3 scallions, thinly sliced

Begin the pancakes: Combine flour, salt, and baking powder in a small bowl. Stir in oil until crumbly. Slowly mix in enough water to create a thin pancake batter. Fold in scallions, and cover. Let batter rest 15 minutes before cooking.

Make the tofu: Cut tofu into 1-inch cubes and pat dry. Heat about 1/4 inch oil in a deep skillet or wok, and fry tofu until golden brown on all sides. Drain on paper towels and set aside.

Make the sauce: Heat oil in a skillet over medium heat. Add chili powder, onion, and salt; sauté 1 minute. Add squash, corn, and a dash of soy sauce; sauté 1 to 2 minutes. Mash half of the beans. Add mashed and unmashed beans to vegetable mixture, and stir to combine. Season lightly with soy sauce, and add water. Stir in fried tofu. Cover and simmer 5 to 7 minutes.

Finish the pancakes: Heat 2 to 3 tablespoons sesame oil in a large skillet over medium heat. Drop batter by spoonfuls to make 3-inch pancakes. Cook until golden brown, turning to brown both sides. Drain on paper towels, and place pancakes in a warm oven while cooking the remaining batter. Make 8 to 10 pancakes.

To serve: Place 1 or 2 pancakes on 4 to 8 individual plates. Top generously with tofu and black bean sauce. Sprinkle with scallions. Serve hot.

Makes 4 main-course servings or 8 starter servings

Dried Tofu and Winter Squash Stew

Tofu has a character that can be relaxing to the body. Sweet winter squash also helps the body relax. Stewing makes us feel calm and centered, its long simmering creating the perfect comfort food. Put them all together, and you have created one of the finest destressers of all time.

6 slices dried tofu

1 onion, cut into large dice

1 parsnip, cut into 1-inch chunks

1 small to medium unpeeled butternut squash, cut into 1-inch pieces

Soy sauce

1 to 2 teaspoons brown rice syrup

1-inch piece fresh ginger, grated and juice extracted (page 188)

1 cinnamon stick

1 to 2 teaspoons kuzu dissolved in about 1 tablespoon cold water

Soak tofu in enough water to cover until tender, about 10 minutes. Drain and squeeze excess liquid from the slices, and cut into cubes.

Layer onion, parsnip, and squash in a deep pot. Add tofu and ½ inch of water. Sprinkle lightly with soy sauce. Cover, and bring to a gentle boil over medium heat. Add rice syrup, ginger juice, and cinnamon stick. Cover, reduce heat to low, and simmer until squash is soft, about 25 minutes. Season lightly with soy sauce, and remove cinnamon stick. Cover and simmer 5 minutes. Stir in kuzu mixture, and cook, gently stirring, until a thin glaze forms over stew. Transfer to a serving bowl and serve hot.

Makes 4 to 6 servings

Sesame-Encrusted Tofu on Soba

In this splendid main course, mild-mannered tofu is cooked sweet and spicy, coated in sesame seeds, and sautéed to infuse it with vitality. Then there are soba noodles made from buckwheat, the most strengthening grain of all, mixed in with sweet carrots for rooted focus and light watercress for fresh flexibility. And so delicious.

2 to 3 tablespoons mirin

2 teaspoons toasted sesame oil

2 teaspoons soy sauce

1 tablespoon brown rice syrup

1-inch piece fresh ginger, grated and juice
extracted (page 188)

Grated zest and juice of 1 lemon

Juice of 1 orange

1 pound extra-firm tofu, drained and cut
into 8 slices

3 to 4 tablespoons tan sesame seeds

2 tablespoons arrowroot

Light sesame oil

8 ounces soba noodles

1 carrot, cut into fine matchstick-size
pieces

1 small bunch watercress, sliced into
1-inch pieces

1 red onion, cut into thin half-moon slices

Combine mirin, toasted sesame oil, soy sauce, rice syrup, ginger juice, lemon zest and juice, and orange juice in a small bowl. Arrange tofu in a shallow baking dish, and pour juice mixture over. Marinate tofu 15 to 20 minutes. Drain, and reserve marinade.

Combine sesame seeds and arrowroot in a shallow dish. Dredge one side of the tofu slices in sesame seed mixture. Add enough light sesame oil to just cover the bottom of a large skillet. Heat over medium heat. Add tofu, sesame side down, and fry until golden. Turn and brown the other side. Drain well on paper towels.

Meanwhile, bring a large pot of water to a boil over high heat. Add noodles, and cook until tender but firm to the bite, about 10 minutes. Drain and rinse noodles well. Transfer noodles to a large bowl.

Bring a medium pot of water to a boil over high heat. Add carrot, watercress, and onion separately, in the order listed, and blanch until crisp-tender, 30 to 60 seconds. Drain vegetables well, and add to noodles. Pour reserved marinade over the top, and mix well.

To serve, arrange noodles and vegetables on a serving platter, and top with tofu slices. Serve warm.

Makes 4 to 6 servings

Tempeh with Lotus Root and Sauerkraut

The perfect autumn stew . . . hearty and warming, yes, but that's not all. This dish has perfect autumn energy, too. Tempeh, a fermented soy product, has a substantial texture and an energy in the body. The lotus root, a many-chambered tuber vegetable, is beneficial to our lung function, balancing moisture and increasing our breathing capacity. Add the long-pickled sauerkraut, fresh ginger, stewed onions, and cabbage, which nourish the digestive tract, and you have one hearty autumn dish that will warm your insides come winter.

Safflower oil

8 ounces tempeh, cut into 1-inch cubes

1 onion, cut into thick wedges

¼ head green cabbage, shredded

1 small lotus root, halved lengthwise and cut crosswise into ⅛-inch-thick slices

½ cup sauerkraut, drained well, rinsed if too salty

1-inch piece fresh ginger, grated and juice extracted (page 188)

Soy sauce, to taste

1 to 2 teaspoons kuzu dissolved in about 2 tablespoons cold water

About ¼ cup minced flat-leaf parsley, for garnish

Heat about 1 inch of oil in a deep skillet over medium heat until wooden chopstick tips, submerged in oil, draw lots of tiny bubbles around them. Add tempeh and fry until golden brown. Drain on paper towels.

Layer onion, cabbage, lotus root, and tempeh in a deep skillet. Add ½ inch of water. Cover, and bring to a boil over medium heat. Reduce heat to low, and simmer until cabbage is quite limp, about 15 minutes. Add sauerkraut and ginger juice, and season lightly with soy sauce (remember the salt in the sauerkraut). Cover, and simmer 5 to 7 minutes. Stir in kuzu mixture, and cook, stirring, until a thin glaze forms over stew. Transfer to a bowl, and garnish with parsley.

Makes 4 to 6 servings

Corn Crepes with Savory Tempeh

The rich, substantial nature of tempeh is the perfect complement to these light, sunny crepes. For a spring or early summer meal, the marriage of the hearty filling to the airy crepes balances us for the alternating cool and warm weather so common this time of year. Plus, tempeh is a protein and tends to be heavier in the body, so the sunshine nature of corn will prevent lethargy and infuse us with vitality.

Corn Crepes
¾ cup whole wheat pastry flour
¼ cup yellow cornmeal
Generous pinch sea salt
About 2½ cups plain rice or soy milk
Light sesame oil

Savory Tempeh
3 to 4 teaspoons light sesame oil
4 ounces tempeh, coarsely crumbled
¼ cup spring or filtered water
Soy sauce
1 onion, diced
1 carrot, diced
2 cups thinly sliced button mushrooms
3 to 4 dried shiitake mushrooms, soaked until tender, thinly sliced
1 cup plain rice or soy milk

½ teaspoon ground dried rosemary
1 to 2 teaspoons kuzu dissolved in 2 tablespoons cold water

Onion-Ginger Gravy
½ sweet onion, finely diced
2 cups spring or filtered water
About 1 teaspoon soy sauce
½-inch piece fresh ginger, grated and juice extracted (page 188)
1 teaspoon kuzu dissolved in about 1 tablespoon cold water

Begin the crepes: Combine flour, cornmeal, and salt in a medium bowl. Mix in rice milk to form a thin pancake batter. Set aside 15 minutes before cooking.

Make the tempeh: Heat oil in a skillet over medium heat. Add tempeh, and sauté, stirring occasionally, until golden. Add water, season lightly with soy sauce, and simmer 5 to 7 minutes over low heat. Stir in onion, carrot, and mushrooms. Gently stir in rice milk and rosemary. Season lightly with soy sauce, cover, and simmer until mushrooms are very tender, about 10 minutes. Stir in kuzu mixture, and cook, stirring, until mixture thickens, 3 to 4 minutes. Set aside to cool.

Finish the crepes: Lightly oil a small cast-iron skillet or crepe pan, and heat over medium. Add ¼ cup of batter to hot pan, turning pan to coat evenly with batter. Cook until edges loosen and center of crepe is covered with pin-point-size bubbles. Gently flip crepe and cook other side until set, 1 to 2 minutes. Transfer to a kitchen towel to cool. Repeat with remaining batter. Cover cooked crepes with another towel to keep them moist while cooking the others.

Make the gravy: Simmer onion, water, soy sauce, and ginger juice over low heat for 3 to 4 minutes. Stir in kuzu mixture and cook, stirring, until gravy thickens slightly, about 3 minutes.

To serve: Spoon some tempeh mixture onto center of each crepe and roll to enclose. Place, seam side down, on a platter. Repeat with remaining crepes and filling. Serve topped with warm gravy.

Makes 6 to 8 crepes

Asian Sautéed Tempeh and Root Vegetables

Keeping warm and vibrant in cold weather seems to challenge so many of us. Well, no more. Drawing warm energy deep into the body is the primary job of this dish; that it is rich and delicious is a splendid bonus. The real beauty of this dish is that we're bringing together substantial tempeh, centering carrot, and strengthening burdock, sautéing them over high fire and then long-simmering them for deep warmth and enduring stamina.

2 teaspoons toasted sesame oil
1 cup matchstick-sized burdock pieces
Pinch sea salt
1 cup matchstick-sized carrot pieces
8 ounces tempeh, cut into 1-inch cubes
    (see Note)
Soy sauce, to taste
1-inch piece fresh ginger, grated and juice
    extracted (page 188)

Heat oil in a skillet over medium heat. Add burdock and salt; sauté, stirring, until shiny with oil, about 1 minute. Spread burdock evenly over bottom of skillet; top with carrot and then tempeh. Add enough water to just cover burdock. Cover and cook over medium-low heat 5 to 7 minutes. Season lightly with soy sauce, and add ginger juice. Cover, and cook until all liquid has been absorbed into the dish, 5 to 7 minutes. (If any liquid remains at this point, remove cover, and continue cooking until liquid is absorbed.) Stir gently to combine, and transfer to a serving platter. Serve immediately.

Makes 4 to 6 servings

Note

For added richness and warmth, you may lightly fry the tempeh before adding it to the recipe.

Tempeh-Stuffed Escarole

This special dish is a take-off on a dish that I loved as a child. My mother made the best stuffed escarole, but it was stuffed with seasoned meat. My version is not only healthier but has interesting energy. Escarole is a bitter green with light, flexible energy. Filled with substantial, warming tempeh and vitality-packed pine nuts, it makes a main course that will leave you feeling energized and flexible, with endurance to burn.

> 2 teaspoons extra-virgin olive oil
>
> 1 sweet onion, diced
>
> Pinch sea salt
>
> 3 to 4 tablespoons golden raisins, soaked 15 minutes in ⅔ cup spring or filtered water
>
> ½ cup pine nuts
>
> 2 tablespoons capers, drained and rinsed
>
> 4 ounces tempeh, coarsely crumbled
>
> Soy sauce
>
> 1 medium head escarole

Heat oil in a deep skillet over medium heat. Add onion and salt; sauté until limp and beginning to brown, about 5 minutes. Drain raisins, reserving the soaking liquid. Add pine nuts, raisins, and capers to skillet, and cook 2 minutes, stirring, to prevent pine nuts from burning. Add tempeh, season lightly with soy sauce, and cook, stirring frequently, until tempeh is lightly browned, 7 to 10 minutes. Transfer mixture to a bowl; set skillet aside—you'll be using it again.

Rinse and drain escarole. Without removing any leaves, open the head, exposing all layers of leaves. Spoon tempeh filling into escarole, filling it as abundantly as possible. Gather leaves into a head and tie with kitchen string to secure escarole and filling. Lay stuffed head on its side in reserved skillet. Add raisin-soaking water and season lightly with soy sauce. Cover, and bring to a boil over medium heat. Reduce heat to low and simmer, turning once, until escarole is tender, 10 to 12 minutes. Add more water to pan if it dries out.

Transfer escarole to a serving platter, and remove string. Cut into wedges, and serve hot.

Makes 3 or 4 servings

Stir-Fried Tempeh with Bitter Greens

Tempeh loves to be paired with bitter greens. Here's how it works . . . Tempeh is a soy product, meaning it has a natural richness as well as protein. The bitter greens have an astringent quality that is invaluable in aiding the body in digesting protein and fat (which is why these delicate greens are so great sautéed). Together, they create a recipe for stamina and vitality; the greens, while providing flexibility, help us assimilate the protein of the tempeh, so we can use the fuel more efficiently—without giving us a heavy lethargy in the process.

2 teaspoons extra-virgin olive oil

1 red onion, thin half-moon slices

Soy sauce

1-inch piece fresh ginger, grated and juice
    extracted (page 188)

¼ teaspoon chili powder

1 carrot, cut into matchstick-size pieces

1 cup fine matchstick pieces daikon

8 ounces tempeh, cut into thin 1-inch-long
    slices

½ bunch broccoli rabe, rinsed well, cut
    into 2-inch slices

Heat oil in a deep skillet or wok over medium heat. Add onion and a dash of soy sauce; stir-fry 1 to 2 minutes. Add ginger juice and chili powder, and stir well. Add carrot, daikon, and a dash of soy sauce; stir-fry 1 to 2 minutes. Stir in tempeh and a dash of soy sauce; stir-fry until lightly browned, 2 to 3 minutes. Stir in broccoli rabe, season lightly with soy sauce, and add a small amount of water to steam the rabe. Cover, and steam over medium heat until rabe is bright green, 3 to 4 minutes. Stir gently to combine, and transfer to a serving platter. Serve immediately.

Makes 4 to 6 servings

GLORIOUS VEGETABLES

I MUST TELL you that I have a hard time understanding people who tell me how much they dislike shopping for food. I am as delighted by produce sections of markets, with their bins spilling over with fresh, colorful vegetables and fruits, as most people are by specialty boutiques! For me, exploring produce aisles of natural foods stores and farmers' markets is a treat. The bad news is that I live in the real world and have a busy life just like everybody else and can't spend my days wandering open-air markets. What I do is shop once a week for the bulk of my produce needs, supplementing the more delicate ingredients, like leafy greens, with a second trip in between. That way, I'm as ensured as I can be that the food I'll be cooking is as fresh as I can manage.

Lots of people these days talk about the importance of eating your vegetables. The vitamins, minerals, and other nutrients are so important to us. Paying attention to all this information will give you a whole new respect for lowly broccoli. Plants that make up the vegetable kingdom have an even more important job than nourishing our bodies. They supply the planet with oxygen. They purify the air of carbon dioxide through photosynthesis, making oxygen available to us. We humans, on the other hand, absorb oxygen and dispel carbon dioxide in its place. Perfect balance.

Plants also have the unique talent of transforming sunlight's energy into chemical energy—energy we can use; plus, they can store this energy up for later use, like little reservoirs. And here's the interesting part—this stored energy, when consumed by humans or animals, turns into fuel, usable fuel—vitality.

Plants are also the true origin of protein, carbohydrates, and other complex food molecules—the vital basic components necessary to create and sustain our life. So without plants, life as we experience it would not exist. Makes you think about cauliflower a little differently.

On the planet, we take life from many plant families. Flowering plants, which include plants with roots, stems, leaves, flowers, and fruit, provide much of our nutrition. Then there are nonflowering plants, which include ferns, mosses, algae, and fungi, which we use a bit less for food. The lovely sea plants provide us with incredible amounts of vitamins and minerals and make up a small part of our nutrition.

Did you know that the word *vegetable* comes from the Latin verb *vegere,* meaning "to animate or enliven"? The flowering plants, those that provide the bulk of our nutrition, are the most highly developed of the seed plants. This group of plant life contains more varieties than all the other groups combined. Most of the vegetable-type plants we, as humans, consume are seed plants. Many of these vegetables can be consumed in their entirety, although we use only parts of others, depending on the energy and nutrients we want and need at any given time.

I keep my refrigerator stocked with a wide variety of vegetables, so that I can vary my meals and the energy we get from those meals. From Earth energy, I choose winter squash, green cabbage, rutabaga, and parsnips. From Metal energy, there are cauliflower, cucumbers, onions, carrots, leeks, daikon, and ginger. From Water energy, there are burdock and sea plants. From Tree energy, there are celery, broccoli, Brussels sprouts, chives, and lemons. And then there's Fire energy, giving me dark leafy greens, fresh corn, fresh herbs, radicchio, endive, and lettuce.

With a supply of basics on hand—such as root vegetables and leafy greens—plus a few exotics or specialties for adding sparkle to my cooking, a block of tofu, and tempeh, I can walk in the door and put a meal together without a second thought.

RAVISHING ROOTS

Candied Parsnip and Carrot Tatin

A splendid sweet-and-savory side dish, this cake is smothered in caramelized, sweet root vegetables, topped with an orange-scented glaze, bringing together the most delicious complementary flavors and energies. The deeply grounding energy of roots is gentled—sweetened, if you will—by the long simmering and the glaze, while the tender cake relaxes the body, creating a calm, centered energy.

¼ cup plus 2 teaspoons corn oil

4 carrots, halved lengthwise

4 parsnips, halved lengthwise

Soy sauce

¼ cup brown rice syrup

Grated zest and juice of 1 orange

2 ½ cups whole wheat pastry flour

Generous pinch of sea salt

2 teaspoons baking powder

2 teaspoons tan sesame seeds

1 teaspoon dried basil

1 teaspoon crushed dried rosemary

½ to 1 cup plain rice or soy milk

Preheat oven to 350F (175C).

Heat 2 teaspoons of the oil in a 10-inch ovenproof skillet over high heat. (I like cast iron for this recipe.) Stir in carrots and parsnips, season lightly with soy sauce, and cook, stirring, until shiny with oil. Arrange vegetables in a decorative pattern, covering bottom of skillet. Add rice syrup and orange zest; reduce heat to medium. Cook until liquid forms a glaze and vegetables are brown, about 15 minutes. Remove from heat, and add orange juice.

Combine flour, salt, baking powder, sesame seeds, basil, and rosemary in a medium bowl. Stir in remaining ¼ cup oil and slowly stir in rice milk to make a smooth, spoonable batter. Spoon batter evenly over cooked vegetables, taking care not to disturb the pattern.

Bake about 35 minutes or until center of cake springs back to the touch. Allow cake to cool in pan about 10 minutes. Run a sharp knife around rim of the skillet to loosen cake. Place a serving platter over skillet, and carefully invert cake and skillet. If any vegetables stick to the pan, replace them on the cake top. Serve warm or hot.

Makes 6 to 8 servings

Harvest Salad

Astrengthening but light salad, it brings together the incredible energy of root vegetables—nothing beats them for centering, grounding, and focus. Their energy is freshened and brightened by blanching and tossing in a richly flavored vinaigrette. Relaxed strength is the perfect combination for facing our stress-filled lives.

Hazelnut Vinaigrette

¼ cup hazelnuts

2 tablespoons minced fresh basil or 1 teaspoon dried

3 to 4 tablespoons minced flat-leaf parsley

2 teaspoons stone-ground mustard

¼ cup extra-virgin olive oil

1 teaspoon brown rice syrup

½ teaspoon soy sauce

Juice of 1 lemon

Salad

1 large parsnip, cut into ¼-inch-thick 1-inch spears

1 large carrot, cut into ¼-inch-thick 1-inch spears

1 large rutabaga, cut into ¼-inch-thick 1-inch spears

1 to 2 turnips, cut into ¼-inch-thick 1-inch spears

1 small daikon, cut into ¼-inch-thick 1-inch spears

3 to 4 fresh scallions, thinly sliced on the diagonal

1 small bunch watercress

Make the vinaigrette: Preheat oven to 325F (165C). Spread hazelnuts in a pie pan. Toast hazelnuts about 20 minutes or until fragrant. Transfer to a paper sack and seal shut. Allow to stand a few minutes to loosen skins. Transfer hazelnuts to a dry towel, and gently rub off skins. Mince nuts. Whisk together all ingredients in a small bowl until well blended.

Make the salad: Bring a large pot of water to a boil over high heat. Add parsnip, carrot, rutabaga, turnips, and daikon separately, in the order listed, and blanch until tender but not soft, 5 to 6 minutes. Transfer vegetables to a large bowl, and add scallions. While salad is still warm, toss with vinaigrette, and marinate at room temperature about 30 minutes. Just before serving, blanch watercress in boiling water about 30 seconds, and cut into bite-sized pieces. Arrange watercress on a serving plate, and spoon marinated vegetables over it.

Makes 6 to 8 servings

Sweet Root Vegetable Stew

There's nothing quite like sweet root vegetables to create calm strength. The energy of root vegetables keeps your feet firmly on the ground, and the sweet glaze and long stewing relax the body, so you can keep a clear head when faced with decisions. Served in cooler weather, this splendid side dish will keep you toasty warm . . . in warm weather, just cut the vegetables into smaller pieces, cook for a shorter period of time, and get your strength, without too much heat.

1-inch piece kombu

1 sweet onion, cut into thick wedges

1 carrot, cut into large irregular pieces

1 parsnip, cut into large irregular pieces

1 small daikon, cut into large irregular pieces

2 cups 1-inch cubes winter squash

Grated zest of 1 lemon

Unfiltered apple juice

Mirin, to taste

Soy sauce

Place kombu on the bottom of a heavy pot. Layer onion, carrot, parsnip, daikon, and squash on top. Top with lemon zest. Add enough apple juice to just cover the bottom of pan. Sprinkle lightly with mirin and soy sauce. Cover, and bring to a gentle boil over medium-low heat. Reduce heat to low, and simmer until vegetables are tender but not soft. Season lightly with soy sauce. Simmer stew, uncovered, until any remaining liquid has been absorbed; apple juice and mirin will reduce to a slightly sticky glaze.

Makes 4 to 6 servings

Herb-Scented Roasted Daikon

I frequently say that daikon is the world's miracle food. Need a blood tonic? Daikon has cleansing properties. Need to rid the body of excess water? Daikon is a gentle, natural diuretic. Need to move stagnant energy in the body? Daikon's peppery taste stimulates your metabolism. Needless to say, this delicious root serves our bodies in many ways and is just as versatile in cooking.

1 large daikon, cut into $1/2$-inch-thick
2-inch-long spears

2 teaspoons extra-virgin olive oil

1 teaspoon dried basil

$1/2$ teaspoon crushed dried rosemary

$1/4$ teaspoon dried thyme

About 2 teaspoons soy sauce

About 2 teaspoons mirin
Small handful fresh parsley, minced

Preheat oven to 350F (175C).

Toss daikon with oil in a medium bowl. Add herbs, and toss to combine. Add soy sauce and mirin, and toss well. Spread seasoned daikon in a shallow baking dish, avoiding a lot of overlap.

Bake, uncovered, stirring occasionally to ensure even cooking, about 40 minutes or until daikon is soft and the edges begin to brown. Toss daikon with parsley, and serve hot.

Makes 4 to 6 servings

Burdock Kinpira

Usually, we make this vitalizing dish with only carrot and burdock, combining the intensely strengthening burdock with the gently strengthening carrot, cooked as a high fire sauté for energy and then simmered for quiet endurance. This version, a powerhouse of energy in its own right, has a few more ingredients and is simply sautéed, giving high energy and enduring stamina.

2 teaspoons toasted sesame oil
½ dried hot chili, seeds removed and
*   minced*
1 small sweet onion, cut into thin half-
*   moon slices*
Sea salt
1 cup fine matchstick-size burdock pieces
1 cup fine matchstick-size carrot pieces
1 cup finely shredded green cabbage
Soy sauce
1-inch piece fresh ginger, grated and juice
*   extracted (page 188)*

Heat oil in a deep skillet over medium heat. Add chili, and sauté for several seconds. Add onion and a pinch of salt; sauté until onion is limp, about 2 minutes. Add the burdock and a pinch of salt; sauté for 2 minutes. Add carrot and a pinch of salt; sauté 1 minute. Stir in cabbage, season lightly with soy sauce, and add ginger juice. Cook, stirring frequently, until cabbage is limp and vegetables are tender but not soft, 3 to 5 minutes. Stir to combine, and serve immediately.

Makes 3 to 5 servings

Winter Vegetable Salad

There's nothing like roasted root vegetables for strength and incomparable sweet taste. Roasting brings the vegetables' natural sugars to the surface, resulting in sweet, succulent, satisfying flavor. But don't let their tenderness fool you; roasting also gives us incredible endurance and keeps us warm. Try this twist on roasted veggies for yet another way to enjoy their brilliance.

Salad

> 1 to 2 pounds Brussels sprouts, trimmed
>   and left whole
> 2 cups 2-inch-long, 1/2-inch-thick pieces
>   daikon
> 2 cups baby carrots
> 3 to 4 stalks celery, cut into 2-inch spears
> 6 to 8 shallots, peeled and left whole
> About 2 teaspoons soy sauce
> About 4 teaspoons light sesame oil
> Grated zest of 1 lemon

Lemon-Ginger Vinaigrette

> 1-inch piece fresh ginger, grated and juice
>   extracted (recipe follows)
> Juice of 1 lemon
> 1/4 cup brown rice vinegar
> 1 teaspoon umeboshi vinegar

> 1 tablespoon brown rice syrup
> 1/4 cup light sesame oil, warmed 1 to 2
>   minutes over low heat

Preheat oven to 375F (190C).

Make the salad: Toss vegetables together in a medium bowl. Drizzle lightly with soy sauce and oil. Stir gently to coat. Add lemon zest, stir gently. Spoon vegetables into a large shallow baking dish, without a lot of overlapping. Cover, and bake 30 minutes. Remove cover, and bake about 15 minutes or until vegetables are lightly browned and just tender but not soft.

Make the vinaigrette: Meanwhile, combine ginger juice, lemon juice, vinegars, and rice syrup in a small bowl. Add sesame oil, and whisk to combine. Set aside 15 minutes to allow the flavors to develop.

To serve: Gently transfer vegetables to a large bowl. Drizzle with vinaigrette, and toss gently to coat. Serve warm.

Makes 4 to 6 servings

GINGER JUICE

Finely grate fresh ginger. Squeeze in cheesecloth to extract the juice.

Sweet-and-Savory Rutabaga

The perfect dish for cool weather, it's warming, relaxing, and sweet. And I love sweet. Like all root vegetables, this dish provides strength and endurance, but the addition of sweet natto miso (sweet grain chutney, not a miso) calms the middle of the body, helping us manage stress with grace.

1-inch piece kombu

2 to 3 small rutabagas, quartered
(unpeeled if organic)

2 teaspoons natto miso

Soy sauce

1 unpeeled Granny Smith apple, cored,
quartered, and quarters halved

About ¼ cup minced flat-leaf parsley, for
garnish

Place kombu on the bottom of a heavy pot. Top with rutabaga. Spoon miso over the top, and sprinkle lightly with soy sauce. Add enough water to just cover bottom of the pot. Cover, and bring to a gentle boil over medium-low heat. Reduce the heat to low, and simmer 20 minutes.

Add apple, season lightly with soy sauce, and simmer, covered, until apples are tender but hold their shape. Uncover, and cook until any remaining liquid has been absorbed into dish. Stir gently to combine. Garnish with parsley.

Makes 2 or 3 servings

Lemony Baby Carrots with Caraway

A splendid side dish, baby carrots are the epitome of spring, keeping us delicately strong, as we let our energy sprout into movement in concert with nature. Smothered in a rice syrup glaze and laced through with tart lemon zest and savory caraway seeds, this is a dish that lifts your spirits while keeping your feet on the ground, as it opens and relaxes a sluggish liver after a long winter of indulgence.

3 cups baby carrots

1 cup spring or filtered water

Dash soy sauce

2 tablespoons corn oil

Grated zest of 1 lemon

1 tablespoon caraway seeds

1 tablespoon brown rice syrup

1 teaspoon fresh lemon juice

1 to 2 teaspoons minced flat-leaf parsley, for garnish

Place carrots in a saucepan. Add water, soy sauce, oil, lemon zest, and caraway seeds. Cover, and bring to a gentle boil over medium-low heat. Reduce heat to low, and cook carrots until crisp-tender. Remove carrots from the cooking liquid with a slotted spoon and set aside.

Increase heat to medium, and boil liquid, uncovered, until reduced by half. Add rice syrup, and cook until a light syrup forms, 3 to 5 minutes. Stir in carrots and lemon juice; serve garnished with parsley.

Makes 4 to 6 servings

Candied Sweet Potatoes and Parsnips with Bitter Greens

This dish is nicely balanced both in flavor and energy. I love it made with garnet potatoes. The intense sweetness makes us feel relaxed, the root vegetables keep our feet on the ground, and the bitter greens give us flexibility and clarity of mind. A sweet nature and sharply focused thinking—who could ask for more?

3 to 4 parsnips, cut into 2-inch irregular
chunks
1 to 2 sweet potatoes, cut into 2-inch irreg-
ular chunks
About 2 teaspoons corn oil
About 2 teaspoons soy sauce
2 tablespoons balsamic vinegar
2 to 3 tablespoons brown rice syrup
Grated zest of 1 lemon
1 bunch bitter greens, such as broccoli
rabe or watercress, rinsed, left whole

Preheat oven to 375F (190C).

Combine parsnips and sweet potatoes in a large bowl. Drizzle lightly with oil and soy sauce. Toss to coat. Transfer vegetables to a large shallow baking dish, without a lot of overlapping. Drizzle vinegar and rice syrup over top, and sprinkle with lemon zest. Cover, and bake 35 minutes. Remove cover, and bake 15 to 20 minutes, or until vegetables are tender and lightly browned.

Meanwhile, bring a large pot of water to a boil. Add greens, and cook until crisp-tender and bright green, about 10 minutes. Drain well, and cut into bite-sized pieces.

To serve, mound vegetables in center of a serving platter. Arrange greens around rim. Serve hot.

Makes 4 to 6 servings

CLOSE TO THE GROUND

Sweet-and-Savory Brussels Sprouts

This is a beautifully simple side dish. Great in cooler weather, this light vegetable stew won't leave you feeling tired and lethargic. Made from vegetables that grow close to the ground, this dish makes you feel calm and centered, as does the stewing. But to make sure you don't become too relaxed, I've laced it through with the summer vitality of corn, to give the dish a bit of energy.

> 6 to 8 pearl onions or shallots, peeled and
>   left whole
> 10 to 12 small Brussels sprouts, trimmed
>   and left whole
> 6 to 8 unsweetened dried cherries, soaked
>   15 minutes in warm water
> ½ cup fresh or frozen corn kernels
> Spring or filtered water, optional
> Soy sauce
> 1 teaspoon kuzu dissolved in 2 table-
>   spoons cold water

Layer onions and then Brussels sprouts in a medium saucepan. Drain cherries, reserving liquid, and add to the pan. Top with corn. Add enough cherry-soaking liquid and/or water to just cover bottom of pan. Sprinkle lightly with soy sauce; cover, and bring to a gentle boil over medium-low heat. Reduce heat to low, and simmer until sprouts are tender, about 25 minutes. Season lightly with soy sauce, and simmer, covered, 5 minutes more. Stir in kuzu mixture, and cook, stirring, until a thin glaze forms over vegetables. Serve warm.

Makes 4 to 6 servings

Variation

Substitute an equal amount of dried apricots or raisins for the cherries in this dish.

Sweet Nishime Squash

Stewing sweet ground vegetables calms us and relaxes our stressed-out psyches. Sweet winter squash relaxes the middle of the body, satisfies our desire for sweet tastes, and creates a calm vitality. Warming in cooler weather, this is the perfect side dish for those bone-chilling winter days.

1-inch piece kombu

1 sweet onion, cut into thick wedges

2 cups 1-inch cubes winter squash

3 tablespoons mirin

3 tablespoons spring or filtered water

Soy sauce

Place kombu on the bottom of a heavy pot. Top with onion, and then squash. Add equal amounts of mirin and water to just cover bottom of pot. Cover and bring to a gentle boil over medium-low heat. Reduce heat to low, and simmer until squash is soft, about 25 minutes. Season lightly with soy sauce, and cook, uncovered, over medium heat until any remaining liquid has been absorbed. Stir gently to combine, and serve warm.

Makes 3 to 5 servings

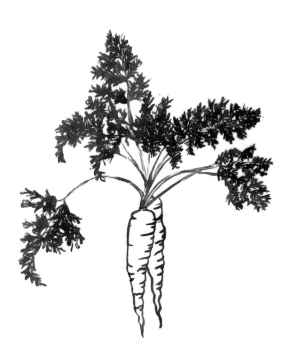

Apple-Stuffed Delicata Squash

If you love sweet taste, this is your dish. Delicata is the perfect name for this squash, with its delicate flavor that is the backdrop for the sweet-and-sour filling of apples, lemon zest, and toasted pecans. Naturally relaxing, this simple dish also packs a vitality punch from the nuts. So relax and enjoy, but rest assured it won't put you to sleep.

1 small to medium Delicata squash,
    halved lengthwise and seeds removed
About 1 tablespoon light sesame oil
½ sweet onion, minced
Sea salt
2 unpeeled Granny Smith apples, quar-
    tered, cored, and diced
Grated zest of 1 lemon
2 teaspoons brown rice syrup
⅔ cup coarsely minced pecans, lightly
    pan toasted (page 131)

Preheat oven to 375F (190C). Lightly oil a shallow baking dish. Lightly brush squash halves with about 1 teaspoon of oil, inside and out. Set aside.

Heat 2 teaspoons oil in a skillet over medium-low heat. Add onion and a pinch of salt; sauté until lightly browned, 7 to 10 minutes. Stir in apples, lemon zest, and rice syrup; cook over low heat about 5 minutes, stirring frequently. Remove from heat, and stir in pecans.

Mound stuffing in squash halves (depending on size of squash, you may have more filling than you need), filling them abundantly. Add about ½ inch of water to the baking dish and cover tightly.

Bake 45 to 60 minutes, until squash is tender. Uncover, and brown edges of squash. Serve hot.

Makes 2 or 3 servings

Spicy Asian Coleslaw

Here is a delicious version of an old-fash-ioned favorite; the heavy creamy dressing has been replaced with a light lemony version. The mild character of green cabbage relaxes the middle of the body, aiding digestion and helping us manage stress. The deeply rooted energy of carrots will draw the energy of the dish deep into the body, giving us strength; the cucumber cools and refreshes, and the spicy dressing moves our body's energy and gives us sparkle.

Salad

2 to 3 cups finely shredded green cabbage

1 carrot, cut into fine matchstick pieces

8 to 10 snow peas, left whole

1 cucumber, peeled and very thinly sliced

½ small head radicchio, shredded

2 to 3 fresh scallions, finely minced

¼ cup sliced almonds, lightly pan toasted (page 131)

Lemon Spice Dressing

2 to 3 tablespoons light sesame oil

½ to 1 teaspoon white miso

1 teaspoon umeboshi vinegar

1 teaspoon mustard powder

1 teaspoon ground ginger

1 teaspoon brown rice syrup

Juice of 1 lemon

Make the salad: Bring a pot of water to a boil over high heat. Add cabbage, carrot, and snow peas separately, in the order listed, and blanch until crisp-tender and bright green, 30 to 60 seconds. When all vegetables are cooked, drain well. Combine with cucumber, radicchio, and scallions in a large bowl.

Make the dressing: Combine oil and miso in a small saucepan, and warm over low heat 1 to 2 minutes. Add remaining ingredients, except almonds, and whisk to combine.

Mix dressing into vegetables, and let stand 15 to 30 minutes before serving to allow flavors to develop. Just before serving, stir in almonds. Serve warm or chilled.

Makes 4 or 5 servings

Brussels Sprouts with Shiitakes, Daikon, and Baby Carrots

A very settling dish, the Brussels sprouts relax the middle organs, making us feel calm and centered. The daikon and shiitake mushrooms combine to cleanse the blood and various organ systems, so they can do their jobs efficiently, calming the body. The baby carrots provide relaxing sweet taste, but their rooted nature will make us feel strong and centered. The ginger increases circulation, efficient body function, and great vitality.

3 or 4 pearl onions or shallots, halved

10 to 12 baby carrots

10 to 12 Brussels sprouts, trimmed and left whole

1 cup ¼-inch-thick half-moon pieces daikon

4 to 5 dried shiitake mushrooms, soaked until tender, thinly sliced

Soy sauce

Mirin, optional

½-inch fresh ginger, grated and juice extracted (page 188)

1 teaspoon kuzu dissolved in about 1 tablespoon cold water

Layer onions, carrots, Brussels sprouts, daikon, and mushrooms, in the order listed, in a deep saucepan. Add ¼ inch of water. Add a dash of soy sauce and mirin, if using. Cover, and bring to a gentle boil over medium heat. Reduce heat to low, and simmer until carrots are tender, about 25 minutes. Season lightly with soy sauce, and add ginger juice; simmer 3 to 5 minutes. Stir in kuzu mixture, and cook, stirring, until a thin glaze forms over vegetables. Serve warm.

Makes 3 or 4 servings

Braised Cabbage with Sesame-Ginger Sauce

Combining the calm, centering, and refreshingly cool energy of green cabbage with the Fire energy of sautéing creates a dish that will give you energy and help you keep your head. The delicately spicy sauce will sharpen your focus.

Cabbage

2 teaspoons light sesame oil

1 sweet onion, cut into thin half-moon slices

Sea salt

1 carrot, cut into fine matchstick-size pieces

½ head green cabbage, cut into thick wedges

¼ head red cabbage, cut into thick wedges

Sesame-Ginger Sauce

½ cup minced fresh ginger

¼ cup spring or filtered water

2 to 3 teaspoons brown rice syrup

2 teaspoons soy sauce

Juice of 1 lemon

1 tablespoon light sesame oil

2 to 3 fresh scallions, thinly sliced on the diagonal, for garnish

Make the cabbage: Heat oil in a deep skillet over medium heat. Add onion and a pinch of salt; sauté until onion is limp, about 2 minutes. Add carrot and a pinch of salt; sauté until shiny with oil. Stir in cabbage wedges. Add enough water to just cover the bottom of the skillet. Sprinkle lightly with salt. Cover, and cook over low heat until cabbage is limp, about 15 minutes. Remove cover, increase heat to medium, and boil away any remaining liquid.

Make the sauce: Mix all ingredients together in a small bowl and pour over cabbage mixture. Stir gently to combine, and cook over low heat, uncovered, until sauce makes a thin syrup, about 5 minutes. Serve hot.

Makes 5 or 6 servings

Spicy Cucumber Ribbon Salad

Mildly flavored and loaded with moisture, cucumbers have the ability to cool and refresh the body, allowing us to manage stress with grace and style. Strengthening carrots and the spicy dressing buoy our spirits, so we can take on the world.

> 2 large cucumbers, preferably organic and
>   unpeeled, halved lengthwise
> 1 carrot, cut into long matchstick pieces
> ⅛ cup brown rice vinegar
> ⅛ cup umeboshi vinegar
> 1 teaspoon toasted sesame oil
> 1 to 2 teaspoons brown rice syrup
> ½ teaspoon soy sauce
> 1-inch piece fresh ginger, grated and juice
>   extracted (page 188)
> 2 to 3 tablespoons black sesame seeds,
>   lightly pan toasted (page 131)

Slice cucumber halves lengthwise into paper-thin ribbons. Combine with carrot in a medium bowl; set aside. Mix together vinegars, oil, rice syrup, soy sauce, and ginger juice to make the dressing. Adjust seasoning to taste. Toss dressing with cucumbers and carrot, and set aside to marinate for about 30 minutes before serving. Just before serving, toss in sesame seeds. Serve at room temperature or chilled.

Makes 3 or 4 servings

TIP

The simplest way to make ribbons is to pull a vegetable peeler the length of the cucumber halves. This will give you the thin delicate slices you want.

Pickled Cucumber and Baked Tofu Salad

Because they both have a cooling effect on our bodies, cucumbers and tofu are a great combination. Lest, however, we get too chilled, a spicy mustard sauce is just the ticket to rekindle our internal heat. Who says you can't make balance?

Baked Tofu
> 4 (¼-inch-thick) slices extra-firm tofu
> 2 teaspoons soy sauce
> 1 teaspoon mirin

Cucumber Salad

1 large cucumber, peeled, halved length-
wise, and cut into very thin half-moon
slices
Generous pinch sea salt
1 carrot, cut into very fine matchsticks
1 red onion, cut into thin half-moon slices

Mustard Dressing

2 teaspoons stone-ground mustard
2 teaspoons sesame tahini
1 teaspoon brown rice syrup
$\frac{1}{2}$ teaspoon soy sauce
$\frac{1}{2}$ teaspoon umeboshi vinegar
Juice of $\frac{1}{2}$ to 1 orange

Make the tofu: Preheat oven to 400F (205C). Place tofu slices in a shallow baking dish, and cover with water. Swirl in soy sauce and mirin, and marinate 10 minutes. Drain off marinade and bake tofu, uncovered, about 25 minutes, or until golden brown.

Turn tofu and brown remaining side, about 7 minutes more. (Or broil the tofu under high heat, but take care not to burn it, for 3 to 5 minutes on each side).

Make the salad: Meanwhile, toss cucumber with salt to remove excess fluid, and place in a strainer in the sink or over a bowl. Bring a small pot of water to a boil over high heat. Add carrot and then onion, separately, and blanch 30 seconds. Drain well. Combine cucumber, carrot, and onion in a medium bowl.

Cool tofu until you can handle it. Using a sharp knife, shred tofu into irregular pieces. Stir into vegetables.

Make the dressing: Whisk all ingredients together in a small bowl until smooth. Add a small amount of water if needed to thin the dressing.

To serve at room temperature, toss cucumber and tofu mixture with the dressing. If serving chilled, refrigerate salad and dressing separately, and mix together just before serving.

Makes 3 or 4 servings

Vegetable Hotpot with Biscuit Topping

Nothing is quite as warming as bubbling stews; they make us feel cozy and nurtured, like snuggling in a soft quilt in front of a roaring fire. Sweet, round vegetables, lightly sautéed and stewed, then baked under flaky biscuits, create a relaxing, nourishing energy that will give us a calm, centered mind and the endurance we need to get through the day with grace.

Vegetable Filling

    2 teaspoons extra-virgin olive oil

    10 to 12 pearl onions or shallots, peeled, left whole

    Pinch sea salt

    2 teaspoons brown rice syrup

    6 to 8 Brussels sprouts, trimmed and halved

    2 small rutabagas, cut into 1-inch chunks

    1 small to medium butternut squash, cut into 1-inch chunks

    1 cup cooked whole chestnuts (see Note)

    Soy sauce, to taste

    3 to 4 tablespoons arrowroot

Biscuit Topping

    1½ cups whole wheat pastry flour

    1½ teaspoons baking powder

    Pinch sea salt

    1 teaspoon dried basil

    ⅛ cup corn oil

    ¼ cup coarsely minced walnut pieces

    ½ cup plain rice or soy milk

    Olive oil

Make the filling: Heat the oil in a deep skillet over medium heat. Add onions and salt; sauté until onions begin to wilt, about 5 minutes. Add rice syrup and simmer, uncovered, over low heat until onions are caramelized, as long as 15 minutes. Add Brussels sprouts, rutabagas, squash, and chestnuts, and stir over high heat 2 to 3 minutes. Add enough water to just cover the bottom of the pan, and season lightly with soy sauce. Simmer, covered, over low heat until vegetables are tender, about 10 minutes. Remove from heat, and gently stir in arrowroot. Transfer mixture to an oiled deep casserole dish. Set aside.

Make the topping: Preheat oven to 375F (190C). Mix flour, baking powder, salt, and basil together in a medium bowl. With a fork or pastry cutter, cut corn oil into flour mixture until it is the texture of wet sand. Stir in walnuts. Slowly stir in rice milk to make a soft dough. Cover loosely, and set aside 10 minutes to allow gluten to relax.

Roll out dough between two sheets of parchment paper or on a floured surface to about ½-inch thickness. Cut into 2-inch rounds with a glass or biscuit cutter (see Tip). Cover top of vegetable mixture with biscuits, allowing filling to peek through. Brush top lightly with olive oil, and bake, covered, 15 minutes. Uncover, and bake 15 to 20 minutes more to brown biscuits. Serve warm.

Makes 4 to 6 servings

Note

For the chestnuts, there are several options. Fully cooked canned or frozen chestnuts are available. Dried chestnuts require soaking 2 to 3 hours and pressure cooking 20 minutes. Fresh chestnuts may be baked or boiled 25 minutes and peeled while warm.

TIP

When cutting out biscuits, just press the cutter into the dough and pull up, without turning the cutter. Turning can remove some of the air needed to make the dough rise, resulting in tough biscuits.

Sweet Onion Tart

Sweet ground vegetables relax the center of the body, helping us keep our cool under fire. This richly flavored onion tart is perfect—browned onions and delicately tart dried cherries nestled in a flaky crust create the perfect nourishment when we're overcome with stress.

Filling

2 teaspoons extra-virgin olive oil

10 to 12 sweet onions, cut into large dice

Soy sauce

1 cup dried cherries, soaked in warm
    water 15 minutes, drained, and halved

2 tablespoons plain rice milk or soy milk

Pastry

1½ cups whole wheat pastry flour

1 teaspoon baking powder

⅛ teaspoon sea salt

¼ cup corn oil

¼ to ½ cup rice or soy milk

Make the filling: Heat oil in a deep skillet over medium heat. Add onions and a dash of soy sauce; sauté until onions are limp, about 5 minutes. Add cherries and rice milk, and season lightly with soy sauce. Cook over medium heat, stirring occasionally, until onions are browned and beginning to caramelize, about 20 minutes.

Make the pastry: Preheat oven to 350F (175C). Line a baking sheet with parchment paper.

Mix together flour, baking powder, and salt. With a fork or pastry cutter, cut in oil until it is the texture of wet sand. Slowly stir in rice milk to form a stiff dough. Gather dough into a ball and roll out between 2 sheets of parchment paper to a 12-inch round.

To assemble: Transfer round to a baking sheet, allowing excess to hang over edges. Spoon filling onto center of pastry, leaving a 2-inch wide rim of exposed dough. Fold exposed dough over filling, pleating as you go, leaving filling in the center exposed.

Bake for 35 to 40 minutes, or until pastry is golden brown and firm to the touch. Transfer to a serving platter, and allow to cool 10 minutes before slicing.

Makes 8 to 10 servings

Variation

Unsweetened dried cranberries or apricots can be substituted for the cherries.

Butternut Squash and Leek Pie

I love to make this pie on cool autumn days when I have the urge to bake, and my body is craving sweet taste and rich nourishment. Creamy squash and buttery leeks come together with sweet chestnuts to create relaxed energy, endurance, and deep inner warmth.

Filling

2 teaspoons corn oil

2 to 3 leeks, split lengthwise, rinsed well, and thinly sliced

Soy sauce

1 small butternut squash, peeled, seeded, and diced

1 cup cooked chestnuts (page 201), coarsely minced

3 tablespoons plain rice or soy milk

About ¼ cup coarsely minced walnuts, pan toasted (page 131), for garnish

Walnut Pastry

1½ cups whole wheat pastry flour

Pinch sea salt

½ cup walnuts, finely minced

¼ cup walnut or corn oil

About 4 tablespoons spring or filtered water

Make the filling: Heat oil in a deep skillet over medium heat. Add leeks and a dash of soy sauce; sauté until limp, about 5 minutes. Add squash and a dash of soy sauce; sauté, stir-ring, until mixed in with leeks and shiny with oil. Stir in chestnuts and rice milk, and season lightly with soy sauce. Cover, and simmer over low heat until squash is soft, about 15 minutes. Remove cover, and simmer until sauce reduces and thickens.

Make the pastry: Meanwhile, preheat oven to 350F (175C). Oil a rectangular tart pan with a removable bottom. Combine flour, salt, and walnuts in a medium bowl. With a fork or pastry cutter, cut in oil until it is the texture of wet sand. Slowly mix in water until dough gathers into a firm ball. Roll dough between 2 sheets of parchment to create a rectangle that is about 1 inch larger than pan. Transfer rectangle to pan and press, without stretching, to fit into crevices of pan. Trim away excess crust flush with top rim. Pierce in several places with a fork. Fit a piece of foil over crust, pressing for a firm fit. Fill crust with dried beans or pie weights to prevent crust from bubbling. Bake 17 minutes. Remove from oven, lift off foil and beans (you may reuse the beans for pie weights), and allow crust to cool.

To assemble: Spoon filling evenly into cooled pastry. Garnish with toasted walnuts, and let stand about 15 minutes before slicing.

Makes 6 to 8 servings

Note

You may also use a standard pie plate for this recipe.

Balsamic Glazed Vegetable Napoleons

There's something elegant about a napoleon, with its rich filling between delicate flaky pastry layers. It's irresistible. And I love the energy of this dish. You have the strength of roasting, the calm centered nature of sweet vegetables, the cool relaxed character of tofu—all within flaky phyllo, so digestion isn't compromised by too much hard flour. So you have the best of all worlds: great taste, exquisite presentation, and wonderful energy . . . perfection. Serve with a side dish of whole grains and cooked greens for a lovely light meal.

Roasted Vegetables

1 red onion, cut into thin rings

1 to 2 zucchini, thinly sliced lengthwise

1 to 2 yellow summer squash, thinly sliced lengthwise

¼ small butternut squash, thinly sliced lengthwise and peeled

1 tablespoon extra-virgin olive oil, or to taste

Soy sauce, to taste

1 tablespoon balsamic vinegar, or to taste

Tofu Filling

½ pound extra-firm tofu, crumbled

½ teaspoon dried basil

2 tablespoons sesame tahini

2 tablespoons extra-virgin olive oil

Pastry

6 sheets thawed phyllo pastry (see Tip)

About 2 tablespoons extra-virgin olive oil

About ½ teaspoon dried basil

Make the vegetables: Preheat oven to 400F (205C). Oil 2 large baking sheets with sides. Lay vegetables on the baking sheets, overlapping as little as possible. Drizzle with oil, soy sauce, and balsamic vinegar. Bake, uncovered, 25 to 30 minutes, or until vegetables are tender and edges are lightly browned. Set aside to cool, but leave oven on.

Make the tofu filling: Mix tofu, basil, tahini, and oil together in a medium bowl to make a thick paste. (Use a food processor for a smoother texture.) Set aside.

Make the pastry: Place 1 phyllo sheet on a dry, flat surface. Brush lightly with oil and sprinkle with basil. Top with a second phyllo sheet, brush with oil, and sprinkle with basil. Top with another phyllo sheet, and brush with oil. With a sharp knife, divide phyllo sheets in half lengthwise and cut each half into three equal pieces. Repeat with remaining 3 phyllo sheets, giving you 12 layered squares of pastry. Place them on baking sheets, with no overlap, and bake 10 to 12 minutes, until crisp and golden brown. Set aside to cool.

To assemble: Place 1 stacked square on

a plate. Top with a dollop of tofu and then several slices of each vegetable. Add another dollop of tofu, and then press a phyllo square on top. Add a dollop of tofu, vegetables, another dollop of tofu, and top with a phyllo square. Repeat with remaining ingredients to make four napoleons. Serve immediately, garnished with a few roasted vegetables or some minced basil.

Makes 4 servings

Roasted Vegetable Terrine

Roasting vegetables brings their natural sweet character to the surface like no other form of cooking. Roasting also creates great strength, keeping the heat focused, so roasted foods can help us feel strong and warm. This beautiful dish layers roasted vegetables in a savory gelled broth that beautifully complements the intense sweetness of the vegetables.

2 cups spring or filtered water

About 2 tablespoons soy sauce

3 tablespoons agar flakes

*2 leeks, quartered lengthwise and rinsed
   well*

*2 to 3 yellow summer squash, thinly sliced
   lengthwise*

2 to 3 zucchini, thinly sliced lengthwise

2 to 3 carrots, thinly sliced lengthwise

About 1 tablespoon extra-virgin olive oil

10 to 12 basil leaves, shredded

In a small saucepan, simmer water, 1 tablespoon soy sauce, and agar over low heat, stirring occasionally, until agar dissolves, about 20 minutes. Set aside to cool, stirring frequently to prevent setting. It should be cooled to warm before proceeding with the terrine.

Preheat oven to 400F (205). Lay vegetables on one or two baking sheets, keeping them as flat as possible, trying to avoid overlapping. Sprinkle lightly with oil and remaining soy sauce. Bake, uncovered, 20 to 25 minutes, or until vegetables are soft and their edges are browned.

Lightly oil a 9 × 5-inch loaf pan. Press a large piece of plastic wrap into pan, smoothing along sides and into corners, allowing excess to hang over sides. Oil plastic wrap.

To assemble terrine, spoon a little agar broth over the bottom of loaf pan. Begin layering roasted vegetables and basil decoratively along full length of pan, continuing until all ingredients are used. Gently pour enough broth over vegetables to just cover. Set aside until firmly set. Cut into thick slices, and serve at room temperature on a bed of fresh or lightly cooked greens.

Makes 6 to 8 servings

Mustard Pickled Sweet Vegetables

Pickles play an important part in whole foods cooking. They create good digestive fortitude by providing live bacteria essential to the health of the flora that reside in our intestines. And strong intestines mean "guts"; the strength of character that we all need to face life's challenges. This is just one of many pickle recipes—try varying the vegetables to create your own.

2 to 3 unpeeled cucumbers, quartered lengthwise

½ head cauliflower, broken into florets

1 small daikon, cut into ½-inch thick, 3-inch-long spears

1 carrot, cut into ½-inch thick, 3-inch-long spears

2 sweet onions, quartered

½ cup plus 1 teaspoon sea salt

1 cup brown rice syrup

1 cup umeboshi vinegar

1 cup brown rice vinegar

5 to 6 tablespoons whole wheat pastry flour

3 tablespoons powdered mustard

To prevent spoilage, wash vegetables well in cold water before pickling. Mix vegetables and ½ cup salt in a large bowl. Add enough water to cover. Stir gently to dissolve salt. Cover and refrigerate overnight.

Drain vegetables, rinse well, and drain again. It's really important to rinse vegetables thoroughly. Set aside.

Mix rice syrup and vinegars in a saucepan, and cook over medium heat until the syrup is thoroughly dissolved, about 7 minutes. Set aside to cool.

Transfer vinegar mixture to a large, heavy saucepan. Whisk in flour, mustard, and remaining salt, and bring to a boil over medium heat, stirring frequently to prevent lumps. Stir in vegetables, reduce heat, and simmer 20 to 25 minutes. Transfer entire mixture to a large bowl and cover. Refrigerate 6 to 8 hours or overnight.

To serve, drain and transfer vegetables to a serving platter. Pickles will keep, refrigerated in sealed jars, for about a week. Eat only a small amount each day.

Makes 8 to 10 cups of pickled vegetables

LOVELY LEAFIES

Red and Green Medley

A combination of sweet and bitter greens, they are sautéed to infuse them with even more of the vitality they already give us. Delicate, flexible, and rich in calcium, iron, and folic acid, this is a side dish that everyone should have. Add to that the stimulation of ginger, making for good circulation, and you have a dish that creates strong, clean blood and a flexible attitude.

> 2 teaspoons light sesame oil
>
> 1 red onion, cut into thin half-moon
>   slices
>
> 4 to 5 slices fresh ginger, cut into very fine
>   matchsticks
>
> Soy sauce
>
> 1 small head radicchio, shredded
>
> 1 small bunch kale, sliced into bite-sized
>   pieces

Heat oil in a deep skillet or wok over medium heat. Add onion, ginger, and a dash of soy sauce; sauté for 1 to 2 minutes. Add radicchio and a dash of soy sauce; sauté until just limp. Stir in kale, season lightly with soy sauce, and sauté until kale is limp and a rich, deep green, about 5 minutes. Transfer to a serving platter, and serve immediately.

Makes 3 or 4 servings

Stir-Fried Cauliflower and Mustard Greens in Lemon-Sesame Sauce

The mild character of cauliflower is the perfect complement to the strong flavor of mustard greens. High in calcium and iron, mustard greens have a sharp taste that gives us clarity of mind and focused thinking. The creamy sesame sauce adds a rich flavor and helps us relax.

Vegetables

> 2 teaspoons light sesame oil
>
> 1 small leek, split lengthwise, rinsed well,
>   and cut into 1-inch slices
>
> Grated zest of 1 lemon
>
> Soy sauce
>
> 1/2 head cauliflower, broken into small
>   florets
>
> 1 bunch mustard greens, cut into bite-
>   sized pieces

Lemon-Sesame Sauce

> *¼ cup sesame tahini*
>
> *1 teaspoon brown rice syrup*
>
> *¼ teaspoon soy sauce*
>
> *½ teaspoon umeboshi vinegar*
>
> *Juice of 1 lemon*
>
> *About 3 teaspoons black sesame seeds,*
> *lightly pan toasted (page 131),*
> *for garnish*

Make the vegetables: Heat oil in a deep skillet or wok over medium heat. Add leek, lemon zest, and a dash of soy sauce; stir-fry 1 to 2 minutes. Add cauliflower and a dash of soy sauce; stir-fry 1 to 2 minutes. Add greens, season lightly with soy sauce, and stir-fry until limp and a rich deep green.

Make the sauce: Mix all ingredients, except sesame seeds together in a small bowl until smooth and creamy. Just before serving, stir sauce into cooked vegetables, and garnish with sesame seeds. Serve immediately.

Makes 3 or 4 servings

Steamed Greens Medley

I t doesn't get easier than this one, and the vitality you get is priceless. Greens give us vascular strength and strong red blood cells. They are rich in calcium, iron, folic acid, and vitamin C. Cooking the greens in moist, hot air gives them tremendous vitality and retains much of their nutritive value, helping us feel relaxed and cool.

Greens keep their nutritive value best if cooked whole, so the only time I slice them before cooking is when sautéing. (It's hard to slice sautéed greens.)

> *2 to 3 leaves Chinese cabbage, rinsed and*
> *left whole*
>
> *3 to 4 leaves kale, rinsed and left whole*
>
> *3 to 4 leaves collards, rinsed and left*
> *whole*
>
> *1 small bunch watercress, rinsed and left*
> *whole*

Bring about 1 inch of water to a boil in a large, deep pot over high heat. Cook each type of greens separately, in the order listed, to maintain their individual characters. Cook greens until limp and dark green, 2 to 3 minutes each. Drain, and slice into bite-sized pieces. You may also steam greens in a bamboo steamer over a skillet of boiling water.

Mix greens together, and serve warm, at room temperature or lightly chilled.

Makes 3 or 4 servings

Warm Escarole and Shiitake Salad

Escarole is a delicate bitter green that sharpens our focus and clears our thinking. Shiitake mushrooms cleanse the blood and are reputed to balance blood pressure. Simple and strong.

Salad

> 2 teaspoons extra-virgin olive oil
>
> 1 red onion, cut into thin half-moon slices
>
> 1/2 teaspoon chili powder
>
> Soy sauce
>
> 5 to 6 dried shiitake mushrooms, soaked until tender, thinly sliced
>
> 1 head escarole, rinsed well, sliced into 1-inch pieces

Dressing

> 2 tablespoons balsamic vinegar
>
> 2 teaspoons brown rice syrup
>
> 2 teaspoons sesame tahini
>
> 1/2 teaspoon soy sauce
>
> 1 teaspoon umeboshi vinegar
>
> Juice of 1/2 lemon

Make the salad: Heat oil in a deep skillet over medium heat. Add onion, chili powder, and a dash of soy sauce; sauté until limp, about 2 minutes. Add mushrooms and a dash of soy sauce; sauté for 3 to 4 minutes. Add escarole, season lightly with soy sauce, and sauté until limp and deep green, 5 to 7 minutes.

Make the dressing: Whisk all ingredients together until combined.

To serve: Mix dressing into hot escarole mixture, transfer to a serving platter, and serve immediately.

Makes 4 or 5 servings

Watercress, Pear, and Pecan Salad with Candied Cranberries

This salad is a symphony of flavors and energies. The delicate peppery taste of watercress is the perfect backdrop to the sweet pears and cranberries, crunchy pecans, and the sweetly spicy mustard dressing. A delicious starter or side course, this dish will leave your guests feeling chatty and vital, with the light freshness of the greens supporting the sweet relaxation of the pears and cranberries. Add the pecans and dressing and you create a social energy that will make any dinner party a hit.

Salad

1 to 2 bunches watercress, rinsed, left
   whole

2 ripe pears

3 to 4 tablespoons mirin

1 cinnamon stick

1 cup unsweetened, dried cranberries

2 to 3 tablespoons brown rice syrup

Grated zest of 1 lemon

Pinch sea salt

1 teaspoon fresh lemon juice

Dressing

¼ cup extra-virgin olive oil, warmed over
   low heat 2 to 3 minutes

3 tablespoons umeboshi vinegar

1 tablespoon brown rice syrup

2 teaspoons stone-ground mustard

To Serve

⅔ cup pecan pieces lightly pan toasted
   (page 131)

Make the salad: Bring a pot of water to a boil over high heat. Add watercress, and blanch until bright green and crisp-tender, 30 to 60 seconds. Drain well, and place in a bowl of ice water to stop the cooking. Slice thinly, and set side.

Halve and core pears. Arrange halves in a deep skillet and add about ¼ inch of water. Add mirin and cinnamon stick. Cover, and bring to a gentle boil over medium heat. Reduce heat to low, and simmer until pears are tender but not mushy, 15 to 20 minutes. Remove pears from skillet and set aside to cool.

Add cranberries, rice syrup, lemon zest, and salt to a small saucepan. Cook over medium heat until syrup foams. Stir in lemon juice, transfer to a small plate, and set aside.

Make the dressing: Whisk together all ingredients until smooth.

To serve: Arrange equal amounts of watercress on 4 individual salad plates. Cut each pear half into a fan shape by making long thin slices from blossom end to within ½ inch of stem end. Press gently to fan. Place pears on top of watercress. Surround each pear with pecans and candied cranberries. Just before serving, spoon some dressing over top. Serve immediately.

Makes 4 servings

Phyllo Bites

This is a delightful starter course or side dish. Easy to make, richly flavored, and loaded with vitality, these little beauties pack a punch—rich in calcium, magnesium, and vitamin C. They're beautiful, they're delicious, and they keep us flexible and clear headed. What could be better?

About 4 tablespoons extra-virgin olive oil
1 small bunch kale, stemmed, rinsed, and
*   thinly sliced*
Pinch sea salt
6 to 8 sun-dried tomatoes, soaked until
*   tender, minced*
6 to 8 oil-cured black olives, pitted and
*   minced*
1 teaspoon dried basil
6 sheets phyllo dough, thawed
Freshly ground nutmeg

Preheat oven to 400F (205C). Line a baking sheet with parchment paper.

Heat 2 tablespoons of the oil in a skillet over medium heat. Add kale and salt; sauté 1 minute. Add tomatoes, basil, and olives, and sauté until greens are limp and a rich deep green. Transfer to a medium bowl and set aside.

Keep phyllo covered with a damp towel to prevent drying. Lay a phyllo sheet on a flat, dry work surface, with the short side directly in front of you. Brush lightly with olive oil. Sprinkle very lightly with nutmeg. Top with another phyllo sheet and brush lightly with oil. Spread one-third of kale mixture across the short edge of the phyllo. Roll jelly-roll style, folding in the edges as you roll to form a tight cylinder. Transfer roll to the prepared pan, leaving room for two more rolls. Repeat with remaining ingredients to make a total of 3 rolls.

Brush each roll lightly with olive oil. With a sharp knife, make angular slits in the rolls to release steam and mark slices. Bake 12 to 15 minutes, or until the rolls are golden and crispy. Allow rolls to cool slightly before slicing at an angle into bite-sized pieces. Arrange, cut side up, on a serving platter. Serve warm.

Makes 18 pieces; 6 to 8 servings

Spicy Sautéed Collard Greens

Sautéing leafy green vegetables enhances their naturally vitalizing nature. Greens give us great flexibility, and so does cooking with oil. Bring the two together with the high fire of a sauté, and you have created a dish that's bursting with energy but won't leave you nervous and edgy. The lemon's astringent quality aids the body in digesting the oil.

2 teaspoons light sesame oil
½ dried hot chile, seeded and finely
   minced
1 sweet onion, cut into thin half-moon
   slices
Soy sauce
1 bunch collard greens, rinsed and thinly
   sliced
1 lemon, quartered

Heat oil in a deep skillet over medium heat. Add chile, onion, and a dash of soy sauce; sauté 1 to 2 minutes. Add collards, and season lightly with soy sauce; sauté just until the greens are limp and a rich deep green. Serve with lemon wedges.

Makes 3 or 4 servings

SPLENDID SEA PLANTS

Marinated Kombu Salad

There's nothing quite like kombu for light, upward energy and lots of minerals. High in glutamic acid (the basis of monosodium glutamate), kombu aids the body in digesting protein and fat. Kombu is used in Asia in shampoo for lustrous hair and in lotion for soft skin. Combined with crunchy, blanched vegetables and a spicy dressing, this dish softens the body and makes us feel energized—with great skin and hair.

10 (3-inch) strips kombu, soaked until tender, thinly sliced

8 to 10 baby corn, split lengthwise

1 carrot, cut lengthwise, then into thin diagonal half-moons

8 to 10 snow peas, trimmed, strings removed, left whole

2 stalks broccoli, broken into florets

3 to 4 fresh scallions, sliced thinly on the diagonal

1-inch piece fresh ginger, grated and juice extracted (page 188)

3 tablespoons balsamic vinegar

½ teaspoon umeboshi vinegar

1 teaspoon soy sauce

4 tablespoons toasted sesame oil

1 teaspoon brown rice syrup

Juice of 1 orange

Orange slices, for garnish

Bring a pot of water to a boil. Cook vegetables separately, in the order listed, until just tender: kombu, corn, and carrot, 2 minutes each; snow peas, 1 minute; and broccoli, 3 minutes. Drain well and combine in a large bowl. Stir in scallions.

Prepare the marinade by whisking ginger juice, vinegars, soy sauce, oil, rice syrup, and orange juice together in a small bowl. Pour marinade over hot vegetables, and stir well. Set aside to marinate at room temperature for 1 to 2 hours, stirring frequently. Serve at room temperature or lightly chilled, garnished with orange slices.

Makes 3 or 4 servings

Sesame Hiziki Salad

Hiziki is loaded with calcium, vitamin C, iron, folic acid, magnesium, and other

vitamins and minerals that help make strong bones, lustrous hair, healthy blood, and smooth organ function. And in this salad, hiziki's strong flavor is nicely complemented by sweet, relaxing vegetables and a rich sesame dressing.

Salad

1 teaspoon light sesame oil

½ cup dried hiziki, rinsed 2 to 3 times and soaked until tender

Soy sauce, to taste

½ small leek, rinsed well, thinly sliced

1 carrot, cut into fine matchstick pieces

1 cup fine matchstick-sized winter squash pieces

¼ cup fresh or frozen corn kernels

Creamy Sesame Dressing

¼ cup sesame tahini

1 to 2 teaspoons brown rice syrup

1 teaspoon mirin

½ teaspoon soy sauce

Juice of 1 lemon

Juice of 1 lime

To Serve

About 2 teaspoons tan sesame seeds, lightly pan toasted (page 131), for garnish

Make the salad: Heat oil in a small skillet over medium heat. Add hiziki and season lightly with soy sauce. Sauté 1 minute. Spread evenly over skillet, and add enough water to half-cover. Bring to a boil, uncovered. Reduce heat to low, and simmer, covered, 15 minutes. Add leek, carrot, squash, and corn. Cover, and simmer until vegetables are tender, about 15 minutes. Remove cover, increase heat to high, and cook away any remaining liquid.

Make the dressing: Whisk all ingredients together in a small bowl until smooth.

To serve: Add dressing to vegetables, and toss until combined. Stir in the sesame seeds, and transfer to a serving plate. Serve warm.

Makes 2 or 3 servings

Arame with Dried Daikon and Ginger

This is a deep-cleansing and energizing dish. Arame, a good source of calcium, magnesium, and other minerals, helps make strong blood. The dried daikon and shiitake travel deep into the body to get rid of any fat and protein that may have accumulated in various organ systems. The ginger improves circulation.

6 to 8 thin slices fresh ginger, fine matchstick pieces
½ cup dried arame, rinsed several times and soaked 5 minutes, until tender
½ cup dried daikon, rinsed and soaked until tender
2 dried shiitake mushrooms, soaked until tender, thinly sliced
Spring or filtered water
Soy sauce

Layer ginger, arame, daikon, and mushrooms in a saucepan. Add enough water to half-cover ingredients. Add a dash of soy sauce. Cover, and bring to a boil over medium heat. Reduce heat to low, and simmer 40 minutes. Season lightly with soy sauce, and simmer 5 minutes more. Remove cover, increase heat to medium, and allow any remaining liquid to cook away. Stir gently, and transfer to a serving bowl.

Makes 4 or 5 servings

Nori Condiment

This is a special condiment designed for creating strong blood and overall vitality. Richly cooked, it is traditionally served in small amounts with whole grains. It is especially good for relieving fatigue or just keeping your vitality high.

6 to 8 sheets untoasted nori
Soy sauce, to taste
Spring or filtered water

Shred nori into small pieces, and place in a small saucepan. Season lightly with soy sauce, and add enough water to generously cover nori. Bring to a boil, uncovered, over medium heat. Reduce heat to low, and cook, uncovered, until nori is creamy and all liquid has been absorbed, about 20 minutes. Serve about 1 tablespoon over cooked grain. The condiment will keep, refrigerated, for several days.

Makes about 1 cup

KILLER DESSERTS THAT WON'T KILL YOU

I READ AN interview with Maida Haetter, the idol of every dessert maker, back when I was learning to cook. Her words have stayed with me to this day. The interviewer asked her if she loved cooking as much as she loved baking and making desserts. She replied, with her characteristic wit, that she liked cooking just fine—it was like the warmup to a baseball game.

I have always loved to make desserts, even working at it professionally at one point in my career. As much as I enjoy all aspects of cooking, delicious and beautiful desserts really bring out my creative side, with cooking serving as the opening act.

And so you can imagine my dismay when I changed my style of eating to whole foods. No sugar, no milk, no butter, no refined flours, which meant no crème caramel, no buttercream frostings, no custards. And—I thought—no desserts, unless I was supposed to consider those hockey-puck cookies and paperweight muffins I had found in natural foods stores to be a treat. It was a grim thought.

So I struggled with healthy dessert recipes that tasted like, well, healthy desserts—not worth the work and certainly not worth eating. And then one day, as I threw yet another batch of cookies in the trash, I had an epiphany (one of many in my life—often when I'm in the kitchen). Why was I struggling so much? I was a pastry maker. The ingredients may have changed, but the techniques remained the same. I didn't need to reinvent the wheel. This wasn't rocket science. We're talking cookies here. So I took a deep breath, pulled out some of my most cherished recipes from my own career and my mother's kitchen, and went to work.

I made a lot of discoveries as I experimented. I found that I didn't like the flavor that apple juice gave as a sweetener, except in apple cake or apple pie. I fell in love with whole wheat pastry flour, made from a softer wheat, yielding a lighter end product, yet retaining its whole-grain flour status. I began my passionate affair with whole-grain sweeteners—rice syrup and barley and wheat malts—sweeteners that don't drastically alter the glucose balance in the blood. I discovered the wonder of grain, nut, and soy milks. And all of my playing in the kitchen paid off. I rediscovered delicious, sweet, decadent (tasting) desserts that didn't compromise my commitment to healthy eating. I could, once again, make killer desserts—but they wouldn't kill me. Life was good again.

I made an even more important discovery. I discovered that we need dessert—yes, *need* dessert. In whole foods cooking, we say that nothing is arbitrary, that everything is done for a reason, that everything will have an effect on us—how we look, feel, and act. It's no different with dessert. It, too, has a purpose in our lives. Just like broccoli.

Dessert (good-quality dessert, at least) works to relax the body; to open up our energy; and, most important, to give us satisfaction. Dessert makes us really happy (at least when we're not feeling guilty about it). Dessert can relieve tension in the body; relax tight muscles; and, in small amounts and eaten regularly, can actually help us eat less and not crave sweets. Think about it. On a deadline at work? Exhausted? Stressed? Depressed? In most cases, we reach for sweets, naturally, in an attempt to release the tension and lift our spirits.

Does eating dessert really help you eat less? It works like this. Just because you deprive yourself of dessert, it doesn't mean that your body doesn't want or need richness. And in the body's search for satisfaction, you will eat more food. But treat yourself to a good-quality dessert a few times a week, and you'll find that you spend fewer nights with your head in the refrigerator looking for just the right something to satisfy you.

So go ahead, indulge yourself with a cookie or two, a slice of pie, maybe even a custard-filled tart. Made from whole, natural ingredients, dessert can serve your needs for richness, satisfaction, and unparalleled joy . . . at least where food is concerned.

Ginger-Poached Pears

The delicate sweet taste of pears is showcased in this simple and beautiful dessert. To gentle the effect of the fruit sugar on our blood chemistry, the pears are poached in a lightly spiced broth—ginger for strength, cinnamon for warmth, and lemon to aid the body in assimilating the sugars. The overall effect is a dessert that relaxes and nourishes the body.

1-inch piece fresh ginger, thinly sliced
4 ripe pears with stems
1 cinnamon stick
Grated zest of 1 lemon
¼ cup mirin
¼ cup brown rice syrup

Place ginger on the bottom of a pot that will hold the pears. Take a thin slice off the bottom of each pear so it will sit flat. Arrange pears in pan on top of ginger. Add enough water to cover pears; add cinnamon stick, lemon zest, mirin, and rice syrup. Cover, and bring to a boil. Turn off heat, remove cover, and drape cheesecloth over the surface of the water to keep pears submerged. Cool to room temperature. Remove pears and arrange, on flat ends, on a plate.

Strain pear-cooking liquid, reserving 2 cups. Bring reserved liquid to a boil over medium heat, and boil until reduced by half and slightly thickened.

Spoon thickened sauce over pears, and serve immediately.

Makes 4 servings

Spiced Pecan Baked Apples

Baking fruit introduces a strengthening energy that is the perfect complement to the strong sweetness that is the nature of fruit. Eating a lot of raw fruit can leave us feeling tired and weak—and chilled. Fruit is mostly sugar and water. Cooking, especially baking, introduces the vitality of fire for strength and warmth, gentles the sugars, and creates a satisfying sweet dessert. In this dish, the nuts add lots of energy, making them the perfect complement to the relaxed fruit. Now you know why fruit and nuts go so well together.

6 large apples, (Delicious, Golden Delicious, or Rome)

1 cup pecan pieces

1/3 cup raisins

1/4 cup unsweetened shredded coconut

2 tablespoons brown rice syrup

Grated zest and juice of 1 lemon

Grated zest of 1 orange

1/4 teaspoon powdered ginger

About 6 tablespoons fruit-sweetened apricot preserves

6 whole pecans

1 cup unfiltered apple juice

2 teaspoons corn oil

Preheat oven to 375F (190C).

Core apples, but do not peel. Cut a thin slice off the bottom of each apple so it will sit flat. With a sharp paring knife, make a 1-inch-wide × 1-inch-deep hollow in the top of each apple. Arrange apples in a deep baking dish.

Coarsely mince pecan pieces, raisins, and coconut. Mix together in a medium bowl. Stir in rice syrup, lemon and orange zests, and ginger. Fill hollow of each apple abundantly with pecan mixture. Spoon a dollop of preserves over top of each apple, and press a whole pecan on top of preserves.

Combine apple juice and oil in a saucepan, and cook over medium heat 2 to 3 minutes. Remove from heat, and stir in lemon juice. Spoon into the baking dish around apples. Cover loosely with foil.

Bake, basting every 10 minutes with the juice, about 35 minutes, or until apples are tender. Serve warm, with any remaining juices spooned over top.

Makes 6 servings

Asian Pears in Ginger Syrup

Asian pears have a delicate flavor that screams to be eaten fresh. But optimal health comes from minimizing lots of simple sugars, like fruit sugar in our diet. So what do we do? We make a spiced, warm syrup that when poured over sliced fruit will cook it just enough to gentle the sugars but not harm the splendid natural taste of the fruit.

¼ cup spring or filtered water
1 tablespoon fine matchstick-size pieces
   fresh ginger
1 cup brown rice syrup
2 tablespoons mirin, optional
Grated zest and juice of 1 lemon
1 teaspoon kuzu, dissolved in 1 table-
   spoon cold water
4 Asian pears
4 to 6 mint sprigs, for garnish

Combine water and ginger, and simmer 5 minutes. Add rice syrup; mirin, if using; and lemon zest. Cover, and simmer 10 minutes, stirring occasionally, to develop the flavors. Stir in kuzu mixture, and cook, stirring, until syrup thickens slightly. Stir in lemon juice.

Slice each pear into thin rounds. Arrange slices on individual plates, and spoon hot syrup over the top. Garnish with mint sprigs and serve immediately.

Makes 4 to 6 servings

Lemon Gingerbread Trifles

Creamy lemon pudding layered with spicy gingerbread creates a most satisfying dessert without being too heavy. Light and sweet, this temptation can be enjoyed without guilt or compromise to your health. Too many floury desserts can leave us feeling and looking heavy. But this treat lets us enjoy the satisfaction of flour with only a taste; I love desserts like this one.

Gingerbread

2 cups whole wheat pastry flour

2 teaspoons baking powder

⅛ teaspoon sea salt

1 teaspoon powdered ginger

½ teaspoon cinnamon

¼ teaspoon nutmeg

¼ teaspoon allspice

¼ cup corn oil

½ cup Eden Wheat Malt or brown rice
    syrup

1 teaspoon pure vanilla extract

¾ to 1 cup Eden Rice & Soy Blend or
    vanilla rice or soy milk

Lemon Pudding

2 cups plain amasake

2 teaspoons mirin

1 vanilla bean, split lengthwise and pulp
    removed

Grated zest of 1 lemon

2 tablespoons kuzu dissolved in about 3
    tablespoons cold water

Juice of 1 lemon

To Assemble

1 to 2 cups frozen raspberries, thawed
    and pureed

Grated lemon zest, for garnish

Make the gingerbread: Preheat oven to 350F (175C). Lightly oil and flour a 9 × 5-inch loaf pan.

Combine flour, baking powder, salt, and spices in a medium bowl. Mix in oil, wheat malt, and vanilla. Stir in enough rice and soy blend to form a thick, smooth cake batter. Spoon batter evenly into prepared pan.

Bake about 45 to 60 minutes, or until center of loaf springs back to the touch or a toothpick inserted into center comes out clean. Cool in pan about 10 minutes. Invert pan to remove gingerbread to a wire rack. Cool completely.

Make the pudding: Mix amasake, mirin, vanilla pulp, and lemon zest in a saucepan. Warm through over low heat. Stir in kuzu mixture, and cook, stirring, until pudding thickens, 3 to 4 minutes. Remove from heat, and stir in lemon juice.

To assemble: Cut 4 slices of gingerbread (you will have more gingerbread than needed, so indulge yourself), and cube slices. Begin trifles by layering gingerbread cubes in each of 4 wineglasses or parfait dishes. Add a layer of lemon pudding, and then add a thin layer of raspberry puree. Repeat layers to fill glasses, ending with raspberry puree. Garnish with lemon zest. Chill thoroughly before serving.

Makes 4 servings

The Best Rice Pudding

One of the greatest sweet treats ever—delicious, creamy, satisfying, and delicate—this rice pudding is comfort in a cup. Long-simmered in rice milk, it can satisfy any sweet tooth and not compromise your commitment to healthy eating. Serve it warm, and it makes you cozy in cool weather; serve it chilled, and you feel refreshed on the hottest summer day.

Cook this very slowly; you can't speed up the cooking process if you want the best result. It's worth the time. Garnish with fresh berries, toasted nuts, or coconut.

> 1½ cups Eden Rice & Soy Blend or vanilla rice or soy milk
> 1 cup plain or almond-flavored amasake
> ½ cup white basmati, Arborio, or sushi rice, unrinsed
> ½ cup brown rice syrup
> 1½ cups unsweetened flaked coconut
> 2 vanilla beans, split lengthwise and pulp removed

Combine all ingredients in a saucepan, and place on a flame deflector over the lowest possible heat. Cook pudding slowly, without letting it come to a boil, stirring frequently to prevent sticking, 2 hours or more. Rice will soften slowly, and pudding will thicken naturally. Spoon into individual dessert bowls. Serve warm or chilled.

Makes 4 to 6 servings

Lemon Stars

Taken from a sweet cream cheese dough, these delectable cookies are richly satisfying yet incredibly light, so they won't weigh you down; plus, soft cookies are easier to digest. Add to that the sparkle of lemon zest and the energy of poppy seeds, and you have created a cookie that will make you feel vital.

> *2 cups whole wheat pastry flour*
>
> *1 teaspoon baking powder*
>
> *Pinch sea salt*
>
> *2 to 3 tablespoons poppy seeds*
>
> *¼ cup corn oil*
>
> *4 ounces firm tofu*
>
> *1 teaspoon umeboshi paste*
>
> *Grated zest of 1 lemon*
>
> *1 teaspoon pure vanilla extract*
>
> *¾ cup brown rice syrup*

Combine flour, baking powder, salt, and poppy seeds in a large bowl. Puree the oil, tofu, and umeboshi paste in a food processor fitted with the metal blade or in a blender until smooth. Fold tofu mixture into flour with lemon zest, vanilla, and ½ cup of the rice syrup. Stir until combined into a soft dough. If dough seems dry, add lemon juice or rice milk for moisture. Divide dough in half and pat each piece into a thick disk. Wrap each disk in plastic wrap, and chill 1 hour or longer.

Preheat oven to 350F (175C). Line a baking sheet with parchment paper.

Remove 1 dough disk from refrigerator, and divide it in half. Return one piece to refrigerator. Roll remaining piece out on a lightly floured surface to a ⅛-inch thickness. With a star-shaped cookie cutter, cut out cookies and transfer to prepared pan.

Bake 10 to 12 minutes, or until golden on edges and firm; do not overbake, or cookies will become quite hard as they cool. Repeat with remaining dough.

To glaze lemon stars, heat remaining ¼ cup rice syrup over high heat until it foams. Quickly spoon over warm cookies.

Makes about 4 dozen

Peanut Butter Marvels

These chewy treats are quite decadent; I reserve them for special occasions or gifts. Although chocolate is not the best choice of sweets, a small bit now and then can satisfy your desire for it without going overboard, making you feel nourished, relaxed, and happy. And forget carob, it won't fool anybody; it's higher in sugar and causes more allergic reactions than does chocolate. So if you're going for it, go for good-quality, nondairy chocolate, then relax and enjoy.

1 cup unsalted, unsweetened, chunky peanut butter

½ cup Eden Wheat Malt or brown rice syrup

¼ cup corn oil

2 tablespoons barley malt

2 teaspoons pure vanilla extract

1½ cups whole wheat pastry flour

1½ teaspoons baking powder

½ cup rolled oats

¼ cup unsweetened flaked coconut

¼ to ½ cup Eden Rice & Soy Blend or vanilla rice or soy milk

⅔ cup nondairy, malt-sweetened chocolate chips

Preheat oven to 350F (175C). Line 2 baking sheets with parchment paper.

Beat together peanut butter, wheat malt, oil, barley malt, and vanilla in a medium bowl until smooth. Mix flour, baking powder, oats, and coconut in a separate bowl. Add flour mixture to peanut butter mixture, and mix into a soft dough, adding rice and soy blend as needed to make a soft dough. Fold in chocolate chips.

Drop rounded tablespoonfuls of dough onto prepared pans, pressing lightly and rounding, leaving a small space between cookies. Bake 15 to 18 minutes, or until cookies are light golden and firm. Transfer to wire racks, and cool completely.

Makes about 2 dozen

☯

Pine Nut Crescents

A tradition growing up in my house, this soft, chewy cookie was like eating a miniature cake, and so rich. My healthier version maintains the delicate texture, but loses the eggs, a lot of the fat, and all of the simple sugar. Plus, soft, cakelike cookies are easy on the digestive tract, allowing us to enjoy them without feeling heavy and lethargic. Served with hot tea, these treats make a nice light ending to a hearty meal.

¾ cup blanched almonds

1 cup rolled oats

Pinch sea salt

1 teaspoon baking powder

¼ cup corn oil

½ cup brown rice syrup

About ½ cup whole wheat pastry flour

1 to 2 cups pine nuts

Preheat oven to 350F (175C). Line a baking sheet with parchment paper.

Place almonds in a food processor fitted with the metal blade and grind into a fine meal. Transfer to a medium bowl. In the same processor, grind oats into flour. Mix into almond meal. Stir in salt and baking powder. Mix in oil and rice syrup to make a sticky dough. Slowly add flour to make dough hold together, but it should still stay sticky.

Spread pine nuts on a floured surface. Using floured hands, roll dough into 1-inch balls. Roll cookies in pine nuts. Place cookies on prepared pan, spacing them about 1 inch apart. Press them into disks.

Bake for 12 to 18 minutes, or until cookies are golden and slightly puffed. Transfer to a rack, and cool completely.

Makes 18 to 20 cookies

Hamantaschen

A cookie traditionally used in the celebration of Purim, this cookie has come to symbolize the emotions of that Jewish holiday—pure merriment and joy. Just one look at this festive, richly filled pastry, and you'll know what I mean. Although tradition calls for a poppy seed or prune filling, modern hamantaschen are filled with apricots or cherries (my personal favorite). No matter what the filling, these soft, delicious pastries will leave you happy and relaxed.

Pastry

2 cups whole wheat pastry flour

2 teaspoons baking powder

⅛ teaspoon sea salt

2 teaspoons grated lemon zest

¼ cup FruitSource (granulated brown rice syrup)

⅓ cup corn oil

½ to ⅔ cup Eden Rice & Soy Blend or vanilla rice or soy milk

Dried Cherry Filling

1½ cups unsweetened dried cherries, soaked in warm water until tender and drained well

⅓ cup fresh orange juice

1 teaspoon brown rice syrup

Grated zest of 1 orange

Pinch sea salt

Make the pastry: Process flour, baking powder, salt, lemon zest, and FruitSource in a food processor fitted with the metal blade until combined. Add oil, and pulse 45 to 50 times, or until texture of wet sand. Do not overmix. Slowly pour rice and soy blend down feed tube, pulsing until dough gathers into a ball. Wrap dough in plastic wrap, and chill 1 hour.

Make the filling: Combine all ingredients in a saucepan. Simmer over low heat until a thick, stewlike consistency, 7 to 10 minutes. Transfer to a bowl, and cool completely before making cookies.

To assemble and bake: Preheat oven to 350F (175C). Line 2 baking sheets with parchment paper.

Roll out half of the dough on a floured surface or between parchment sheets to a ¼-inch thickness. With a 3-inch cookie cutter or glass, cut out rounds of dough. Transfer rounds to the prepared pans, leaving about ½ inch between cookies. Spoon a teaspoon of filling into center of each round. Fold up and pinch edges to form triangular-shaped cookies, with filling peeking out of center. Pinch dough firmly, so seams don't come open. Repeat with remaining dough and filling.

Bake cookies about 20 minutes, or until lightly golden and firm. Cool on baking sheet 5 minutes, and then transfer to wire racks to cool completely.

Makes about 24 cookies

Nutty Shortbread

There's nothing quite like a buttery, rich cookie to satisfy a sweet tooth . . . and it doesn't come better than shortbread. Traditionally a butter dough, my version delivers rich, tender cookies without compromising our rich, tender health. Putting nuts in your cookies adds energy, making you feel social and friendly.

1¾ cups whole wheat pastry flour

Pinch sea salt

½ cup corn oil

½ cup brown rice syrup

1 teaspoon pure vanilla extract

2½ ounces pecan pieces, lightly oven
    toasted (page 159) and coarsely
    minced

2 to 3 tablespoons FruitSource
    (granulated brown rice syrup)

Preheat oven to 325F (175C). Line 1 or 2 baking sheets with parchment paper.

Mix flour and salt in a medium bowl. Cut in oil until texture of wet sand. Stir in rice syrup and vanilla to make a stiff dough. Fold in pecans. Wrap dough in plastic wrap and chill 1 hour or longer.

To make cookies, roll out dough on a lightly floured surface to a ¼-inch thickness. Using a 2½ to 3-inch round plain or fluted cookie cutter, cut out cookies, and transfer to prepared pans. Sprinkle lightly with FruitSource.

Bake for 15 to 18 minutes, or until cookies are golden and just firm, not hard. If you overbake, cookies will harden as they cool. Transfer cookies to a rack and cool completely.

Makes about 20 cookies

Apple-Cranberry Crisp

Sweet and tart fruit covered by a tender, cakelike topping is one of the most wonderful, homey desserts. Easy to make, delicious, and beautiful, you get it all with this one. Baking the fruit gentles its simple sugars, and the topping gives you the satisfaction of flour without eating too much of it. The tart flavor of the cranberries balances the sweet apples perfectly.

Fruit Filling

3 to 4 Granny Smith apples, peeled, cored, and thinly sliced

¾ cup unsweetened dried cranberries

1 tablespoon corn oil

2 tablespoons arrowroot

2 tablespoons brown rice syrup

Topping

½ cup rolled oats

1 cup whole wheat pastry flour

⅛ teaspoon sea salt

1 teaspoon baking powder

½ teaspoon ground ginger

1 teaspoon ground allspice

¼ cup corn oil

½ cup brown rice syrup

About ½ cup Eden Rice & Soy Blend or vanilla rice or soy milk

½ cup coarsely minced pecans

Preheat oven to 350F (175C). Lightly oil a 9-inch-square baking dish.

Make the filling: Mix apples and cranberries with oil until coated. Stir in arrowroot and rice syrup, and spread evenly in prepared pan.

Make the topping: Combine oats, flour, salt, baking powder, and spices in a medium bowl. Mix in oil and rice syrup to make a soft dough. Slowly mix in rice and soy blend to make a thick, spoonable batter. Fold in pecans. Spoon topping, by dollops, over surface of fruit, covering almost completely, but allowing some fruit to peek through.

Bake about 30 minutes, or until fruit is bubbling and topping is golden and firm. Serve warm.

Makes about 8 servings

Apple Streusel Tart

Pies are among our culture's favorite desserts. We love everything about pie: flaky crust, rich fillings, sweet toppings, ease of preparation, and—best of all—the homey, comfortable energy of them. We love a piece of apple or pumpkin pie in cold weather, and nothing says summer to us quite like blueberry, cherry, or peach pie.

Pastry

1¾ cups whole wheat pastry flour

⅛ teaspoon sea salt

½ cup corn oil

About ¼ cup spring or filtered water

Streusel Topping

1½ cups whole wheat pastry flour

½ cup coarsely minced pecans

¼ cup FruitSource (granulated brown rice syrup)

2 tablespoons corn oil

Apple Filling

6 unpeeled Granny Smith apples, cored and thinly sliced

2 tablespoons corn oil

Pinch sea salt

Grated zest and juice of 1 lemon

2 tablespoons arrowroot

3 tablespoons brown rice syrup

Preheat oven to 350F (175C). Lightly oil a 13-inch tart pan with a removable bottom, taking care to oil all crevices.

Make the pastry: Combine flour and salt in a medium bowl. Cut in corn oil until texture of wet sand. Slowly mix in water until dough just gathers together; do not overmix. Gather dough into a ball, cover with a damp towel, and let it rest 5 minutes to relax the gluten. Roll dough out between 2 sheets of parchment paper into a 14-inch round. Gently transfer to prepared pan and, without stretching dough, press it into pan, fitting it into all crevices. Pierce in several places with a fork.

Bake 8 to 10 minutes, or until pale golden. Set aside, leaving oven on.

Make the topping: Combine all ingredients in a small bowl to form a coarse, granular texture. Set aside.

Make the filling: Mix apples, oil, salt, lemon zest and juice, arrowroot, and rice syrup in a large bowl.

To assemble and bake: Spread filling evenly over partially baked shell. Crumble topping over filling, covering completely. Bake 45 to 50 minutes, or until apples are soft and topping is golden and crunchy. Cool about 15 minutes before slicing.

Makes 10 to 12 servings

Pecan Squares

Rich nuts smothered in thick, sweet syrup, nestled atop a buttery shortbread—does this sound like the impossible dream in healthy cooking? Not anymore. My take on this rich, special-occasion dessert employs the nuts, rich syrup, and buttery crust, but it's made from whole-grain flour, rice syrup, and cold-pressed oils. The best-quality ingredients make the best desserts. Another wonderful thing about this treat (if decadent taste isn't enough for you) is that bringing together the nuts with the brown rice syrup creates marvelous energy, but the complex sugar won't leave you with the jitters.

Crust

3 cups whole wheat pastry flour

1½ teaspoons baking powder

¼ teaspoon sea salt

⅔ cup corn oil

¾ cup brown rice syrup

1 teaspoon pure vanilla extract

Pecan Topping

¼ cup corn oil

1½ cups brown rice syrup

¼ cup Eden Rice & Soy Blend or vanilla rice or soy milk

4 cups coarsely minced pecans

Make the crust: Combine flour, baking powder, and salt in a medium bowl. Stir in corn oil, rice syrup, and vanilla to make a stiff dough. Press dough into a lightly oiled 10 × 15-inch jelly-roll pan. Refrigerate at least 1 hour before baking.

Preheat oven to 375F (190C). Bake crust 12 minutes, or until golden. Set aside, leaving oven on.

Make the topping: Combine oil and rice syrup in a saucepan. Cook over medium heat until mixture foams lightly, 3 to 4 minutes. Remove from heat, and whisk in rice and soy blend. Stir in pecans.

To finish: Spread filling evenly over crust. Bake 25 to 30 minutes, or until topping is bubbling and starting to firm up. Cool completely, and cut into 1½-inch squares.

Makes about 5 dozen

Peach and Berry Cobbler with Lemon Biscuits

With juicy peaches and succulent berries at their peak, this lemony spiral-shaped biscuit-topped cobbler is the perfect finale to any summer meal, from leisurely brunches to midday garden lunches to evening feasts. Homey and comfortable, this is a dessert to relax your guests and create a social atmosphere.

Fruit Filling

2 to 3 pounds ripe peaches, halved, pitted, and cut into ½-inch wedges

4 to 5 cups fresh berries (blackberries, blueberries, raspberries, or a mixture)

Grated zest and juice of 1 lemon

2 tablespoons corn oil

Generous pinch sea salt

2 to 3 tablespoons arrowroot

2 to 3 tablespoons brown rice syrup

Lemon Biscuits

2 cups whole wheat pastry flour

2 teaspoons baking powder

⅛ teaspoon sea salt

Grated zest of 1 lemon

¼ cup FruitSource (granulated brown rice syrup)

¼ cup corn oil

½ teaspoon pure lemon extract

½ to ⅔ cup Eden Rice & Soy Blend or vanilla rice or soy milk

About ⅔ cup fruit-sweetened apricot preserves

Preheat oven to 350F (175C). Lightly oil a 13 × 9-inch baking dish.

Make the filling: Mix peaches, berries, lemon zest and juice, oil, salt, arrowroot, and rice syrup in a large bowl. Spread evenly in prepared pan, and set aside.

Make the topping: Combine flour, baking powder, salt, lemon zest, FruitSource, oil, and lemon extract in a food processor fitted with the metal blade. Pulse 45 to 50 times or until texture of wet sand. Do not overmix. Slowly add rice and soy blend through the feed tube, pulsing until dough gathers into a ball. Roll out dough between 2 sheets of parchment paper to a ¼-inch-thick rectangle. Trim edges to even out shape. Spread a thin layer of preserves over dough. With a sharp knife, divide dough in half lengthwise, creating 2 long rectangles. Starting at a long side, roll each rectangle, jelly-roll style, to form 2 cylinders. Slice cylinders into 1-inch pieces, and arrange pieces, cut side down, on top of fruit filling, covering completely. Cover loosely with foil.

Bake for 25 minutes. Remove foil, and bake 25 to 30 minutes more, or until filling is bubbling and biscuits are golden and firm. Serve warm.

Makes 8 to 10 servings

Orange-Scented Steamed Pudding

You can have your cake and eat it too. For optimum health, it is best to use baked flour products in small quantities. They can tax our digestion, making us tired, if eaten in excess. That's what makes steamed cakes so great; you get the satisfaction of eating cake, but because they're steamed, they're moist and easy to digest. Rich, with a warm energy, this is a dessert that can satisfy the most discerning sweet tooth.

2 tablespoons fruit-sweetened orange
marmalade
1 tablespoon brown rice syrup
2 cups whole wheat pastry flour
2 teaspoons baking powder
⅛ teaspoon sea salt
Grated zest of 1 orange
¼ cup corn oil
½ cup brown rice syrup
About ¾ cup Eden Rice & Soy Blend or
vanilla rice or soy milk
¼ cup coarsely minced walnuts, optional

Lightly oil a 1-quart pudding basin.

Mix marmalade and rice syrup in a small bowl and spoon evenly over bottom of the basin. Set aside.

Combine flour, baking powder, salt, and orange zest in a medium bowl. Mix in oil and rice syrup. Slowly stir in rice and soy blend to make a thick, smooth cake batter. Do not overmix. Fold in walnuts, if using. Spoon batter evenly into basin, taking care not to move marmalade mixture.

Lightly oil cover of basin. Seal tightly. If using a basin with no cover, cut a piece of parchment paper about 1 inch larger than basin. Wet parchment paper and wring out. Cover basin with paper, top with foil, and seal tightly. Place sealed basin in a pot large enough for it to comfortably fit. Add water to come halfway up basin's side. Cover pot, and bring to a boil. Reduce heat to medium-low. Steam pudding for 2 hours, checking water after 1 hour, adding more as needed. It's important to maintain the water level so pudding will be moist.

Carefully remove basin from pot and allow to stand, undisturbed, for 10 minutes. Remove cover, and loosen the edges with a knife. Place a plate over basin, and carefully invert pudding onto plate. The marmalade and rice syrup will create a glaze that will run down sides of pudding, covering it completely. Allow pudding to cool slightly before slicing.

Makes 6 to 8 servings

TIP

Any cake recipe you love can be steamed instead of baked. You can eliminate the glaze and frost just as you would any other cake.

Raspberry-Hazelnut Torte

A special-occasion, decadent, multilayered cake that will, once and for all, shatter the myth that whole foods are boring and tasteless. A dessert like this moist cake with its creamy filling and rich nuts conveys the message that this day, this event, is truly special and to be remembered. I like to serve a beautiful cake like this one perched on a high pedestal dish, garnished with fresh berries and flowers—the perfect illustration of the joy of the occasion.

Raspberry Filling
1 cup fresh or thawed frozen raspberries
1 cup fruit-sweetened apricot preserves

Frosting
2 cups almond amasake
½ cup Eden Rice & Soy Blend or vanilla rice or soy milk
¼ cup brown rice syrup
3 tablespoons brewed grain coffee (see Tip)
3 tablespoons agar flakes
1 tablespoon kuzu dissolved in about 2 tablespoons cold water

Cake
1 cup hazelnuts, toasted and skins rubbed off (recipe follows)
3 cups whole-wheat pastry flour
1 teaspoon brewed grain coffee (see Tip)
1 tablespoon baking powder
⅛ teaspoon sea salt
¼ cup corn oil
½ cup Eden Wheat Malt or brown rice syrup
1 teaspoon pure vanilla extract
¾ to 1 cup Eden Rice & Soy Blend or vanilla rice or soy milk

To Serve
Toasted hazelnuts and fresh raspberries, optional

Make the filling: Press berries and preserves through a fine sieve into a bowl. Stir to blend, and chill at least 1 hour or overnight.

Make the frosting: Combine amasake, rice and soy blend, rice syrup, grain coffee, and agar in a saucepan. Cook over low heat, stirring frequently, until agar has dissolved, 15 to 20 minutes. Do not boil. Stir in kuzu mixture, and cook, stirring, until mixture thickens, about 3 minutes. Transfer to a heat-resistant bowl, cover with plastic wrap, and set aside until firm, about 1 hour. (You may prepare this ahead. Cool frosting to room temperature before refrigerating, covered.)

Make the cake: Preheat oven to 350F (175C). Lightly oil and flour 3 (9-inch) round cake pans. Cut 3 pieces of parchment paper the size of pans, lightly oil them, and lay on pan bottoms.

Place hazelnuts, flour, grain coffee, baking powder, and salt in a food processor fitted with the metal blade. Process until nuts are ground into a fine meal. Transfer flour mixture to a medium bowl. Stir in oil, wheat malt, and vanilla. Slowly mix in rice and soy blend to make a smooth cake batter. Spoon equal amounts of batter into prepared pans.

Bake for 30 to 35 minutes, or until the cakes are golden and the centers spring back to the touch. Cool cakes in pans about 5 minutes before turning out onto wire racks. Peel parchment paper away from cakes and cool completely.

To assemble the torte: Place 1 cake layer on a serving platter and the remaining layers on pieces of foil. Spread a thin layer of filling over each cake top. Allow it to set up 10 minutes. Whip frosting to loosen. Spread a layer of frosting over each layer. Position a layer on top of the layer on the platter, and top with third layer. Spread remaining frosting over top

and sides of torte. Garnish with hazelnuts and raspberries, if desired. Cut into wedges.

Makes 8 to 10 servings

TOASTING HAZELNUTS

Spread nuts on a baking sheet, and toast in a preheated 350F (175C) oven for about 20 minutes, until fragrant. Transfer nuts to a paper sack, and let cool to loosen the skins. In small amounts, transfer nuts to a kitchen towel and gently rub away skins.

TIP

To brew grain coffee, add 1 tablespoon granules to 1 cup water, and simmer about 2 minutes to dissolve.

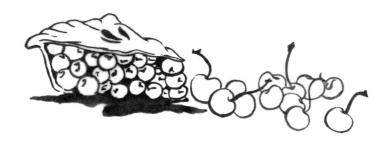

Walnut-Pear Cake with Lemon Sauce

Walnuts and pears seem to go together; their complementary flavors blend so well, you can hardly imagine one without the other. This old-fashioned dessert sets the stage for a relaxed evening of socializing, with the pears calming everyone's energy but maintaining just enough sparkle from the lemons and vitalizing walnuts to keep the conversation active.

Lemon Sauce

¼ cup brown rice syrup

1½ cups amasake

Grated zest of 1 lemon

1 vanilla bean, split lengthwise and pulp removed

1 tablespoon kuzu dissolved in about 2 tablespoons cold water

1 teaspoon fresh lemon juice

Walnut-Pear Cake

1¼ cups brown rice syrup

3 tablespoons spring or filtered water

2 large pears, peeled, cored, and thinly sliced

2 cups whole wheat pastry flour

1 tablespoon baking powder

⅛ teaspoon sea salt

¼ cup corn oil

Grated zest of 1 lemon

3 tablespoons mirin

1 teaspoon pure vanilla extract

About 1 cup Eden Rice & Soy Blend or vanilla rice or soy milk

½ cup coarsely minced, lightly pan-toasted (page 131) walnut pieces

Make the lemon sauce: Warm rice syrup, amasake, lemon zest, and vanilla pulp in a saucepan over low heat. Stir in kuzu mixture and cook, stirring, until mixture thickens, about 3 minutes. Remove from heat, and stir in lemon juice. Transfer to a heat-resistant bowl, cover with plastic wrap, and refrigerate until chilled.

Make the cake: Preheat oven to 350F (175C) Lightly oil a 2 × 9-inch round cake pan.

Combine ¾ cup of the rice syrup and water in a saucepan. Cook over medium heat until mixture foams. Spoon over bottom of prepared pan. Arrange pear slices decoratively over syrup.

Combine flour, baking powder, and salt in a medium bowl. Stir in oil, remaining ½ cup rice syrup, lemon zest, mirin, and vanilla. Slowly stir in rice and soy blend to make a thick, smooth cake batter. Do not overmix. Fold in walnut pieces. Spoon batter evenly over pears, taking care not to disturb the pattern too much.

Bake for 35 to 45 minutes, or until the center of the cake springs back to the touch or a toothpick inserted into center comes out clean. Cool cake in pan for 10 minutes. Invert onto a serving platter. Leave pan over cake 1 minute before removing it to prevent pears from sticking; if they do, simply replace them on top of cake.

To serve: Whisk sauce to loosen, and slice cake into wedges. Serve warm cake on a pool of cool lemon sauce.

Makes 8 to 10 servings

Gingered Pumpkin Cake with Sweet Cranberry Sauce

Traditionally a holiday treat, this delicate cake will be a hit on your table all winter long. Ever wonder why pumpkin is so great during the holidays? Sure it's in season, but think about its energy—calm, centering, lightly sweet. Pumpkin provides the right touch of relaxed energy during our stress-filled holiday season. So go ahead, kick off your shoes, put your feet up, and enjoy.

Cake

2½ cups whole wheat pastry flour

½ cup yellow cornmeal

4 teaspoons baking powder

¼ teaspoon sea salt

½ teaspoon ground ginger

½ teaspoon ground cinnamon

½ teaspoon freshly grated nutmeg

¼ cup corn oil

½ cup Eden Wheat Malt or brown rice syrup

1 cup unsweetened cooked or canned pumpkin puree (see Tip)

About 1 cup Eden Rice & Soy Blend or vanilla rice or soy milk

½ cup coarsely minced pecan pieces, lightly oven toasted (page 159)

Cranberry Sauce

1 cup amasake

1 cup fresh cranberries, sorted, rinsed, and drained

Pinch sea salt

3 tablespoons Eden Wheat Malt or brown rice syrup

2 teaspoons kuzu dissolved in about 1 tablespoon cold water

To Serve

Fresh cranberries, for garnish, optional

Make the cake: Preheat oven to 350F (175C). Lightly oil and flour a 10-inch Bundt pan.

Combine flour, cornmeal, baking powder, salt, and spices in a large bowl. Stir in oil, wheat malt, and pumpkin. Slowly mix in rice and soy blend to make a thick, smooth cake batter. Fold in pecans. Spoon batter evenly into prepared pan.

Bake for 35 to 40 minutes or until the center of the cake springs back to the touch. Cool cake in the pan about 10 minutes. Invert onto a serving plate.

Make the sauce: Combine amasake, cranberries, salt, and wheat malt in a saucepan. Cook over low heat until cranberries pop and amasake is warmed through. Stir in kuzu mixture, and cook, stirring, until mixture thickens, about 3 minutes.

To serve: Spoon some sauce onto individual dessert plates. Top with a wedge of cake. Garnish with a few fresh cranberries, if desired.

Makes 10 to 12 servings

<table>
<tr><td>

TIP

To make your own unsweetened pumpkin puree, cut a butternut squash or sugar pumpkin in half and remove seeds and fibrous material. Lightly oil squash and bake in a preheated 400F (205C) oven until quite soft. Cool enough to handle and scoop flesh from skin. Puree squash in a food processor fitted with the metal blade until smooth. Press through a fine strainer to make a smoother puree. Freeze any puree you do not use in the recipe. Homemade puree tastes sweeter than the unsweetened canned puree.
</td></tr>
</table>

Mocha Cake with Chocolate Ganache

Arich coffee-flavored cake smothered in a chocolate glaze is a decadent treat. I am a firm believer that we need decadence now and then, otherwise life becomes a grim endurance. Spicy and moist, this cake will satisfy your need for richness without compromising your idea of healthy eating, because here's the real treat—it has no white sugar or heavy dairy fats, but just enough chocolate to make you purr.

Cake

2½ cups whole wheat pastry flour

1 tablespoon baking powder

⅛ teaspoon sea salt

1 tablespoon grain coffee granules

¼ cup corn oil

½ cup Eden Wheat Malt or brown rice syrup

1 teaspoon pure vanilla extract

½ cup nondairy, malt-sweetened chocolate chips

1 cup amasake or vanilla rice or soy milk

Ganache

⅔ cup nondairy, malt-sweetened chocolate chips

¼ cup amasake or vanilla rice or soy milk

2 tablespoons Eden Wheat Malt or brown rice syrup

To Serve

Apricot Roses, optional (recipe follows)

Make the cake: Preheat oven to 350F (175C). Lightly oil and flour a 10-inch Bundt pan.

Combine flour, baking powder, salt, and grain coffee in a large bowl. Mix in oil, wheat malt, and vanilla. Warm chips and amasake together until chips melt. Stir into flour mixture to make a thick, smooth cake batter. Spoon evenly into prepared pan.

Bake for about 35 minutes, or until the center springs back to the touch. Cool cake in the pan for about 10 minutes. Invert onto a serving plate. Cool completely before frosting.

Making the ganache: Place chips in a heat-resistant bowl. Heat amasake and wheat malt until very foamy over medium heat. Pour over chips, whisking to make a creamy, smooth ganache. Cover and chill to thicken slightly, about 30 minutes.

To serve: Loosen ganache with a whisk (if too thick, rewarm) and spoon over cake, allowing chocolate to run down sides of the cake. Decorate with Apricot Roses, if desired.

Makes 10 to 12 servings

Apricot Roses

For 4 apricot roses, you will need 16 dried apricots (unsulfured, from a natural foods store). Roll and flatten 4 apricots to form 2-inch circles. Lay a flattened apricot on a dry surface. Lay a second one on top, overlapping by about ¾ inch. Overlap third and fourth apricots in the same way. Press bottom edges together with a rolling pin. Roll up row of apricots as tightly as possible. Press base flat with your fingers, and trim flat with a sharp knife. Insert a toothpick into base, trimming to leave about ¼ inch exposed. Holding "rose" by base, gently fold petals open to form a rose shape. Press the rose into top of cake, inserting exposed toothpick into cake to hold it in place. Roses will keep, in a sealed container at room temperature, for about a week.

Fresh Fruit Gâteau

This cake is the ultimate messenger, heralding the cry "This is an occasion to be remembered!" I love to serve this on a pedestal dish mounded high with fresh summer fruits to celebrate a special festive time. The tender vanilla cake is smothered in creamy custard frosting topped with brightly colored fruit and dripping with a rich, caramel glaze. All these ingredients come together to create a joyful energy just right for any celebration.

Cake
5 cups whole wheat pastry flour

5 teaspoons baking powder

¼ teaspoon sea salt

½ cup corn oil

1 cup brown rice syrup

2 teaspoons pure vanilla extract

2 to 2¼ cups Eden Rice & Soy Blend or
vanilla rice or soy milk

Vanilla Cream
2½ cups amasake

4 teaspoons brown rice syrup

3 tablespoons kuzu dissolved in ¼ cup
water

2 teaspoons pure vanilla extract

To Assemble
1 cup coarsely minced pecan pieces,
lightly oven toasted (page 159)

3 to 4 cups soft fruit, such as whole raspberries, blueberries, cherry halves,
sliced strawberries, or peach slices

Glaze
½ to 1 cup brown rice syrup

Make the cake: Place oven racks in center of oven, and preheat oven to 350F (175C). Lightly oil and flour 2 (9-inch) round cake pans.

Combine flour, baking powder, and salt in a large bowl. Stir in oil, rice syrup, and vanilla. Slowly stir in rice and soy blend to make a smooth, spoonable batter. Do not overmix. Divide batter between prepared pans.

Bake for 35 to 40 minutes, or until light golden and the center springs back to the touch. Cool cakes in pans for 10 minutes. Turn out onto wire racks to cool completely.

Make the vanilla cream: Warm amasake and rice syrup over low heat. Stir in kuzu mixture, and cook, stirring, until thick, 3 to 4 minutes. Stir in vanilla. Set aside to cool, whisking occasionally to keep custard loose and smooth. Cool to room temperature.

To assemble: Using a sharp, serrated knife, cut-off top of one cake layer to make it level. Place this layer on a serving platter. Spread with a generous layer of cooled vanilla cream and top with pecan pieces. Place remaining cake layer on top. Spread top with vanilla cream, letting it slip down sides of cake. Top cream with a decorative pattern of soft fruit; be generous, fruit should be high and abundant.

Make the glaze: Heat rice syrup over high heat until it foams. Immediately spoon over fruit to glaze, allowing syrup to run down sides of cake. Allow cake to stand for about 30 minutes before slicing, to set glaze.

Makes 10 to 12 servings

Sweet Fruit Pizza

This is a comfortable, rustic dessert that is just perfect for those casually lazy get-togethers. The flaky biscuit crust is a wonderful complement to the sweet, succulent summer fruit mounded on the surface. Topped with an apricot glaze, this homey tart is the picture of summer, giving us a light, fresh energy just right for the season.

Pizza

2½ cups whole wheat pastry flour

3 teaspoons baking powder

⅛ teaspoon sea salt

½ cup plus 1 tablespoon corn oil

½ cup brown rice syrup

½ to ⅔ cup Eden Rice & Soy Blend or vanilla rice or soy milk

1 small plum, halved, pitted, and thinly sliced

1 to 2 unpeeled peaches, halved, pitted, and thinly sliced

½ cup fresh raspberries

½ cup thinly sliced strawberries

½ cup blueberries or blackberries

Glaze

½ cup fruit-sweetened apricot preserves

2 tablespoons brown rice syrup

Make the pizza: Preheat the oven to 350F (175C). Line a 10-inch pizza pan with parchment paper or lightly oil.

Combine flour, baking powder, and salt in a food processor fitted with the metal blade. Add ½ cup oil and ¼ cup of rice syrup; pulse 45 to 50 times, or until texture of wet sand. Slowly add rice and soy blend through the feed tube, and pulse until dough gathers into a ball. Roll dough between 2 sheets of parchment to a 9- to 10-inch round. Place in prepared pan.

Lightly brush dough with remaining 1 tablespoon oil. Arrange fruit abundantly, keeping berries toward center (so their juices don't run). Drizzle remaining ¼ cup rice syrup over fruit.

Bake 25 to 30 minutes, or until fruit is lightly browned and bubbling. Remove from oven and transfer to a serving plate.

Make the glaze: Heat preserves and syrup over high heat until mixture foams. Quickly spoon over warm pizza, and allow to stand for about 15 minutes to set the glaze. Slice into wedges.

Makes 8 to 10 servings

Fruitcake Cups

These little jewels are tiny, moist cakes dotted with dried fruit and nuts. Baked in mini muffin tins, they make a perfect-sized dessert. They're delicate and lightly sweet, with a relaxing, warming, spicy energy that make them the perfect snack with tea on a chilly winter day.

Fruitcake

2 cups whole wheat pastry flour

½ cup yellow cornmeal

2 teaspoons baking powder

⅛ teaspoon sea salt

½ teaspoon ground ginger

¼ teaspoon ground cinnamon

¼ teaspoon ground allspice

¼ cup corn oil

½ cup brown rice syrup

¾ to 1 cup Eden Rice & Soy Blend or
    vanilla rice or soy milk

½ cup dried currants

½ cup minced dried apples

½ cup minced dried cherries

½ cup coarsely minced pecans, lightly
    oven toasted (page 159)

Glaze

½ cup fruit-sweetened apricot preserves

2 tablespoons brown rice syrup

Preheat oven to 350F (175C). Lightly oil and flour a 24-cup mini muffin pan.

Combine the flour, cornmeal, baking powder, salt, and spices in a large bowl. Mix in oil and rice syrup. Stir in rice and soy blend to form a smooth, thick cake batter. Fold in dried fruit and pecans. Spoon batter into prepared cups, filling them three-quarters full.

Bake 25 to 30 minutes, or until the cakes are raised and spring back to the touch. Cool in pan for about 5 minutes. Carefully remove cakes from the pan, and transfer to a wire rack to cool completely.

Make the glaze: Slip a piece of parchment paper under rack. Combine preserves and rice syrup in a saucepan, and cook over high heat until mixture foams. Quickly spoon over cakes, allowing excess to run down sides. Let stand for about 10 minutes to set the glaze before serving.

Makes 24 mini cakes

Dried Cherry and Sweet Pear Pie

This richly flavored pie has the texture of mincemeat, but with a twist. Sweet, ripe pears are cooked with lightly tart dried cherries and earthy spices, creating a symphony of flavors bursting on your tongue, with the sour flavor of the cherries balancing the sugar of the pears. Laced through with nuts, this pie is rich, with a relaxed yet vital energy just perfect for holiday feasts, midwinter dinner parties, or even tea time.

Filling

6 to 7 ripe pears, halved, cored, and cut
into chunks

Juice of 1 lemon

2/3 cup brown rice syrup

1 cup spring or filtered water

1 cup unsweetened dried cherries

1/2 cup raisins

1/2 teaspoon ground cinnamon

1/2 teaspoon ground allspice

1/2 teaspoon freshly grated nutmeg

Generous pinch sea salt

2 to 3 tablespoons mirin

1 cup coarsely minced walnut or pecan
pieces

2 teaspoons white miso

1 to 2 tablespoons kuzu dissolved in

about 2 tablespoons cold water

Double-Crust Oat Pastry

2 cups whole wheat pastry flour

1/2 cup rolled oats

1/8 teaspoon sea salt

1/2 cup corn oil

2 teaspoons brown rice syrup

About 4 to 6 tablespoons cold spring or fil-
tered water

Make the filling: Combine pears, lemon juice, rice syrup, water, cherries, raisins, spices, and salt in a large saucepan. Stir in mirin, and bring to a boil, covered, over medium heat. Reduce heat to low, and simmer until fruit is soft, about 45 minutes. Stir in nuts. Remove a small amount of liquid and use to dissolve miso. Stir miso and kuzu mixtures into the pot, and cook, stirring, until thickened, 3 to 4 minutes.

Make the crust: Preheat oven to 325F (165C).

Combine flour, oats, and salt in a medium bowl. Stir in oil and rice syrup until texture of wet sand. Slowly stir in enough water so dough just gathers into a ball. Cover, and set aside 5 minutes to relax the gluten.

Divide dough in half, and roll each piece between 2 sheets of parchment paper to a 10-inch circle. Gently fit 1 circle into a 9-inch pie plate. Pierce in several places with a fork.

To assemble and bake: Spoon filling into pie shell. Slice remaining dough circle into thin strips. Laying them over the filling, weave strips to form a lattice top. Fold edges of bottom crust up over edge, crimping with lattice pieces to seal. Crimp between your fingers, forming a decorative rim.

Bake for 45 to 60 minutes, or until filling is bubbling and set and crust is golden.

Makes 8 to 10 servings

The Best Pecan Pie

There's nothing quite like pecan pie . . . rich, decadent, incredibly delicious; we view it as positively sinful. What if I told you that, while rich, pecan pie could create vital energy. After all, nuts are tiny seeds that grow into trees! That's a lot of energy. The energy from the nuts is gentled by delicate, sweet grain malts, all nestled in a whole-grain short-bread crust. Indulgence isn't all bad.

One-Crust Pastry

1½ cups whole wheat pastry flour

¼ cup FruitSource (granulated brown rice syrup)

Generous pinch sea salt

⅓ cup corn oil

About ¼ cup Eden Rice & Soy Blend or vanilla rice or soy milk

Pecan Filling

1 cup brown rice syrup

½ cup barley malt

¼ cup amasake

3 tablespoons corn oil

2 tablespoons agar flakes

2 teaspoons pure vanilla extract

2½ to 3 cups coarsely minced pecans

Make the pastry: Combine flour, FruitSource, and salt in a medium bowl. Mix in oil until texture of wet sand. Slowly stir in rice and soy blend, mixing just until dough gathers into a ball. Cover, and set aside 10 to 15 minutes to relax the gluten.

Make the filling: Combine rice syrup, barley malt, amasake, oil, and agar in a saucepan. Cook over low heat, stirring frequently, until agar dissolves, 15 to 20 minutes. Increase heat, and cook mixture until very foamy. Remove from heat, and whisk in vanilla. Stir in pecans.

To assemble and bake: Preheat oven to 350F (175C).

While filling cooks, roll out dough between 2 sheets of parchment paper to a 10-inch circle. Transfer circle to a 9-inch pie plate, forming it to sides and bottom without stretching. Turn excess crust up over edge, crimping with your fingers to form a decorative rim. Pierce in several places with a fork. Spoon filling evenly into pie shell.

Bake for about 1 hour, or until the pie is set. If the pie still seems soft (but not loose) after 1 hour, remove from oven; it will set as it cools. Cool completely before slicing.

Makes 8 to 10 servings

Pumpkin Squares

Pumpkin pie filling atop a flaky biscuit crust—I prefer these creamy little squares to a traditional pumpkin pie. Bite-sized, rich and spicy, these are perfect with a hot cup of tea, providing a relaxed, calming energy from the pumpkin, but the energizing spices create a lovely chatty quality just perfect for a social gathering.

Biscuit Crust

1½ cups whole wheat pastry flour

1 teaspoon baking powder

Pinch sea salt

¼ cup corn oil

2 tablespoons brown rice syrup

¼ to ½ cup Eden Rice & Soy Blend or
vanilla rice or soy milk

Pumpkin Filling

2 cups unsweetened pureed butternut
squash or sugar pumpkin

1 cup amasake

¼ cup brown rice syrup

2 tablespoons agar flakes

1 teaspoon pure vanilla extract

½ teaspoon ground ginger

¼ teaspoon ground cinnamon

¼ teaspoon freshly grated nutmeg

Pinch sea salt

2 tablespoons kuzu dissolved in ¼ cup
cold water

Pecan Topping

¼ cup brown rice syrup

1 cup coarsely minced pecan pieces

Make the crust: Preheat oven to 350F (175C). Lightly oil a 9- or 10-inch square baking dish.

Combine flour, baking powder, salt, oil, and rice syrup in a food processor fitted with the metal blade. Pulse 40 to 50 times or until texture of wet sand. Slowly add rice and soy blend through the feed tube, and pulse until mixture gathers into a ball. Press dough evenly into prepared dish.

Bake 12 minutes. Set aside, leaving oven on.

Make the filling: Combine all ingredients except kuzu mixture in a saucepan. Cook over low heat, stirring frequently, until agar dissolves, 15 to 20 minutes. Stir in kuzu mixture and cook, stirring, until mixture thickens, about 3 minutes. Spoon filling evenly over partially baked crust.

Make the topping: Cook rice syrup over high heat until it foams. Stir in pecan pieces and spoon over filling.

Bake the squares: Bake for 30 minutes, or until edges of filling are set. The center will still be soft but will set as it cools. Cool completely before cutting into bars.

Makes 12 to 16 bars

Spicy Apple-Pear Pie

Autumn spells pie season to me. You can just smell the earthy spices and sweet fruit melting together in the oven, encased in a warm, flaky crust. Tree fruit, like apples and pears, are at their peak during late summer and autumn and provide us with a delicate, sweet, relaxing nature. Cooking them, especially baking, gentles the effect of their sugars on the bloodstream, creating a dessert that satisfies without making our blood chemistry a mess.

Double-Crust Pastry

2½ cups whole wheat pastry flour

⅛ teaspoon sea salt

½ cup corn oil

About 4 tablespoons cold spring or filtered
water

Filling

3 to 4 medium-sized ripe pears, peeled,
cored, and thinly sliced

3 to 4 medium-sized apples, peeled,
cored, and thinly sliced

2 to 3 tablespoons corn oil

3 tablespoons arrowroot

¼ cup brown rice syrup

1 teaspoon ground ginger

Grated zest and juice of 1 lemon

Generous pinch each ground cloves,
ground nutmeg, and ground allspice

Make the pastry: Place a rack in the center of oven, and preheat oven to 325F (175C).

Combine flour, salt, and oil until the texture of wet sand. Slowly stir in enough water so the dough just gathers into a ball. Cover, and set aside 5 minutes to relax the gluten.

Divide dough in half, and roll each piece between 2 sheets of parchment paper to a 10-inch circle. Gently fit 1 circle into a 9-inch pie plate. Pierce in several places with a fork.

Make the filling: Combine all ingredients in a large bowl.

To assemble and bake: Spoon filling into pie shell, mounding fruit in center.

Gently place remaining dough circle on top of filling. Roll edge of bottom crust up over top crust and press edges together to seal. Roll to edge of pan, and crimp decoratively to seal. Pierce top crust in several places to allow steam to escape.

Bake for 45 to 60 minutes, or until filling is bubbling and crust is golden brown.

Makes 8 to 10 servings

Blueberry Galette

This beautiful rustic tart makes a splendid ending to any summer meal. Filled to the brim with succulent, sweet berries, nestled in a free-form crust, this tart looks as casual as leisurely summer days. The cooling energy of blueberries is enhanced by the sparklingly fresh flavor of lemon.

Crust

2 cups whole wheat pastry flour

1 teaspoon baking powder

⅛ teaspoon sea salt

¼ cup corn oil

¼ to ½ cup spring or filtered water

Blueberry Filling

6 cups blueberries

4 tablespoons brown rice syrup

2 tablespoons arrowroot

2 teaspoons corn oil

Grated zest of 1 lemon

Juice of ½ lemon

Glaze

½ cup brown rice syrup

2 teaspoons corn oil

Make the crust: Preheat oven to 350F (175C). Line a 10-inch pizza pan with parchment paper or lightly oil. A lightly floured baking stone also works great with this recipe.

Combine flour, baking powder, and salt in a medium bowl. Stir in oil until texture of wet sand. Mix in water until dough gathers into a ball. Roll out dough on a floured surface to a 12-inch circle, about ⅛-inch thick. Transfer dough to prepared pan or stone.

Make the filling: Mix all ingredients together to coat berries.

To assemble and bake: Spoon filling onto center of dough, leaving about 1 inch of dough exposed around rim. Carefully fold edges of dough up over filling, pinching to form pleats and leaving about a 6-inch opening in center of filling exposed.

Bake for 30 to 35 minutes, or until the crust is golden brown and firm and the filling is bubbling. Remove from oven, and carefully transfer pie to a cooling rack.

Make the glaze: Combine rice syrup and oil in a saucepan and cook over high heat until mixture foams. Quickly brush over crust to glaze. Cool completely before slicing.

Makes 8 to 10 servings

NATURAL HOME REMEDIES

SOMETIMES WE NEED a quick fix for an acute symptom, a jump-start to get energy moving, or a little concentrated help for a chronic condition.

There are lots of over-the-counter products that we're more than willing to spend billions of dollars on to prevent indigestion, get rid of a headache, relieve a stuffy nose, break up chest congestion, mask our aches and pains, get rid of spots and pimples, and diminish wrinkles. Right in your kitchen you have the ingredients to create gentle remedies to fix these same conditions. Instead of just masking symptoms and covering flaws, these simple recipes relieve the symptoms and help get to the root of the problem.

Sweet Vegetable Tea

This warm, delicately sweet drink will help soften tightness that forms in the middle of the body—spleen, stomach, pancreas—from overconsuming heavy animal protein. This tea is also helpful for relaxing tight, tense muscles. For best results, drink a cup a day for two to three weeks—that will be enough to get your body to respond.

Note that there is no seasoning in this recipe. That is so the vegetables will bleed their entire flavor and nutrients into the broth.

¼ cup finely diced sweet onion
¼ cup finely diced green cabbage
¼ cup finely diced winter squash
¼ cup finely diced carrot
4 cups spring or filtered water

Layer the vegetables in a saucepan in the order listed. Add water and bring to a boil, uncovered, over medium heat. Boil tea for 2 minutes. Reduce heat to low, and simmer for 15 minutes. Strain out vegetables.

Drink tea hot or warm. Keep refrigerated for up to 3 days, and rewarm it before drinking.

Makes 4 servings

Carrot-Daikon Drink

This spicy, pungent tea is designed to help dissolve hardened fat deposits that have accumulated deep within various organs, inhibiting their function. Working deep in the body to restore balance, this drink also adds minerals to create strong blood quality.

Its spicy flavor is also a great kick-start for losing some weight. For the best results, take this tea every other day for two weeks, then stop for two weeks. You may repeat again, if needed.

½ cup finely grated carrot
½ cup finely grated daikon
1 cup spring or filtered water
Dash of soy sauce
⅓ sheet toasted sushi nori, shredded
⅓ umeboshi plum

Combine carrot, daikon, and water in a saucepan. Bring to a gentle boil, uncovered, over medium heat. Reduce heat to low, and simmer for 3 to 4 minutes. Add soy sauce, simmer for 2 to 3 minutes. Stir in nori and umeboshi plum; simmer for 1 minute.

Drink tea and eat vegetables while tea is quite hot.

Makes 1 serving

Ume-Sho-Bancha

This simple tea is the absolute best remedy for indigestion, upset stomach, and most headaches. Traditionally used to strengthen digestion, especially when making the transition to a healthier diet, many other benefits come to the surface with its use: better circulation, relief from fatigue or weakness, and a restoration of overall well-being. For the best results, use only as needed—fix a cup when you have indulged a bit too much. But remember; this tea isn't a license to making indulgence a way of life.

> *1 teaspoon kuzu dissolved in 2 teaspoons*
>   *cold water*
> *1 cup spring or filtered water*
> *½ umeboshi plum, finely minced*
> *½ teaspoon soy sauce*

Add kuzu mixture and water to a saucepan. Bring to a boil over medium heat, stirring constantly until liquid thickens, about 3 minutes. Reduce heat to low, and stir in umeboshi plum. Add soy sauce, and simmer for 2 to 3 minutes.

Drink while hot.

Makes 1 serving

Variation

Adding ⅛ teaspoon fresh ginger juice (page 188) helps create body warmth by improving circulation.

Azuki Bean Tea

Got puffy bags under your eyes? Then this tea is for you. Puffy, swollen eyes indicate that the kidneys are becoming flaccid, overcome by too much liquid, sugar, or even fruit juices. Little red azuki beans help regulate kidney function, restoring moisture balance in the body. For best results, take this tea two to three times a week for about a month. You'll enjoy clearer eyes and feel incredibly vitalized.

> *¼ cup azuki beans, sorted and rinsed well*
> *½-inch piece kombu*
> *1 cup spring or filtered water*

Place beans, kombu, and water in a saucepan. Bring to a boil, uncovered, over medium heat. Reduce heat to low, and simmer for about 30 minutes. Strain out beans.

Drink liquid while hot.

Makes 1 serving

Note

You may continue cooking the beans to use in soups or stews.

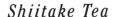

Shiitake Tea

If you have dark circles under your eyes, they could be a sign that your kidneys need a boost. Dark circles mean that your kidneys are becoming constricted and dry (you probably have low back pain, too) as the result of too little liquid, too much salt, too much stress, or too much strenuous activity. This simple tea is designed to regulate kidney moisture, softening the organs so they can do their job efficiently. For the best results, take this tea two or three times a week for about a month. You should see a difference in your eyes and feel more vitalized as a bonus.

1 dried shiitake mushroom
1 cup spring or filtered water
Dash soy sauce

Soak mushroom in water until tender, about 20 minutes. Finely mince and place, with soaking water, in a saucepan. Bring to a boil, uncovered. Reduce heat to low, and simmer 10 to 15 minutes. Add soy sauce, and simmer 2 to 3 minutes.

Drink liquid and eat mushroom while hot.

Makes 1 serving

Note

This tea can also be quite effective in relaxing overall tension or tightness in the body.

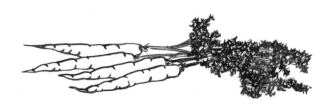

Black Soybean Tea

Effective for both occasional and chronic constipation, this tea is also helpful in warming the body by creating intestinal fortitude. Black soybeans have always been prized for their restorative powers, and this tea is no exception. For occasional constipation, take the tea before bed. To correct a chronic condition, take the tea two or three times a week for about a month, while increasing your intake of whole grains and vegetables.

¼ cup black soybeans, sorted and rinsed
  well
½-inch piece kombu
1 cup spring or filtered water

Combine beans, kombu, and water in a saucepan. Bring to a boil, uncovered, over medium heat. Reduce heat, and simmer for about 30 minutes. Strain out beans.
  Drink liquid while hot.

Makes 1 serving

Note
You may continue cooking the beans to use in soups or stews.

Fresh Lotus Root Tea

This unique vegetable works wonders for our respiratory health. Many-chambered and astringent in quality, this humble tuber has the ability to free our lungs of accumulated congestion and ease the discomfort of coughs and chest colds. For best results, take this tea for three days in a row, at the beginning or even while in the throes of a cold. Use this tea only when needed, as its astringent quality can make you feel too dry.

½ cup grated fresh lotus root
Dash soy sauce

Squeeze grated lotus root to extract juice. Place juice in a saucepan with an equal amount of water. Add a dash of soy sauce. Bring to a gentle boil over medium heat, reduce heat, and simmer 2 to 3 minutes. The tea should have thickened.
  Drink while hot.

Makes 1 serving

Note
A few drops of fresh ginger juice can be helpful for particularly stubborn congestion.

Dried Lotus Root Tea

Fresh lotus root is most effective (see Fresh Lotus Root Tea, opposite), but if it is not available, you can use the dried form.

1/3 ounce dried lotus root
1 cup spring or filtered water
Dash soy sauce

Soak lotus root in water until soft. Mince finely. Combine lotus root, water, and soy sauce in a saucepan. Bring to a boil over medium heat. Reduce heat to low, and simmer for 15 minutes. Strain the liquid.

Drink while hot.

Makes 1 serving

☯

Powdered Lotus Root Tea

All versions of lotus root are available in natural foods stores and some Asian markets. See Fresh Lotus Root Tea (see opposite) for the symptoms that indicate its use.

1 teaspoon lotus root powder
1 cup spring or filtered water
Pinch sea salt

Combine all ingredients in a saucepan. Simmer over low heat for 3 to 5 minutes but do not boil.

Drink while hot.

Makes 1 serving

☯

Kombu Tea

Kombu has so many benefits for the body: strengthening blood quality, dissolving hardened animal fats, restoring nervous system function, and promoting calmness and clear thinking. For the best results, take this tea two or three times a week for two to three weeks.

3-inch piece kombu
4 cups spring or filtered water

Place kombu and water in a saucepan. Cover, and bring to a boil. Reduce heat to low, and simmer until the liquid reduces by half, 10 to 15 minutes.

Drink 1 cup while hot. You may reheat any remaining tea for another serving.

Makes about 2 servings

☯

Daikon-Ginger Tea

Designed to aid in <u>lowering fever</u> by inducing sweat, this tea also helps relieve the symptoms of minor food poisoning. It is strong, so take it only once or twice a day for no more than two days.

2 cups prepared kukicha (bancha) tea

3 tablespoons grated fresh daikon

¼ teaspoon grated fresh ginger

1 tablespoon soy sauce

Heat tea until quite hot. Mix remaining ingredients together in a bowl. Pour hot tea over top, and stir.

Drink as much as possible while hot. Wrap yourself in a blanket to induce perspiration.

Makes 1 serving

TIP

For children, limit this tea to ½ cup per day. For babies, use a tea made from ½ grated Granny Smith apple, 1 cup water, and 1 pinch sea salt simmered together about 10 minutes.

for food poison ↑

Daikon Tea

A mild remedy <u>for ridding the body of excess liquid</u>, it is useful for relief of premenstrual fluid retention, swollen ankles and fingers. For fluid retention, take this tea once a day for three days, take five days off, then repeat if needed. Repeat no more than three cycles. This tea also <u>helps the body digest fat and protein.</u> Taken soon after a meal, you'll see a major difference in how you digest fried foods and fish.

½ cup grated daikon

1 cup spring or filtered water

Dash soy sauce

Squeeze daikon to extract juice. Combine juice with water in a saucepan. Bring to a gentle boil over medium heat. Reduce heat to low, add soy sauce, and simmer for 1 minute.

Drink while hot.

Makes 1 serving

For fluid retention

Ginger Compress

This relaxing compress aids the body in dissolving hardened fats, moving stagnant energy, and stimulating blood circulation, while warming and energizing the body. It is most commonly used on the low back to relax and strengthen the kidneys, making us feel vitalized the next day. Because this compress is quite stimulating, it is not generally recommended for use on people with serious conditions, such as cancer.

1 gallon water
4- to 5-inch piece fresh ginger

Bring water to a boil in a soup pot. While water is heating, grate ginger to make a tennis-ball-sized mound. Reduce heat to low to stop the boiling. Place ginger in a piece of cheesecloth or thin cotton. Wrap ginger and tie in a knot. Squeeze ginger sack into hot water, and place sack in the pot. Simmer for about 5 minutes; do not boil.

Lay a thin towel over the part of the body you are treating, for example, the low back for treating the kidneys. Dip another towel in the hot ginger water, wring out tightly, and lay over the thin towel. Cover with yet another dry towel to keep in the heat. Change the ginger towel when it no longer feels hot. Repeat compress until skin turns bright pink. You may do a ginger compress two or three times a week, as desired. You may use the ginger water two or three times, as long as you are careful not to boil it as you reheat it.

Makes 2 to 3 treatments

Salt Pack

This is an excellent remedy for relieving stiffness in various parts of the body as well as sore muscles. It's also quite effective in relieving stomach cramps, diarrhea, and joint pain. The salt is great at holding heat and has the energy to strengthen and energize.

2 pounds salt
1 cotton pillowcase

Heat salt in a stainless-steel skillet over medium heat until very hot. Wrap salt in the pillowcase.

Apply pack to affected area until it cools. You may reuse the salt until it turns gray (about 4 times), at which point it will no longer hold heat. You may repeat this remedy as needed.

Makes 3 to 4 treatments

Tofu Plaster

Not just for eating, tofu's cooling energy is an essential ingredient in your kitchen's first-aid kit. It's incredibly effective at drawing the fire out of a minor burn, fever, and even sunburn. In many cases, its cooling energy is more effective than ice. The plaster can be stored in the refrigerator for up to 1 week.

1 pound tofu
Unbleached white flour

Mash tofu into a coarse cream. Mix in enough flour to form a cohesive paste.

Apply directly to affected area, and cover with a towel or secure with a cotton strip. Change plaster when it becomes hot.

Makes about 3 cups

TIP

For quick relief of minor kitchen burns, apply a piece of tofu directly to the burn, again changing it as it grows hot. You may also use green cabbage leaves, changing them as they grow hot.

THE BODY SCRUB

A body scrub is the most amazing remedy in the world—and you don't have to cook a thing. If you take showers, you can do this one. This remedy activates circulation and promotes clear, soft skin by helping eliminate toxins.

Quarter fold a cotton washcloth (or use a cloth spa glove from the pharmacy). Using hot water, wet the cloth and begin to scrub the entire body (without soap), rubbing briskly until all the skin turns pink. Be sure to include your hands and feet, but avoid the face and, for women, the breasts and, for men, the genitals. At first, you'll notice that your skin turns a mottled pink. As the body breaks down accumulated, hardened fats, your skin will turn a uniform, rosy pink in minutes.

One month of daily faithful scrubbing and you'll notice that you no longer have dry skin and that your skin is as soft as it has ever been.

A GLANCE IN THE MIRROR
A DIAGNOSTIC PRIMER

A LOOK IN the mirror can tell us a lot about our health. Skin tone, lines, bumps, spots, dots, and wrinkles—or lack of them—reveal a great deal. Some of these factors reflect the vitality of our constitution, which are the traits we're born with; not much can be done with those. Most of what we see on a day-to-day inspection, however, reflects the quality of our daily diet and its effect on our organ strengths and weaknesses, letting us know what we need to work on and what is working just fine.

Visual diagnosis, especially applied to our own faces and bodies, leads us beyond the limits of the modern science definition of diagnosis. This art is much more than a tool for treating illness or determining when something is wrong. A skill like this, developed with practice and use, can help us understand ourselves, our lives, why we behave as we do, and how we fit into the scheme of nature. By simply sharpening our instinctive powers of observation, we can learn to really see ourselves. And here's the best part of visual diagnosis—it requires no technology and no equipment. We use the tools we were born with: our eyes, ears, nose, sense of touch, instinct, and intuition. The more closely we observe ourselves, and act on those observations, the more we can refine our health.

Asian medicine—the traditional healing practices—is among the most ancient forms of healing the body. Unlike the modern medicine of the Western world, Asian medicine views the body as a whole, never fragmenting diagnosis. The art of diagnosis involves more than treating specific symptoms. In most cases, modern medical practitioners look at particular symptoms and specific pain, skin disorders, or organ enlargement. In Asian medicine, the standard practice includes observation of a person's diet, lifestyle, physical activity, attitude, emotional well-being, and living environment, as well as the specific complaint. Using this approach, the practitioner can get a total picture of the client, increasing his or her ability to get to the root of the problem, rather than just artificially eliminating a particular symptom.

By honing your own skills of observation and understanding how your body works, you become an active partner in your health and vitality. Whether you rely on a doctor or an acupuncturist for treatments of any kind, the more you know, the more involved you are, the better equipped you are to maintain your own health.

The art of diagnosis uses physiognomy— the features of the face and general lines of the body—as its primary tool. The basic idea behind diagnosis is that every person is a walking, talking history of his or her development, heritage, environment, diet, and lifestyle. The strengths and weaknesses of our constitution, as well as what we create through our life choices, determine how we look, feel, and act on a daily basis. Our skin color, stance, hair texture, wrinkles, tone of voice, even emotional behavior are all external illustrations of the condition of our organs, blood, nervous system, and bone structure.

Not surprisingly, according to Asian diagnosis, a healthy diet is the key to our health and vitality. Our diet can either make us alert, responsive, and flexible or it can leave us rigid, fearful, tense, exhausted, and unable to see our way clearly.

When observing for health, there are three beginning steps. First, take a look at your total environment: Do you live in a peaceful home? Work at a stressful job? Live in a chaotic home? Surround yourself with order or disarray? Do you live in a city or in the country? By the sea or in the mountains?

Second, consider your physical and emotional being. Is your hair shiny, your skin flawless, and your nails healthy? Is your body flexible and able to respond? Or are you always surprised when you look in the mirror and find yet another wrinkle, pimple, bump, spot, or dot on your face? Are bad hair days a way of life? Do you spend a small fortune on creams and lotions to help your nails grow strong and healthy? Does exercise leave you tired, with stiff, sore muscles? Are there areas of your body that are perpetually tight and tense? Are you vibrant, energetic, enthusiastic, alert, happy, and positive? Or are you tired, listless, negative, and depressed? Are you frequently out of sorts? Do you live on an emotional roller coaster?

Third, look at the details. What are the specific symptoms, if any, you may be experiencing on any given day? Did you get a pimple on your cheek, not your chin? Is your hair limp today? Do you have pain in specific places of the body? Do you have a headache, upset stomach, and tight or loose bowels? How do these symptoms differ from what you experienced yesterday?

HOW TO START

Traditional diagnosis looks at the total body—from face to hands and feet, to posture, tone of voice, body language, and so on. For the purposes of self-diagnosis and for the maintenance of your own health and vitality, we'll concentrate on the face and hair. Keen observation of your own face can be a great help in keeping your day-to-day health on point.

The Face

Before we look at actual points of diagnosis, it's important to see where certain facial traits come from. The constitutional development of our facial structure depends on our parentage and our mother's diet. For instance, narrow eyes can mean a more yang or contracted constitution, whereas rounder eyes are indicative of a more yin or expansive person, by nature. Flat noses and thin lips can indicate a yang constitution, whereas a more protruding nose and full lips might indicate a

more yin nature. A wide, chiseled jaw can indicate a yang nature, but a gentle chin can show a more yin constitution. Large ears can indicate a hearty constitution. Fair coloring can represent a more relaxed constitution, and darker coloring may mean a tighter and more contracted constitution. So you can see, many factors come into play that influence our constitution, which determines our basic facial structure. After that, the face we have is a face that we create with our daily diet and lifestyle.

Seeing the Face

We can see, just by keen observation, how all of our organs are functioning in the features of the face. In their observation of human development, Asian healers determined that as organs were developing in the body, features were developing on the face simultaneously. So we can understand the state of our organs by observing how our face changes day to day (see page 275).

The Hairline

Starting at the top of the face, the hairline shows us the condition of the bladder. This area should be clear and free of blemishes. If excessive perspiration pools here or pimples break out, the bladder is overcome by too much fluid, sugar, and fat in the diet. Altering your intake of liquid, oil and fat (even vegetable quality), and sugar will restore the vitality of this area of the face.

The Forehead

Our forehead represents the condition of our circulatory system and large intestines. Healthy organ function shows as smooth, slightly shiny, firm skin, free of wrinkles, pimples, or spots. Any malfunction, weakness, accumulation of fat, or even constipation will show as imperfections in this area of the face. For instance, when we raise our eyebrows, a few horizontal wrinkles will appear. When we relax our forehead again, the lines should disappear, regardless of age. Wrinkles remaining in the forehead indicate that the intestines are overworked, from overeating or too much liquid intake. A simple diet change—even just eating a bit less—can change this condition very quickly.

If you develop pimples on the forehead, it indicates that the intestines are overcome with fat. Even excess vegetable fats and oils can cause this problem. Dryness on the forehead indicates that digestive function is sluggish, even constipated. Too much animal protein, especially cured meats like luncheon or smoked meats, eggs, or an excess of hard baked flour products in the diet can cause this condition. A bit more fiber and moisture in the diet from whole grains, beans, and vegetables will restore your skin to healthy luster.

The Eyebrows

The eyebrow shape is determined by the bone structure of the face and so is constitutional. The eyebrows indicate natural strength and are reputed to reflect our longevity. They develop like this: during the first trimester, the section closest to the nose develops; during the second, the center; and during the last, the outer tips. So the theory is that the mother's diet during pregnancy is key to the length and quality of life. Contracted, dense foods in the mother's diet, such as animal protein, dense fats, heavy salt, and hard cheese will cause our eyebrows to slant in toward the nose. Vegetarian diets create eyebrows that slant downward at the outer ends. The eyebrows resulting from a balanced diet are even and nicely arched, not too extreme in either direction.

The length and thickness of the eyebrows is also determined before birth. Long eyebrows indicate a long, healthy life. Thick eyebrows indicate strong vitality. Naturally thin eyebrows indicate a delicate constitution. Eyebrows will alter after birth only if there are dramatic changes in our health, thinning or even disappearing. And as we age, our eyebrows will thin if we grow infirm or weak. They will maintain their vitality if we maintain ours, with activity, interest in life, and maintenance of health.

The Eyes

It is said that the eyes are the windows to the soul. The eyes are, indeed, a true reflection of our overall health, showing every detail of how well our organs are functioning. The eyes and the digestive and nervous systems form at the same time during embryonic development, meaning that the eyes reflect the condition of the liver, intestines, and nervous system—essentially all of our bodily functions.

The shape of the eyes is determined in the womb. Most women have rounder eyes than men do, reflecting a softer, feminine exterior that hides a more contracted, strong interior. Rounder eyes on men indicate a sensitive artistic nature. In general, men are born with narrower eyes, indicating a strong, active constitution, with a harder, more muscled exterior. Women born with narrower eyes are fairly athletic.

The study of the eyes can be a lifelong pursuit, but for the daily purpose of keeping track of your own health, you'll want to examine the eye whites, pupils, and irises. The eyes should be clear and vibrant, with clear whites, responsive pupils, and sharp irises.

In the white of the eye, most of us show a couple of blood vessels. That's pretty normal, even though any broken vessels indicate an imbalance somewhere in the body. If you see six or more broken vessels in the whites of your eyes, you are seeing the beginning signs of illness. Yet these lines can change daily, influenced strongly by what we are eating. For example, if you eat animal protein, ice cream, alcohol, or other extreme foods, your eyes will most likely show broken blood vessels in the whites, reflecting stress on the stomach, liver, and intestines. A diet rich in whole grains, beans, and vegetables results in clear whites of the eyes.

Small brown or black spots in the whites of the eyes can reflect more serious stagnation. These spots indicate sluggish energy in the body that is beginning to accumulate in various organs, with results like cysts, kidney stones, or poor circulation.

If the whites of the eyes appear cloudy yellow, this is an indication of mucus forming in the gallbladder, owing to an excess of soft fat in the diet. This is quite common, even in people who eat a plant-based diet, if they are consuming lots of dairy, fried foods, or even vegetable fats. If the whites appear to be cloudy bluish gray, the energy in the kidneys is sluggish from too much animal fat, eggs, shellfish, or salt. If the color is a cloudy brown, this indicates that the majority of your organs' functions are becoming sluggish. With any of these symptoms, a diet change is in order to restore the eye whites to their natural clarity.

The pupil of the eye should be clearly defined and quick to respond to stimulation, not remaining dilated or constricted when the light level changes. The ability of the pupil to respond indicates how well our autonomic nervous system is working. If the nervous system has grown weak or sluggish, the pupil response to stimulation will be slow or impaired. A diet rich in animal fat and protein, hot stimulating foods, alcohol, and caffeine will cause the pupils to respond erratically. Balancing the diet with natural, whole foods, like whole grains, beans, and vegetables, will bring things back into focus.

The iris is similar to the whites of the eyes, revealing an overall state of health. The study of the iris is a complex and fascinating journey, but for our purposes, I'll just give general guidelines. If you look closely at the eye, you'll notice a thin border encircling the pupil. This border indicates the state of the nervous system, and in good health, it will be sharply defined. Any cloudiness here could mean that the nervous response is sluggish. Around the outer rim of the iris, you'll notice another thin border, which again indicates a strong nervous system if clearly defined. An appearance of a milky white or gray rim around the iris is an indication that your cholesterol is high.

Finally, the iris is similar to the whites of the eyes in that any spots or dots not part of your eye color can indicate sluggish organ function, cysts, or kidney stones. Balancing the diet with more grains and vegetables will return the eyes to their natural bright alertness.

The Eyelids

Even your eyelids tell you something about your health. First, there's blinking. A healthy person blinks four times each minute—more frequent blinking indicates that you are eating a bit too much sweet food, caffeine, or other stimulants, making the eyes sensitive to light. Less than four blinks each minute indicates a diet that is dense and includes animal protein, fat, and salt.

Examining your eyelids can tell you even more, especially if you're feeling a bit off. Gently pull down the lower lid, exposing the skin under the eyeball. This area should be moist and a healthy pink. If pale, you could be anemic. Dark leafy greens and a few sea vegetables can improve your blood quality quickly. If this area is bright red, your body could be battling some kind of infection. Home remedies can be helpful here or a visit to your family doctor. If you see any defined spots here, the body is accumulating hard fat in organ tissue. Increasing your intake of fiber (from whole grains and vegetables) while reducing the accumulating fat will restore organ efficiency.

Your upper eyelids reflect the condition of the liver. They should be firm and supple. If they grow loose and begin to droop, the liver is growing flaccid from too much fat and sugar in the diet. Refining the diet to include more whole grains and vegetables will help the skin return to its natural firmness.

The tiny hollows at the inner corners of each eye should be open and clear, free of mucus. If sticky, yellow liquid accumulates here in the morning, your diet is a bit too high in cheese, eggs, or even vegetable oil. If the liquid is whitish, animal and milk proteins are accumulating in the body.

If the tender skin under your eyes either looks as though you were on the receiving end of a large fist or is so puffy your eyes look like slits, your kidneys need your attention. With appropriate dietary changes, you may never need concealer or cold cucumber slices again.

If you have puffiness under the eyes, it is an indication of sluggish kidney function. Soft, puffy flesh means that the body is taking in more fluid than the kidneys can handle. You may also be taking in too much salt or soft dairy fat, like ice cream or yogurt, causing the body to retain fluid. The kidneys are growing loose and flaccid or sluggish with accumulated fat, making them unable to contract and expel fluids. By addressing your diet, you will restore the efficiency of kidney function, making a change in your appearance that will be remarkable.

Harder puffiness indicates that the kidneys are growing hard from accumulating tougher fat. Usually, consuming animal protein, chicken, eggs, shellfish, and hard salty cheese causes this condition. Even simply reducing your intake of these foods will return your eyes to normal. Both of these conditions are usually accompanied by a pale, washed-out complexion, fatigue, and low back pain. Tired kidneys make you look and feel tired and achy.

And then there are the dark circles. Any discoloration under the eyes means that the circulation of blood through the kidneys is growing sluggish, making the kidneys hard, tight, and dry. In most of us, this appears as reddish purple coloring. Usually, this is the result of a diet of dense foods, animal protein, hard salty foods, eggs, shellfish, and excessive amounts of hard baked flour products and nuts. In more serious conditions of kidney impairment, the area under the eye will look darker purple and maybe even show broken vessels. This occurs if the condition is ignored and a diet change isn't made. If the kidneys don't get relief, a painful, tight low back will occur. A diet rich in whole grains, beans, and moisture-rich vegetables is just the ticket to turn you bright-eyed once again, as the kidneys relax and work efficiently.

But what if those circles come from not sleeping well? Why don't you sleep well? Because your kidneys are hard and tight, with impaired function, leaving you unable to rest deeply to rejuvenate the body.

In either case, puffiness or dark circles, a Ginger Compress (page 259) can help restore the kidneys to health.

Any well-defined spots under the eyes can be a sign that kidney stones are forming. Stones are the result of a diet rich in animal fat, salty snacks, eggs, and shellfish. A natural, low-fat diet rich in plant foods and whole grains, especially barley, can help dissolve the stones.

Here's an eye condition that is really interesting. In Japanese diagnosis, this condition is known as *sanpaku,* meaning "three whites." It is a sign of extreme imbalance in the body—one that you don't really want to see—in yourself or anyone you encounter.

At birth, the iris sits partially below the bottom rim of the eye, looking like a sunrise, with the whites of the eyes showing on both sides and on top of the iris. This is normal in infants, and the eyes will roll upward to the position of a mature adult as the child grows. In a healthy adult, the iris sits on the lower rim of the eye, with whites showing on either side. As we age and approach the end of our life, the eyes begin to roll up, showing whites on both sides and below the iris, as the eyes roll back in the head at the end of life.

That is the normal cycle of life. Imbalance comes when you see "three whites" at times of life when they are not a normal progression of the cycle. The most common

Sanpaku

Normal

Reverse Sanpaku

imbalance in our culture is showing three whites on both sides and the bottom of the iris. This is a sign that the body has grown deeply imbalanced and is beginning to weaken, even degenerate. Unfortunately, as we continue to eat a modern, processed diet, devoid of life, this condition grows more common. When the body weakens, our judgment is impaired and we are likely to make poor decisions that can result in accidents. The good news is that this condition is easily turned around, through diet and lifestyle changes that bring the body back into balance.

Reverse sanpaku is the opposite condition, meaning three whites showing on either side and on top of the iris, and is an indication of serious mental imbalance, with a tendency toward violence. And this one's hard to change, because the power to reason and listen is greatly diminished, as the body has become extremely contracted. When the body grows that constricted, energy can no longer enter. On top of that, strong contraction in the body prevents release of energy, and so it builds and builds and finally explodes, many times in the form of violence.

The Nose

The nose will show a great deal about our day-to-day condition. The bridge of the nose reflects the health of our liver function, so if the color is clear and uniform, your liver is doing great. Redness or pimples mean the liver is overworked and aggravated. An oily nose indicates that the liver is overcome with fat that is accumulating in the body. If the bridge of the nose shows broken vessels, then the liver is working hard to filter an excessive intake of alcohol. Of course, it takes time to get the liver to this point; this is not a condition that develops after a glass of wine with dinner.

At the top of the bridge is the area between the eyebrows. This little space tells us a lot. Any vertical creases between the brows mean that the liver is growing tight—from animal fat, alcohol, shellfish, salt, and eggs. Even too much vegetable fat can cause these little wrinkles. The good news is that these little frown or liver lines are as changeable as our diets—eating well eliminates them completely, in some cases overnight. Except in cases of cirrhosis, the liver has the ability to regenerate itself and will be completely renewed within a six-month period.

If you should notice a horizontal line across the top of the bridge of the nose, you might want to consider cutting back the amount of sugar you consume, including granulated sugar, brown sugar, raw sugar, organic sugar, honey, molasses, maple syrup, chemical sweeteners, and even fruit and fruit juice. This line, although small, is big trouble. The pancreas has become hard and tight, unable to regulate blood sugar levels properly. Its ability to release insulin and glucagon is severely impaired. This is not a little wrinkle to ignore. It's time to pay attention to your health.

At the tip of your nose, you are looking at the health of your heart. If the tip of your nose is reddened or enlarged or both (think W. C. Fields), you have an enlarged heart that is working a bit too hard for its own good. This is usually caused by blood vessels becoming constricted from accumulated fat that inhibits blood flow to the heart, making it pump harder and harder. Even a physically active person can show this condition if their diet is rich in animal fat, dairy foods, cheese, eggs, shellfish, caffeine, hot stimulating spices, sugar, and alcohol. A more balanced diet, rich in whole grains, beans, and vegetables and void of so many extreme foods, along with moderate physical activity, will help improve circulation and can right the condition. The Body Scrub (page 260) is incredibly helpful with this condition, as it stimulates circulation.

The Mouth

With the mouth, constitution is again the first consideration. Ideally, the mouth is about the same width as the nose, which indicates balanced organ development. The "rosebud mouth" that we find so appealing is the picture of health and vitality. A wide mouth is an indication of a more delicate constitution, with a naturally weaker digestive system. Interestingly, wide mouths are more

the standard these days, the result of a culture that consistently eats a diet composed of highly processed foods; animal protein; fatty, greasy foods; and sugar—all of which weaken and inhibit digestion.

The area of your mouth just above your lip shows the strength of your reproductive organs. In a healthy woman, this skin is clear, free of hair, and without blemishes or discoloration. Hair on a woman's upper lip (or chin, for that matter) is an indication that the reproductive organs are accumulating more protein than they need and are discharging it as hair. Even women who eat excessive amounts of vegetable protein can see these conditions. Simply cut back a bit on protein, increase your intake of whole grains—especially barley—and use lots of high-fiber vegetables, and you'll never wax or bleach or pluck again. In men, however, you want to see strong, vital facial hair. It indicates efficient processing of protein—and virility.

If this area is discolored, usually grayish (in either sex), it shows that the sex organs are growing sluggish and stagnant, accumulating fat, usually as a result of animal protein, sugar, eggs, and dairy foods. Clearing the diet of these kinds of dense, hard-to-digest foods will clear out the gray color. It may take some time, as the reproductive organs are deep in the body and love to accumulate fat.

Every now and then, you'll notice someone with a horizontal wrinkle across the upper lip that shows mostly when he or she is smiling. In women, this indicates chronic menstrual problems or possibly even fibroids. In men, it can mean that sexual energy is growing weak and the prostate is enlarged. In both cases, this symptom is the result of excess amounts of dairy foods, which can inhibit smooth sexual function. Vertical lines in the upper lips show drying and shriveling reproductive organs and a diminishing sexual appetite—you see this most often in older people, especially if they are no longer in a relationship or have grown inactive in their relationship.

The top lip itself shows the health of the stomach. The lower lip shows the condition of the intestines, and the corners of the mouth show how well the duodenum is working (the exit from the stomach, which is connected to the liver, gallbladder, and spleen).

If the digestive system is growing flaccid and weak, from sugar, tropical fruit, soft dairy, excess liquid, chemical sweeteners, alcohol, or caffeine, the lips will appear overly full, look puffy and swollen. Curiously, what we admire in full lips—what we call seductive or "bee stung"—may, in fact, be an indication of poor digestion.

If, on the other hand, the lips are tight and grow so thin that the pink color seems to disappear, the intestines are growing tight and contracted, dry, and immobile. Yet another symptom of an accumulation of hard animal fat, eggs, poultry, shellfish, hard salty cheese, salty snacks, or even hard dry baked products like pretzels and chips. In both cases, a diet of whole grains, beans, and vegetables will rebalance the intestines and restore their function. The result will be normal-sized lips, equal in size, that reflect your ethnic background.

If you notice that the corners of your mouth crack or break or sprout tiny blemishes, then the valve between the stomach and duodenum has grown sluggish, causing energy to stagnate in the stomach and digestive tract. Cracking is the result of animal protein and salt. Pimples are the result of fat accumulating and trying to discharge.

Dry, chapped lips, especially if it's a chronic condition, indicates an accumulation of hardened fat in the intestines and stomach, preventing moisture from passing from the organs to the body. Simply increasing the amount of fiber in your diet, along with whole grains and vegetables, will change this condition very quickly.

When your face is relaxed, your lips should rest together, for a gently closed mouth. If the lips hang loosely open, it indicates that the body is growing weak and the organs are becoming flaccid, most likely from working too hard to digest food that is inappropriate for you and your lifestyle.

The Chin

The chin reveals the condition of the reproductive system (like the upper lip). A healthy chin matches the color of the rest of the face, is firm, but not tight, and is free of blemishes—and in women, free of hair. Redness, irregularities, or blemishes show that excess fat is hardening and trying to discharge from the sexual organs. A puckered texture can be an indication that fibroids are forming. Caused by animal protein, particularly chicken and eggs, this condition is quite common because of the high volume of poultry we consume.

Pale color indicates soft dairy fat accumulating in the reproductive system, causing sluggish function and lack of sexual vitality. With this condition, if you gently squeeze the chin, you will feel irregular hardness and softness. In both cases, eliminating the foods that cause the trouble and balancing the diet with whole grains, beans, and vegetables will restore normal reproductive function.

The Cheeks

Cheeks reflect the condition of the lungs, so any pimples, redness or broken capillaries that show here indicate inflammation of the tissue, usually as a result of excessive build-up of hardened protein, fat, sugar, or dry flour products in the intestines. The intestines regulate moisture in the body, determining the efficiency of lung function, which relies on proper moisture balance.

Restoring balance to the lungs is a matter of restoring balance to the diet. In the case of redness and pimples, pay attention to the excessive mucus and fluid that have gathered in the lung tissue. Dairy products, animal fat, and sugar will cause this kind of congestion. If the cheeks are dry or flaky, the lungs are dry and tight, from dense proteins, excessive salt, or too many hard flour products. A change in diet that brings more moisture into the body will restore the supple softness to the cheeks.

The Skin

The skin is the largest organ, taking in and letting go of whatever we need. As far as the face goes, we want our skin to be supple and soft, glowing with vitality. We want uniform color; a delicate shininess; and to be free of spots, lines, discoloration, and blemishes. The skin on the face indicates our overall well-being.

Discoloration of the skin is caused by extreme foods and can be easily remedied by rebalancing the diet. Redness anywhere on the face indicates that the heart is overworking, driving broken capillaries to the surface. This can be caused by an excessive intake of animal foods—even fish—or salt. Note that there's a significant difference between a red face and blushing, which is actually quite healthy, reflecting active circulation that responds to stimulation. Brown shadows showing on the face shows that the gallbladder and liver are overworked and aggravated, most likely caused by an excessive intake of eggs, chicken, or shellfish. If the skin takes on a yellow cast, you'd best take care of your liver and pancreas, as they are overworked and unable to keep up with you. Bile is actually being dumped into the blood instead of being excreted, creating jaundice, because the liver is having difficulty discharging excess protein. A diet change that reduces eggs, shellfish, hard fats, and salt and loads up on vegetables will help restore normal organ function and skin color.

Pale, milky skin is caused by dairy food. A very common shade of skin in our modern world, where dairy food rules our diets, this symptom indicates that all of our organs are accumulating dairy fat, with sluggish function. The skin can no longer discharge fat, so it's gathering under the surface of the skin. Because the skin can no longer breathe, it can't take in nutrients or discharge excesses.

A pale yellowish color, however, can be a sign of respiratory difficulties, like asthma or allergies. A complexion with a yellow cast indicates mucus gathering in the lungs and liver, preventing the discharge of protein, causing bile to back up into the blood.

Grayish color on the face is quite common today. It shows that the liver is growing quite hard and swollen, resulting in thick skin that lacks sensitivity. Animal protein and shellfish as well as hard salty dairy products in your diet cause circulation to grow quite sluggish, which over time will weaken the heart and our ability to oxygenate the blood.

Freckles, on the other hand, are an attempt by the body to discharge excess sugar. The expansive nature of sugar draws melanin to the surface of the skin in the form of little spots. Eliminating simple sugars from the diet will help these fade and eventually go away completely. There can be a predisposition to freckling, but our diets can cause them to surface.

Perhaps the most serious condition is indicated by a purple cast to the skin that indicates severe degeneration of the heart and the high probability for an imminent heart attack. This condition arises when a person has ignored all the signs of imbalance in the body, allowing it to deteriorate severely.

The texture of your facial skin is also diet driven. Coarse, rough skin is caused by excessive animal protein, whereas dry, scaly skin can be caused by eggs, salt, fish, shellfish, hard baked flour products, and hard dairy products.

Oily skin is caused by fatty foods, soft dairy (like butter, ice cream, or yogurt), and even vegetable oils. If you struggle with your "T zone" (chin, nose, and forehead), it indicates that the reproductive organs, liver, and intestines are accumulating fat in them, and need your attention. This is more than an inconvenience. Balancing your diet will balance the skin texture, dryness, moisture, and, more important, organ function.

Wet, moist skin, like a damp face or sweaty palms, indicates that the kidneys are overworked and "flooded" with excess moisture. Your diet needs to be balanced—less liquid, especially in the form of soft fats and sugar, with more fiber and salt to dry things up a bit.

Hair

Our culture seems to be obsessed with hair. We spend billions of dollars to make it healthy and shiny. We can apply any amount of gels and liquids to the surface of the hair, but hair, like the rest of the body, is what you eat.

Although we are born with certain characteristics of our hair—color, waviness, texture—we create the rest—oiliness, brittleness, weakness. Our diet determines the day-to-day quality of our hair, including gray hair. As the body ages, its ability to assimilate minerals becomes impaired, and the hair will lose its color and luster. This occurs naturally, to some degree, as we age, so it is normal to see this in older people. Premature gray hair—in people under fifty—is often a sign of malnutrition in the most literal sense. Either digestion is compromised from an inferior diet or the diet is loaded with sugar, which leaches minerals from the body.

Hair reflects the condition of the intestines. Head hair is an outgrowth of the strength of our intestinal flora. Strong, flexible hair is a sign of great intestinal fortitude, and when we have fortitude, we have confidence. That's the connection between great hair days and a great mood. Feeling and looking

good is about feeling strong, not weak or sluggish or dull.

Whether hair is oily or dry is caused completely by diet. Healthy hair is flexible and shiny, able to go several days without washing before feeling dirty. An excess of animal, dairy or vegetable fat, or sugar in the diet causes oily or slick hair. This condition is easily remedied by reducing the intake of extreme foods and including foods that can help clean the digestive tract of accumulating fat and mucus, like barley, daikon, and shiitake mushrooms, as well as other whole grains and vegetables.

Dry, brittle, lifeless hair comes from a dry, brittle diet, rich in foods that tax and constrict the intestines—animal protein, excessive salt, white flour, alcohol, caffeine, hot stimulants, hard cheeses, too little fiber, and lack of moisture. A diet too low in fat can cause this symptom as well. To remedy this condition may take a while, because the hair must grow out, but it can be accomplished by adding more vegetable fat to the diet, reducing extreme foods, and loading up on moisture-rich veggies to create healthy intestinal function.

Baldness is the bane of many men (and in these modern times, more and more women). It is a sign that internal organ function has weakened considerably. Organ function is also reflected on the top of the head, so if you're losing your hair or it's thinning in any of these areas, the corresponding organ is growing weak. Although I have never seen hair grow back, I have heard stories that it does, with a diet change. Either way, premature baldness is a strong sign to pay attention to your health.

These simple diagnostic techniques will help you become aware of what is happening in your body. And you will find that even minor adjustments to your diet and lifestyle will have a dramatic and visible effect.

FACIAL AREAS AND THEIR CORRESPONDING ORGANS

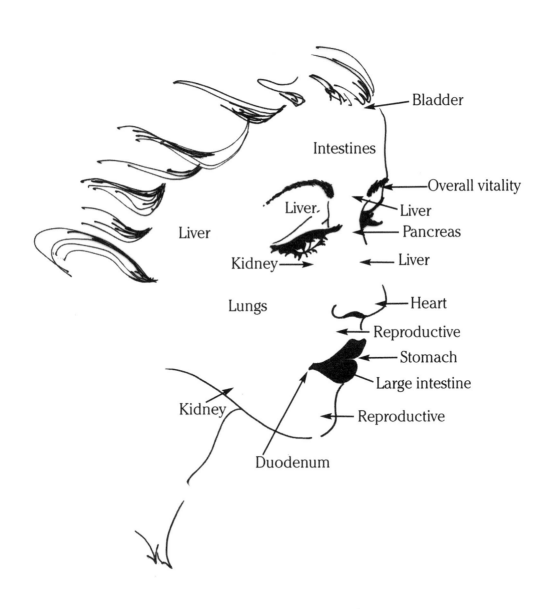

GLOSSARY

Become familiar with the more exotic foods you find in these pages. The more you cook, the more fun you will have experimenting with different foods and flavors. Preparing natural foods can be a wonderful culinary adventure. This section can help you understand what it is you are buying and how to use it to create delicious, healthy meals.

Agar-agar Also called kanten in Asian shops, agar is a gelatin-like food made from various types of red algae. The algae fronds are harvested and dried and boiled in iron kettles. The resulting liquid is allowed to set and is then placed in the sun to dry and bleach. This process takes about 10 days. After drying, the flaky gelatin is finally packaged in bars.

Agar flakes are made from another type of sea vegetable. A more modern product, agar flakes are easier to process and use and have more concentrated bonding properties.

Almonds Fruit kernels of the almond tree. They keep best when purchased in their thin brown skins, which protect their freshness and flavor.

Amaranth A very tiny, brownish yellow seed, high in protein and lysine. It has an earthy, nutty flavor and cooks quite quickly

Amasake A fermented sweet rice drink with the texture of milk. It is a creamy base for custards, puddings, and frostings, not to mention a wonderfully satisfying drink on its own.

Anasazi beans A native American burgundy-and-white bean, similar in taste and texture to pinto beans. Their slightly sweet taste makes them ideal in Mexican-style bean dishes.

Arame A large-leaf sea vegetable, arame is finely shredded and boiled before being dried and packaged for sale. Because it is precooked, it requires far less cooking time than other sea vegetables. One of the milder-tasting sea plants, it is a great source of protein and minerals like calcium and potassium.

Arrowroot A high-quality starch made from a tropical tuber of the same name, used for thickening much the same way as cornstarch is used. Arrowroot has virtually no taste and becomes clear when cooked, making it ideal as a thickener for puddings, gravies, and sauces. Less expensive than kuzu, it can be used interchangeably in recipes.

Azuki beans Azuki beans are small and very compact, with a deep, reddish brown color. These tiny beans are a staple in the Far East. Originally cultivated in Japan and revered for their healing properties, they are quite low in fat and are reputed to be more digestible than most other beans as well as a good source of vitamin B_{12}, potassium, and iron.

Baking powder A leavening agent made up of baking soda, cream of tartar, and either cornstarch or arrowroot. Double-acting baking powder releases carbon dioxide on contact with liquid, creating the air pockets responsible for the light texture in baked goods. Always try to purchase nonaluminum baking powder so that sodium aluminum sulfate is not released into your foods, possibly compromising your health. Baking powder is more perishable than you might think, not lasting to the date on the can. Store in a cool, dry place for the best shelf life.

Balsamic vinegar Italian vinegar made from white Trebbiano grapes. The vinegar becomes a deep, rich amber color during aging in wooden barrels. The best balsamic vinegars are syrupy, a bit sweet, and a little more expensive than other vinegars, but well worth it.

Bancha See *Kukicha*.

Barley Said to be the oldest cultivated grain, barley is native to Mesopotamia, where it was mainly used to make bread and ferment beer. Used by ancient cultures, barley even served as currency in Sumeria. In Europe, barley has been replaced by wheat and rye, but it is still the staple grain of many countries in the Far and Middle East, Asia, and South America. In modern cultures, barley serves to make everything from livestock feed to malted whisky to tea to miso. By itself, however, barley is a great, low-fat grain, chock-full of nutrients. Delicious when cooked with other whole grains and in soups and salads.

Barley malt A sweetener or grain honey made from sprouted barley that is cooked into a sweet syrup. The barley is simply steeped in water and germinated. The sprouted or malted barley is then heated to bring out the flavor and cooked until a thick syrup forms. The syrup contains dextrin, maltose, various minerals, and protein. It adds wonderful depth to baked beans, roasted squash, and savory baked goods.

Beans See individual listings.

Black-eyed peas Medium-size beans with an oblong shape, they have a distinctive black spot on their ivory surface. In the same family as yard-long beans, the pods can indeed grow three feet long. Native to Africa, black-eyed peas were brought to Europe and North America, where they became a staple in cooking, being paired with collard greens for a most delicious supper, nicely complemented with hearty corn bread.

Black soybeans Rounder and more plump than black turtle beans, black soybeans are renowned in Asia for their restorative effects on the reproductive organs. Incredibly sweet and rich, but requiring soaking or roasting and a long cooking time, these beans are well worth the extra effort.

Black turtle beans A sturdy, very satisfying common bean. Earthy and mildly sweet, these beans go well with stronger seasonings, like those commonly used in Brazilian, Caribbean, and Mexican dishes, and make great creamy soups.

Bran A fiber-rich layer just beneath the hull of whole grains that protects the endosperm or germ of the grain. Bran is a great source of calcium, carbohydrates, and phosphorus and is the main reason for eating grains in their whole form.

Brown rice syrup See *Rice Syrup*.

Brown rice vinegar A vinegar traditionally made by the agricultural communities of Japan, it is composed of brown rice, cultured rice (koji), seed vinegar from the previous year, and well water. The vinegar is then fermented for nine to ten months. Brown rice vinegar has a sharp taste and is used for everything from salad dressings to preserving vegetables. It is also commonly used in sushi rice for flavor and for its preservative properties.

Buckwheat (kasha) Also known as Saracen corn, buckwheat was reportedly brought to Europe by the Crusaders from the Middle East, although it originated in the Himalayan Mountains. In botanical terms, buckwheat is not really a grain; it is actually a member of the rhubarb family, with its fruit or groats that resemble tiny, dark-colored nuts.

Grown under adverse conditions in cold weather, buckwheat is very strengthening and warming, containing more protein than most other grains, as well as iron and B vitamins. A natural source of rutic acid, which aids in arterial and circulatory problems, buckwheat is used by many homeopaths for high blood pressure and other circulatory difficulties.

Cooked by itself, buckwheat makes a great porridge, grain dish, or even salad. A very traditional recipe involves sautéing onions and noodles and then tossing them with cooked kasha. Ground into flour, buckwheat is the chief ingredient used to make traditional Japanese soba noodles.

Bulgur (cracked wheat) Made from whole-wheat berries that are cracked into pieces, enabling them to cook quite quickly. A great breakfast cereal, bulgur is most commonly associated with tabouleh, a marinated bulgur salad combining tomatoes, onions, and cucumbers with an aromatic olive oil dressing.

Burdock A wild, hearty plant from the thistle family. According to traditional medicine, this long, dark brown root is renowned as one of nature's finest blood purifiers and skin clarifiers. A strong, dense root vegetable, burdock has a very centering, grounding energy, and is most commonly used in stews and long-simmered sautés.

Cannellini beans Creamy white oval beans most commonly used in the Italian dish pasta e fagioli. Their creamy texture makes them ideal for purees, dips, and creamy soups.

Canola oil Expressed from rapeseeds, this light oil is substantially lower in saturated fats than other oils and also contains omega-3 fatty acids. Virtually tasteless, it is good for baking and salad dressings, but kind of bland for sautéing. Use only organic; conventional oil can be from genetically altered seeds.

Capers Little pickled flower buds, most commonly used in Mediterranean cooking. Salty and briny in taste, they really add flavor to sauces and salads. If they taste too strong for you, simply rinse lightly before use.

Caraway seeds Traditionally used in rye bread, caraway seeds have a distinctive,

hearty taste, making them ideal for seasoning savory stews and other vegetable dishes. Their pungent taste is quite strong, so use sparingly.

Carob Renowned as a substitute for chocolate by natural foods enthusiasts, carob doesn't taste much like chocolate, so true devotees are rarely fooled. Carob is most commonly used in powdered form, which is made from grinding roasted, tropical pods. Its natural sweet taste and dark, rich color are what gained it its reputation as a substitute for chocolate. It is higher in simple sugars than chocolate; I don't really recommend it.

Cashews A tropical nut quite high in fat, with a rich, luscious flavor for creams and nut milks.

Chervil An aromatic herb with lacy fernlike leaves that tastes quite like tarragon. It tastes best when used fresh.

Chestnuts Their rich texture and taste belie the fact that chestnuts are in fact quite low in fat, making them an ideal ingredient in many recipes. At their peak in the fall, fresh chestnuts are a wonderful addition to soups, stews, and vegetable dishes. Their natural sweet taste makes them a great dessert ingredient. Dried chestnuts are available year-round and, with presoaking, achieve as creamy and sweet a taste and texture as their fresh counterparts.

Chickpeas (garbanzo beans) Beige round beans with a wonderful nutty taste and creamy texture when cooked. Traditionally used when making humus, a creamy spread combining chickpeas with olive oil, lemon juice, and a bit of garlic. Also wonderful combined with sweet vegetables or corn and in soups and stews.

Chiles Available fresh and dried, they range from mildly spicy to blazing hot. Remember that the real heat comes from the seeds, so removing them reduces the fire. I recommend you wear rubber gloves when removing seeds so the oil, containing capsaicin, doesn't get on your hands—and then into your eyes when you rub them. It takes several hours, even with washing, to remove the oil, so trust me on this one. Ancho chipotles and jalapeños are the most common varieties used in cooking today.

Chili powder A powdered blend of ground chilies, ranging from mild to hot, combined with oregano, cumin, garlic, and salt. Add it slowly to dishes, adjusting the spicy taste as you go along, so your dish doesn't get too hot. The hot taste increases as you cook it.

Chocolate Do I really need to define chocolate? I suppose not, but perhaps I should define its rare appearances in this book. Energetically, chocolate is highly stimulating and agitating, giving the consumer a great high followed by a very depressing crash of blood sugar. Chocolate also loves stealing minerals from our organs and cells, forcing them to pull minerals from our blood for nourishment, causing everything from cravings to overeating. I reserve the use of chocolate for very special occasions.

Corn Native to South America, corn has been used for over ten thousand years. It has become the staple grain for the entire North American continent. Today, corn is cultivated worldwide and is one of the most popular grains used in cooking.

Corn requires hot summer sun and rain to flourish, and grows quickly. Often eaten by itself as the popular corn on the cob, the grain has practically limitless other culinary uses, including flour, meal, grits, tortillas, syrup, oil, bourbon, and popcorn (from one variety of the grain).

Corn grits A cracked form of dried corn. Corn grits make a great polenta, creamy breakfast cereal, and texturizer for soups.

Cornmeal Dried field corn ground into a coarse flour. Used to make creamier polentas, this flour is most commonly used in cornbreads, tortillas, and corn chips.

Corn oil A golden-colored oil with a rich, buttery taste, ideally suited to whole-grain baking. Its full-bodied texture and light taste give baked goods a moist crumb.

Couscous A staple of North Africa, this rolled durum wheat product has been stripped of its bran and germ, made into a thick paste, steamed and then dried in the form of small granules. It cooks quite quickly, and its starchy texture makes it a great ingredient for loaves, patties, and soups.

Daikon A long, white radish root with a refreshingly clean, peppery taste. Commonly used in salads and side dishes, soups, and stews. Frequently served in Asian restaurants with fish or oily dishes, because it is reputed to aid in the digestion of fat and protein as well as help the body assimilate oil and cleanse organ tissue. Also available in dried, shredded form to be used in various stews and hearty vegetable dishes.

Dulse Dried dulse has a rich, red color, is high in potassium, and comes packaged in large, wrinkled leaves. Its salty, rich taste makes it a great snack right out of the package. Because it is so delicate, it actually requires little or no cooking, just a quick rinse to remove any debris on the leaves. It adds depth of flavor to hearty soups and stews.

Fava beans Available both fresh and dried, favas are used extensively in Mediterranean cooking. These large, chunky beans have a rich, earthy flavor that will remind you of split peas, but they do not get quite as creamy; they retain a soft, potato-like texture.

Flageolets Light ivory beans with a very subtle taste. Highly esteemed in French cooking, these beans are best in simple recipes that showcase their delicate flavor.

Flax seeds Richer than soybeans in omega-3 fatty acids and rich in vitamin E, they have a sweet, nutty flavor. When boiled and whipped with apple juice, they make a good binder and leavener in baked goods, in place of eggs. On their own, flax seeds have a laxative effect on the body and so should be consumed in moderation.

Flour Flour is any ground meal of whole grains. Try to choose only whole-grain flours, because these retain a bit of germ and bran and, therefore, are not completely devoid of nutrients. Also look for stone-ground flours, as these are not processed with extreme heat, which also can destroy nutrients. For the best shelf life, store flour in tightly sealed containers in either the refrigerator or the freezer.

Fu A meat substitute developed by vegetarian Buddhist monks, fu is made of dried wheat gluten. A good source of protein, fu can be used in various soups and stews by simply reconstituting it in water.

Ginger A golden-colored, spicy root vegetable with a variety of uses in cooking. It imparts a mild, peppery taste to food and is commonly used in stir-fries, sautés, sauces, and dressings. Shaped like the fingers of a hand, ginger has the reputation of stimulating circulation with its hot taste. A very popular remedy in Asian medicine for helping with everything from joint pain to stomachaches.

Gluten The protein found in wheat, although it is also found in smaller amounts in other grains, like oats, rye, and barley. When kneaded in dough, gluten becomes elastic and holds air pockets released by the leavener, helping bread to rise. Gluten is also used to prepare seitan, a meat substitute made from wheat gluten.

Great Northern beans Medium-size white beans, they hold their shape very well in cooking, making them ideal ingredients in bean salads as well as in heartier bean dishes that complement their subtle flavor.

Hato mugi barley Also known as Job's tears, this grain is large pearled barley with a beige, translucent skin. A good source of iron, protein, and calcium, hato mugi is reputed in Asia to create beautiful, flawless skin, owing to its ability to cleanse the blood and remove hard fat deposits from beneath the skin.

Hazelnuts (filberts) Shaped like a large chickpea, hazelnuts have a very bitter outer skin that needs to be removed before eating. These guys love chocolate.

Herbs Simply defined, herbs are the leaves and stems of certain plants used in cooking because of their unique, aromatic flavors. Available fresh or dried, herbs add rich, full-bodied taste to soups, stews, and salad dressings, among other things. When using fresh herbs, remember to use three to four times the amount of dried, because drying concentrates their natural flavor. Try to buy your herbs in natural foods stores, because you can be assured that these herbs are not irradiated, as most commercial brands are.

Hiziki (hijiki) Sold in its dry form, hiziki resembles black angel hair pasta. It is one of the strongest-tasting of all sea plants, so soaking it for several minutes before cooking can gentle its briny flavor. Lightly sautéing it in sesame oil before stewing can really bring forth its inherent sweet taste. It is a great companion food to vegetables like carrots, corn, squash, and onions, but it is a bit strong for delicate soups.

Horseradish A root vegetable known for its sharp, hot taste. Actually a member of the mustard family, horseradish adds real zing to any dish. It is truly wonderful freshly grated and stirred into bean dishes or grain salads or served with fish.

Kidney beans Available in a variety of shapes and colors, kidney beans are most commonly recognized in their deep-red all-American shape. Full-flavored and hearty, kidney beans hold up incredibly well in chilies, stews, soups, salads, and casseroles.

Kombu (kelp) A sea vegetable packaged in wide, dark, dehydrated strips that will double in size upon soaking and cooking. Kombu is a great source of glutamic acid, a natural flavor enhancer, so adding a small piece to soups and stews deepens flavor. It is also generally believed that kombu improves the digestibility of grains and beans when added to these foods in small amounts.

Kukicha A Japanese tea made from the stems and twigs of the tea bush.

Kuzu (kudzu) Kuzu is a high-quality starch made from the root of the kuzu plant. A root native to the mountains of Japan (and now in the southern United States), kuzu grows like a vine with tough roots. Used primarily as a thickener, it is reputed to strengthen the digestive tract.

Legumes A large plant family including beans, lentils, peanuts, and peas.

Lentils An ancient legume that comes in many varieties, from common brown-green lentils to red lentils to yellow lentils to Le puys lentils (a tiny sweet French variety that is great in salads). Very high in protein and with a full-bodied, peppery taste, lentils are good in everything from stews and soups to salads and side dishes.

Lima beans Also known as butter beans, these popular white beans are most commonly used in their dried form, although fresh lima beans are exquisite. Lima beans have a very delicate outer skin, so they seem to do best when cooked in salted water (unlike other beans), which helps hold their skin in place. Once the skins loosen, the limas turn to mush—although then you can use them to cream soups or make dips. Baby lima beans are simply smaller, with tougher skins and a sweeter taste.

Maple syrup A traditional sweetener made by boiling sugar maple sap until it becomes thick. The end product is quite expensive, because it takes about thirty-five gallons of sap to produce one gallon of maple syrup. The syrup is available in various grades of quality from AA to B; AA and A are quite nice for sauces and dressings, but I use grade B in baking. I have found the higher grades can result in hard baked goods. I do not often use maple syrup because it is a simple sugar, releasing quickly in the bloodstream, thus wreaking havoc with blood sugar.

Millet Native to Asia, millet is a tiny grain that once equaled barley as the chief staple of Europe. It was very popular in Japan before the cultivation of rice and is still the staple grain of China, India, and Ethiopia. Millet is a tiny round grain grown in cold weather. An effective alkalizing agent, it aids spleen and pancreas function as well as stomach upset. Millet is very versatile, making delicious grain dishes, creamy soups, stews, porridges, stuffings, and loaves. With its sweet, nutty taste and beautiful yellow color, millet complements most foods well but goes best with sweet vegetables, like squash and corn.

Mirin A Japanese rice wine with a sweet taste and very low alcohol content. Made by fermenting sweet brown rice with water and koji (a cultured rice), mirin adds depth and dimension to sauces, glazes, and various other dishes.

Miso A fermented soybean paste used traditionally to flavor soups but prized in Asia for its ability to strengthen the digestive system. Traditionally aged miso is a great source of high-quality protein. Available in a wide variety of flavors and strengths, the most nutritious miso is made from barley and soybeans and is aged for at least two years—this is the miso used most extensively in daily cooking. Other varieties of misos are used to supplement and to create different tastes in different dishes. Miso is rich in digestive enzymes, but these enzymes are quite delicate and should not be boiled. Just lightly simmering the miso activates and releases their strengthening qualities into food.

Mochi Mochi is made by cooking sweet brown rice and then pounding or extruding it to break the grains, a process that results in a very sticky substance. Flat packages of mochi can be purchased in most natural foods stores. Mochi can be used to create creamy sauces, to give the effect of melted cheese, or to make dumplings in soups. It can be simply cut into small squares and pan-fried, creating tiny turnover-like puffs.

Mung beans Tiny pea-shaped, deep green beans, these are most popular in their sprouted forms, although they cook up quickly, making delightful soups, purees, and Indian dahls. Mung bean sprouts are a delicious addition to any salad or stir-fried dish.

Mustard Mustard in a jar is made by blending dried mustard seeds with vinegar and various spices. The best-quality mustards are Dijon or those that have been stone-ground; these are made from coarse seeds and have a rougher texture.

Navy beans Also called pea beans, these are cream-colored, egg-shaped beans that are the quintessential baked bean. They generally require long, slow cooking but hold up well in the pressure cooker. I have found that they do not have a substantial enough flavor for salads, so I use other white beans for those dishes.

Noodles (pasta) Pasta or noodles are made by combining flour, salt, and water into limitless shapes and sizes. Try to choose pastas made from organic flours, preferably whole grain. These are made from the endosperm of the wheat and contain protein and carbohydrates as well as essential fiber, minerals, and B vitamins. However, even refined semolina pastas have a place in a whole foods diet, lending light taste and texture when desired.

Nori (sea laver) Usually sold in paper-thin sheets, nori is a great source of protein and minerals like calcium and iron. Most well-known as a principal ingredient in sushi, nori has a mild, sweet flavor, just slightly reminiscent of the ocean. Great for garnishing grain and noodle dishes or floating in soup.

Nut butters Thick pastes made from grinding nuts. Although rich in fiber and protein, nut butters are also quite high in fat. Nut butters have intense, rich flavors and are great in sauces, dressings, and baked goods.

Nuts See also individual listings. Nuts are true powerhouses of energy. Bear in mind that nuts have the strength to grow entire trees, so imagine what affect they have on us. But they are wonderful in small amounts for taste and richness.

Oats Native to central Europe and used since Neolithic times, oats are rich in B vitamins and contain one of the highest amounts of protein of any grain, as well as iron and calcium. Reputed to have a high fat content (which they do), oats contain soluble gums that bind cholesterol in the intestines, preventing its absorption by the body. Most commonly used in modern cultures as oatmeal, a process by which the oat groats are rolled or steel cut, oats are the most delicious when used in their whole state. I use oatmeal flakes mostly to cream soups and thicken sauces as well as in breads, cookies, and croquettes.

Ocean ribbons A brownish green sea vegetable in the kelp family, normally packaged in long, thin strips—ribbons. It has a sweeter taste than kombu and cooks a bit more quickly.

Oil Oils are rich liquids extracted from nuts, seeds, grains, and olives (the only real fruit oil around). A highly refined food source, oils add a rich taste to foods, making dishes more satisfying and creating a warming, vitalizing energy and soft, supple skin and hair. Try to choose oils that are expelled or cold pressed, because these oils were extracted by pressing and not by extreme heat, which can render oil carcinogenic. I try to limit my oil use to only a few of the more digestible varieties, like toasted sesame, light sesame, corn, and olive oil (usually only extra-virgin, which is the oil extracted from the first pressing of the olives and, therefore, the best quality), occasionally adding safflower and canola oil to a recipe. Oils should be stored in a cool place, but it is not necessary to refrigerate oils to prevent rancidity.

Olives Olives are native to semitropical climates and are used sparingly in cooking to add an appealing punch to grain, vegetables, and bean salads. There are almost limitless varieties available, so you can satisfy your taste by choosing anything from the intensely flavored, oil-cured ripe olives, to purple Greek kalamata olives, to green Spanish olives.

Peanuts Although considered a nut, peanuts are in fact legumes and are a good source of protein. Unlike other legumes, peanuts are very high in fat. Because peanuts are one of the most chemically treated of all crops, try to choose organic peanuts. Peanuts are also prone to a carcinogenic mold called aflatoxin, especially if they are stored under humid conditions, so choose peanuts from the arid climate of the Southwest, like Valencia peanuts, to minimize this risk.

Pecans Among the highest in fat, these nuts are one of the most delicious for baking in cookies, pies, and cakes.

Pine nuts (pignoli) Incredibly luscious nuts that are quite expensive, owing to the labor-intensive process involved in their harvesting from pinecones. High in oil and rich in taste, pine nuts add great depth to pasta and grain pilafs. Roasting them enhances their rich taste, making them delightful in any dish.

Pinto beans The most famous Southwestern bean, pintos were actually named by the Spanish, who used the word meaning "painted" for them, because of the red-brown markings on their beige surface. Their nutty taste holds up well in stews, chilies, and baked bean dishes.

Quinoa A tiny seed-like grain native to the Andes mountains. Pronounced *keen'wah*, this small grain packs a powerhouse of protein and numerous amino acids not normally found in large amounts in most whole grains. Quinoa grains are quite delicate, so nature has coated them with an oily substance called saponin. If the grain isn't rinsed well, it can have a bitter taste. Quinoa has a lovely nutty taste and cooks quickly, qualities that make it a great whole-grain addition to your menus.

Rice The staple grain of most whole foods diets, rice is low in fat and rich in vitamins and minerals like calcium, protein, iron, and B vitamins. Rice as we know it was reportedly cultivated in India, spreading from there to Asia and the Middle East. In its whole form, rice is a near perfect food. High in moisture, rice acts as a gentle diuretic, balancing the moisture content of the body and encouraging the elimination of any excess. Polished or white rice, while delicious on occasion, is pretty much devoid of nutrition and should be enjoyed occasionally with whole rice as the staple grain.

The most common strains of rice include short grain, medium grain, and long grain. Short grain, the hardest and most compact variety, is best suited to cooler, temperate climates, whereas medium- and long-grain rice are used in warmer climates and during the summer months. Other gourmet varieties of rice have become popular in today's cooking. These include Arborio, basmati, Texmati,

wehani, black japonica, and red rice. Sweet brown rice, a glutinous variety of brown rice, is commonly used not only as a grain dish but also in mochi, a cake formed by pounding and drying cooked sweet rice.

There are limitless uses for rice in daily cooking: It can be pressure-cooked, steamed, boiled, fried, baked, roasted, sautéed, and used in breads, sushi, casseroles, pilafs, or stuffings.

Rice milk A creamy liquid made by cooking ten parts water to one part rice for one hour; the resulting rice is pressed through a cheesecloth creating "milk." It is also packaged commercially.

Rice syrup (brown rice syrup, yinnie, rice malt) The Japanese call this "liquid sweetness." Rice syrup is a thick, amber syrup made by combining sprouted barley with cooked brown rice and storing it in a warm place. Fermentation begins, and the starches in the rice convert to maltose and some other complex sugars, making this syrup a wonderfully healthy sweetener. Complex sugars release slowly into the bloodstream, providing fuel for the body rather than wreaking havoc on the blood sugar. Rice syrup's wonderful, delicate sweetness makes it ideal for baked goods and other desserts.

Risotto A generic term for a creamy, almost soupy rice dish native to northern Italy. Traditionally made with a specific short-grain white rice called Arborio rice, the perfect risotto is creamy and soupy, while the rice retains a bit of chewy texture.

Rye The Romans began cultivating this Asian grain, thought to be a weed by the Greeks. By the Middle Ages, rye was a staple grain in most of Europe. As opposed to use in its whole form, rye is most commonly used in flour form to make rich, hearty breads. Similar to wheat in composition, rye is a bit less glutinous and, like wheat, can be used by itself to make breads. Rye is, however, delicious when cooked with rice and makes a great whole-grain dish.

Salt All salt is not the same. The quality of the salt we use is quite important. The best quality of salt to use is white, unrefined sea salt with no additives. Unrefined salts are rich in the trace minerals that are destroyed in processed salt.

Sea vegetables The exotic vegetables that are harvested from the sea coast and rocks along the coast are high in protein and rich in minerals. Readily available in natural foods stores in dehydrated form, sea vegetables are not yet widely used in American cooking but are growing in popularity because of their nutritional benefits and interesting taste.

Seeds In a word, seeds are powerhouses. (Remember that they are the source of entire plants, even trees.) That's a lot of energy in a little seed. They are good sources of protein and calcium, but because of their high oil content, seeds perish relatively quickly and keep best refrigerated. The most popular seeds in natural foods cooking include pumpkin seeds (pepitas), poppy seeds, sunflower seeds, and sesame seeds.

Seitan (wheat gluten) Most commonly called wheat meat, seitan is made from wheat gluten. Made by kneading the bran and starch out of flour, raw seitan is rather bland, so most commercial brands are simmered in savory broth before sale. A wonderful source of protein, it is low in calories and fat and is very popular in Asian mock meat dishes as well as in hearty stews and casseroles.

Sesame tahini A thick, creamy paste made from ground hulled sesame seeds, which is used for flavoring everything from sauces to salad dressings to dips, spreads, and baked goods. Available in natural foods stores and Middle Eastern markets, this paste has a delicate nutty flavor that adds luxurious taste to any recipe.

Shiitake mushrooms Gaining popularity over the last several years for their power to lower cholesterol and cleanse blood, shiitake mushrooms can be found in just about any natural foods store and gourmet shop. They have an intensely earthy taste, so a few go a long way. It is necessary to soak them until tender, 15 to 20 minutes before cooking, and I usually trim off the stems to avoid their bitter flavor. They are wonderful in soups, stews, gravies, and sauces and as in home remedies.

Shiso (beefsteak leaf) A lovely herb with large, reddish leaves. A very popular staple in Japanese cooking, shiso is often used in pickling, most commonly in umeboshi plum pickling. Shiso is rich in calcium and iron.

Shoyu A confusing term because it is the generic term for Japanese soy sauce as well as the term for a specific type of traditionally made soy sauce, the distinguishing characteristic of which is the use of cracked wheat as the fermenting starter, along with soybeans. The best shoyu is aged for at least two years. A lighter seasoning than tamari.

Soba A noodle made from buckwheat flour. Some varieties contain other ingredients, like wheat flour or yam flour, but the best-quality soba are those made primarily of buckwheat flour.

Somen (Japanese angel hair pasta) A very fine, white-flour or whole-grain noodle that cooks very quickly, somen are traditionally served in a delicate broth with lightly cooked fresh vegetables.

Soybeans The base bean for many natural foods products, from miso to soy sauce to tofu and tempeh to soy milk to soy flour. On their own, soybeans are rather bland and hard to digest, so they are more commonly used in other products. When cooked on their own, however—long and slow cooking is the only way—soybeans can be most delicious.

Soyfoods A catchall term for the wide range of foods that have soybeans as their base, including soy milk, tofu, soy flour, tempeh, soy sauce, tamari, shoyu, miso, soy cheese, and soy oil.

Soy sauce Traditional soy sauce is the product of fermenting soybeans, water, salt, and wheat. Containing salt and glutamic acid, soy sauce is a natural flavor enhancer. The finest soy sauces are aged for one to two years, whereas commercial soy sauce is synthetically aged in a matter of days, producing a salty artificially flavored condiment.

Spices Spices are highly aromatic seasonings that come from the seed, root, bark, and buds of plants, whereas herbs are obtained from the leaves and stems. Spices generally give food a very strong taste and energy and should be used sparingly and wisely, because overuse can overstimulate the nervous system, causing irritability and excessive aggression. They can also numb the taste buds. Sparing use of spices, however, can be very helpful in getting energy moving when stagnant or stuck. Spices become stale when kept for more than six months, so it is advisable to buy them in quantities that you will use in that time period. Store spices and herbs in well-sealed containers in a cool, dark place to retain potency.

Split peas These dried peas, most commonly available in yellow and green, make wonderful creamy soups.

Tamari A fermented soy sauce product that is actually the liquid that rises to the top of the keg when making miso. This thick, rich flavor enhancer is nowadays produced with a fermentation process similar to that of shoyu, but the starter is wheat-free. Tamari is richer, with a full-bodied taste, and contains more amino acids than regular soy sauce. I prefer the heavier taste of tamari for heartier, winter cooking.

Tempeh A traditional, Indonesian soy product created by fermenting split, cooked soybeans with a starter. As the tempeh ferments, a white mycelium of enzymes develops on the surface, making the soybeans more digestible as well as providing a healthy range of B vitamins. Found in the refrigerator or freezer section of natural foods stores, tempeh is great in everything from sandwiches to salads to stews to casseroles.

Toasted sesame oil An oil extracted from toasted sesame seeds that imparts a wonderful, nutty flavor to sautés, stir-fries, and sauces.

Tofu (soybean curd) Fast becoming a popular low-fat food in our fat-crazed world, tofu is a wonderful source of protein and is both inexpensive and versatile. Rich in calcium and cholesterol-free, tofu is made by extracting curd from coagulated soy milk and then pressing it into bricks. For use in everything from soups and stews to salads, casseroles, and quiches, or as the creamy base to sauces and dressings.

Udon Flat whole-wheat noodles, much like fettuccine. Udon comes in a variety of blends of flours, from all whole wheat to brown rice to unbleached white flour. I prefer the whole wheat.

Umeboshi plum paste A puree made from umeboshi plums to create a concentrated condiment. Use this sparingly, as it is quite salty. It is a great ingredient in salad dressings and sauces.

Umeboshi plums (ume plums) Japanese pickled plums (actually, green apricots) with a fruity, salty taste. Pickled in a salt brine and shiso leaves for at least one year (the longer, the better), ume plums are traditionally served as a condiment with various dishes, including grains. Ume plums are reputed to aid in the cure of a wide array of ailments—from stomachaches to migraines—because they alkalize the blood. These little red "plums" (made red from the shiso, which adds vitamin C and iron) make good preservatives. The best-quality plums are the most expensive ones, but they are used in small amounts, so one jar will last a long time.

Umeboshi plum vinegar A salty liquid left over from pickling umeboshi plums. Used as a vinegar, it is great in salad dressings and pickle making.

Vanilla (pure vanilla extract) A smoky, smooth flavoring made by extracting the essence from vanilla beans and preserving it in alcohol and water, although nowadays you can obtain vanilla preserved without alcohol. Pure vanilla extract is somewhat expensive, but a small bit goes a long way, so splurge and get the best. By the way, inexpensive, artificial vanilla is made from vanillin, a by-product of making paper.

Vegetable stock A flavorful broth made by simmering any variety of finely cut vegetables until they release their flavor and nutrients into the water. A great base for soups and sauces, a good stock is usually made from a combination of vegetables and small quantities of herbs to create a full-bodied broth.

Vinegar A fermented condiment familiar to most people. There is an entire world of vinegars to explore—and a variety of uses for them, way beyond salad dressings. While lots of vinegars exist, they can be very acidic, so I keep my use to brown rice vinegar, sweet brown rice vinegar (both made from fermented brown rice and sweet brown rice), umeboshi vinegar, balsamic vinegar, and—occasionally—a fruity vinegar like raspberry or champagne.

Wakame (alaria) A very delicate member of the kelp family, wakame is most traditionally used in miso soups and tender salads. It requires only a brief soaking and short cooking time and has a very gentle flavor, so it is a great way to add sea vegetables to your diet.

Wasabi A very potent root, comparable to horseradish in taste. Rather fiery wasabi adds quite a kick as a condiment or as an ingredient, so use it sparingly until you become familiar with its potency.

Wheat Called the staff of life, wheat has been the mainstay of foods in temperate climates since the dawn of agriculture. As long ago as 4000 B.C., Egyptians were cultivating yeast and baking exotic breads for their royalty. From there wheat spread throughout the Roman Empire and eventually to the rest of the world.

There are many strains of wheat, classified according to hardness or softness, which reflects the percentage of protein. Hard winter wheat is high in gluten and is best for breads, whereas softer wheats work best in cakes and pastries. Hard durum wheat and its by-product, semolina, are the principal ingredients in most pasta and macaroni. White flour, bleached and unbleached, has been stripped of most of its nutritional value and makes the soft, puffy pastry and bread commercially produced today.

Whole wheat berries Difficult to digest in their whole form but can be soaked and cooked with other whole grains to create delicious dishes.

Whole wheat flour A flour ground from whole wheat berries that is high in gluten. Good stone-ground flour retains much of its germ and bran and thus much more of its nutrients than its unbleached white counterpart, making it a healthier choice for bread baking.

Whole wheat pastry flour A flour ground from a softer strain of wheat that is low in gluten. It is more finely milled than regular whole wheat flour, making it an excellent choice for pastry, cookie, cake, and muffin baking.

Zest (peel) The thin colored layer of skin on citrus fruit that imparts the fragrant essence of the fruit into cooking.

RESOURCE GUIDE

While you can get quite an array of grains, beans, fresh vegetables, and fruit from your local market and natural foods store, there are a few essential basics that you might not find in your corner store. Don't panic. Cooking your way to the life you want doesn't have to be a hassle. These mail-order resources stock an incredible variety of the finest quality—and, in most cases, organic—ingredients available, as well as access to information, classes, seminars, books, and magazines.

Christina's Choice
Philadelphia, PA
215-551-1430
800-939-3909

Organic macrobiotic and natural food items (imported and domestic), kitchenware and other nonfood items, books, videos, and *Christina Cooks* magazine.

Eden Foods
Clinton, MI
517-456-7424

Organic macrobiotic and natural food items (imported and domestic), nonfood items.

Kushi Institute
Becket, MA
413-623-5741

Seminars, classes, information, books, worldwide directory of resources.

MacroTours
Philadelphia, PA
800-939-3909

Healthy vacation packages to exotic destinations.

The Whole Foods Academy at
The Restaurant School
Philadelphia, PA
215-222-4200

Comprehensive, fully accredited macrobiotic curriculum that includes theory, demonstration, and hands-on study.

BIBLIOGRAPHY

The following volumes have become invaluable to me over the years—and I look to them (and many others) constantly for inspiration and to further my understanding of the laws of nature. I offer my gratitude to all the authors for their wisdom.

Colbin, Annemarie. *The Natural Gourmet*. New York: Ballantine, 1989.

Cottrell, Martha. *AIDS, Macrobiotics and Natural Immunity*. New York: Japan Publications, 1990.

Gagne, Steve. *Energetics of Food*. New Mexico: Spiral Science, 1990.

Kushi, Michio. *Your Face Never Lies*. Garden City, NJ: Avery, 1983.

———. *How to See Your Health*. New York: Japan Publications, 1985.

———. *Nine Star Ki*. Becket, MA: One Peaceful World, 1995.

———, and Aveline Kushi. *Macrobiotic Diet*. New York: Japan Publications, 1985.

McDougall, John. *The McDougall Plan*. Piscataway, NJ: New Century Publishers, Inc., 1983.

Ohsawa, Georges. *You Are All Sanpaku*. New York: Citadel, 1965.

Oski, Frank. *Don't Drink Your Milk*. Syracuse, NY: Mollica Press, 1983.

Sandifer, Jon. *Feng Shui Astrology*. New York: Ballantine, 1997.

Tara, William. *The Magic Mirror*. Boston: Self-published, 1984.

Veith, Ilza. *The Yellow Emperor's Classic of Internal Medicine*. Berkeley, CA: University of California Press, 1949.

INDEX